ZiGGY® on PARADE

Recent *Ziggy* Books

Ziggy . . . A Rumor in His Own Time
A Day in the Life of Ziggy . . .
1-800-ZIGGY
My Life as a Cartoon
The Z Files
Ziggy's Divine Comedy
Get Ziggy with It
The Zen of Ziggy
Ziggy Goes Hollywood
Character Matters

Treasuries

Ziggy's Star Performances
The First 25 Years Are the Hardest!
Ziggy's Friends for Life
Ziggy's Gift
A Little Character Goes a Long Way

ZiGGY on PARADE

A ZiGGY COLLECTiON

by Tom Wilson

**Andrews McMeel
Publishing, LLC**

Kansas City

Ziggy is distributed internationally by Universal Press Syndicate.

07 08 09 10 11 WKT 10 9 8 7 6 5 4 3 2 1

ISBN-13: 978-0-7407-6851-4
ISBN-10: 0-7407-6851-4

Library of Congress Control Number: 2007925458

www.andrewsmcmeel.com

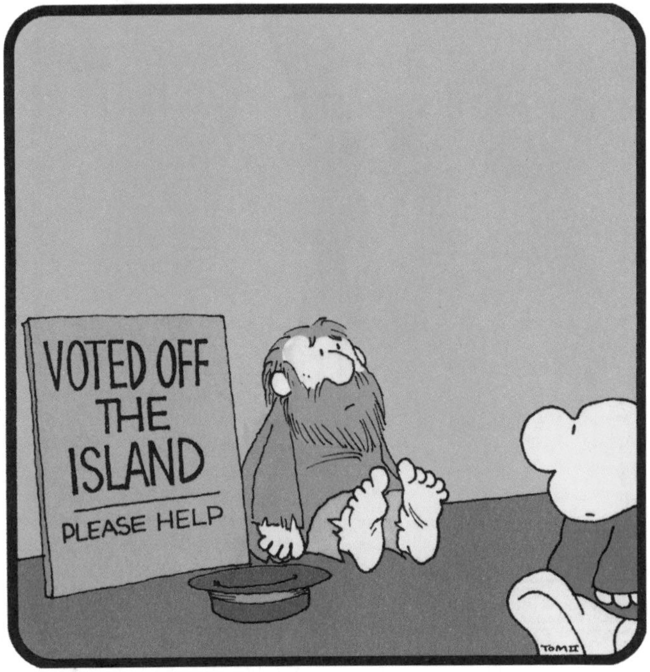
VOTED OFF THE ISLAND
PLEASE HELP
TOM II

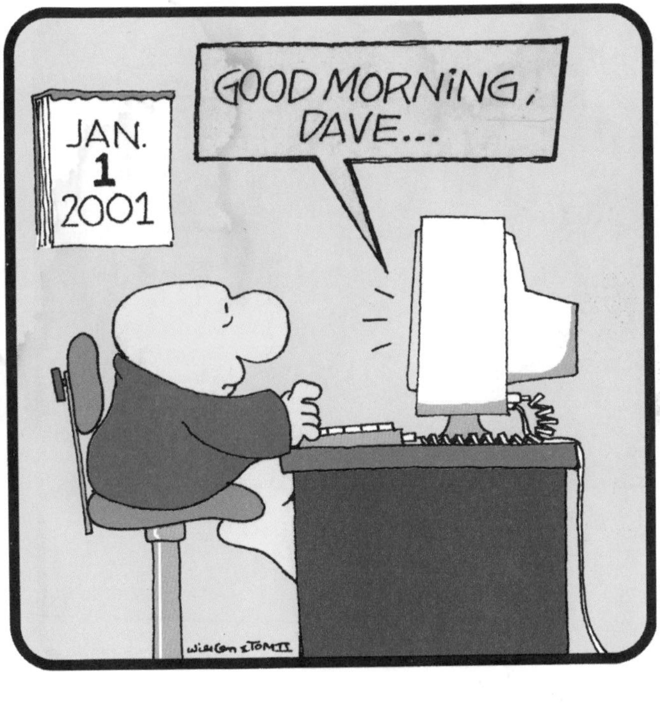
JAN. 1 2001
GOOD MORNING, DAVE...

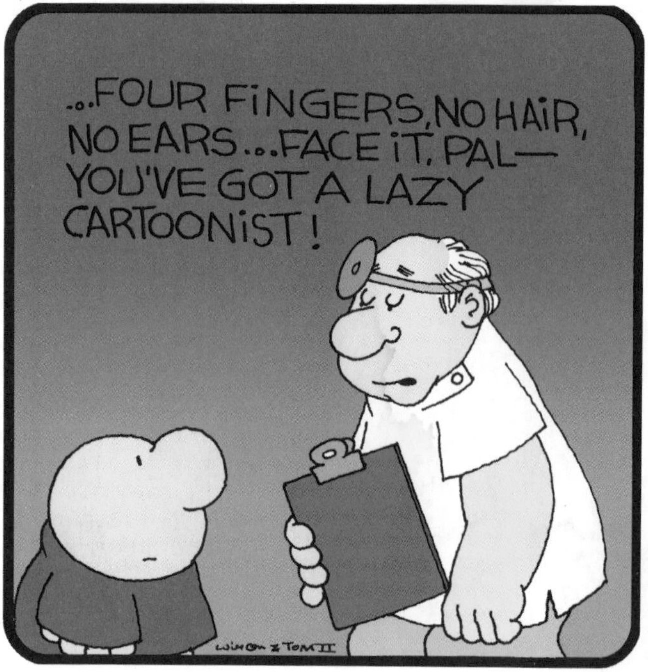
..FOUR FINGERS, NO HAIR, NO EARS...FACE IT, PAL— YOU'VE GOT A LAZY CARTOONIST!
WILSON & TOM II

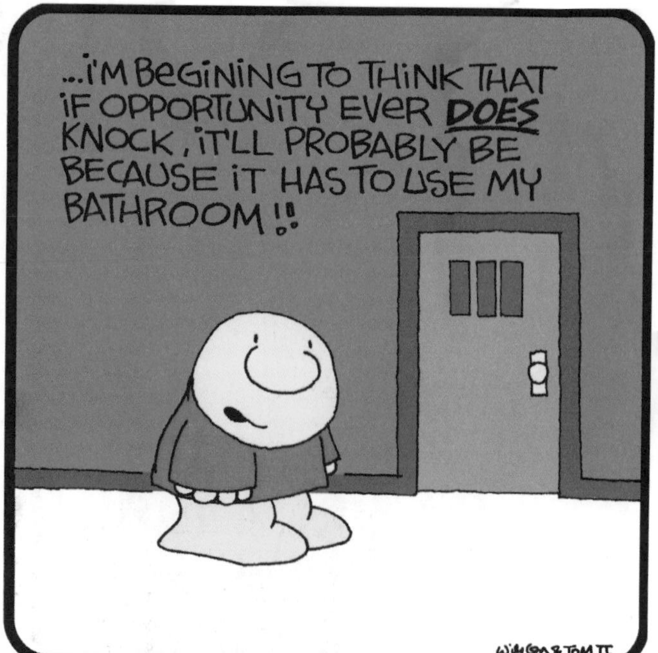
...I'M BEGINING TO THINK THAT IF OPPORTUNITY EVER DOES KNOCK, IT'LL PROBABLY BE BECAUSE IT HAS TO USE MY BATHROOM!!
WILSON & TOM II

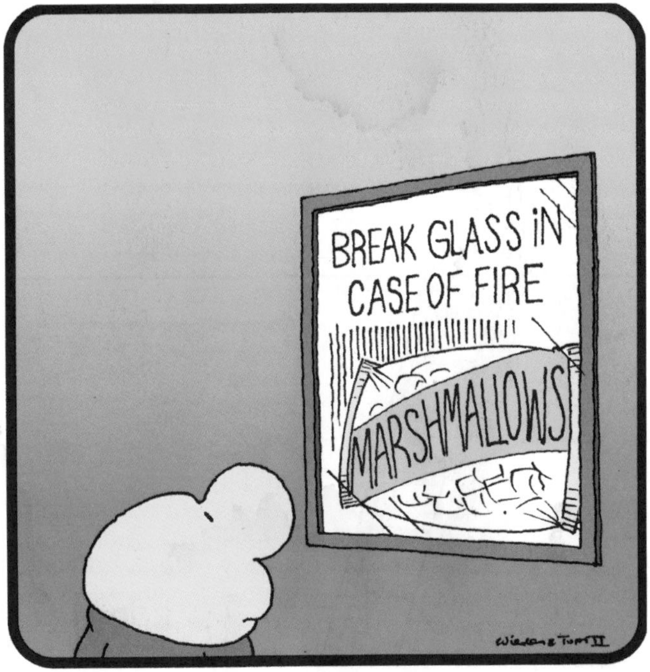
BREAK GLASS IN CASE OF FIRE
MARSHMALLOWS

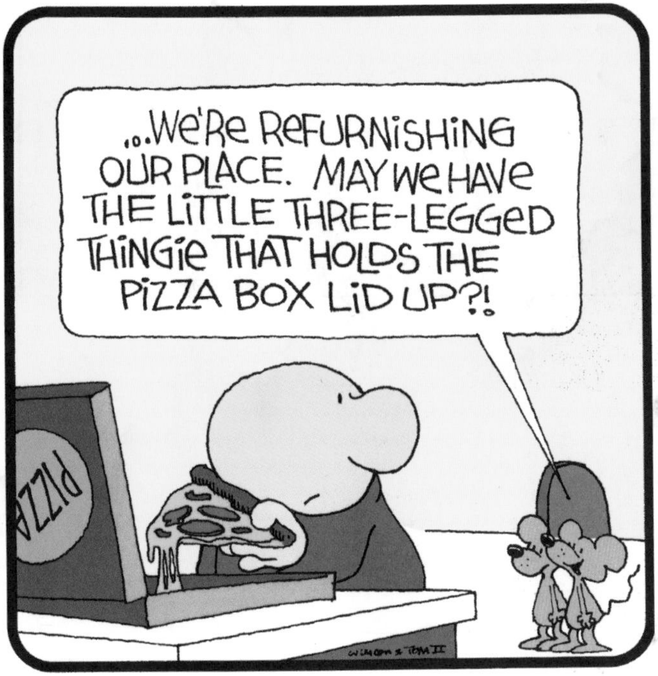
...WE'RE REFURNISHING OUR PLACE. MAY WE HAVE THE LITTLE THREE-LEGGED THINGIE THAT HOLDS THE PIZZA BOX LID UP?!
PIZZA

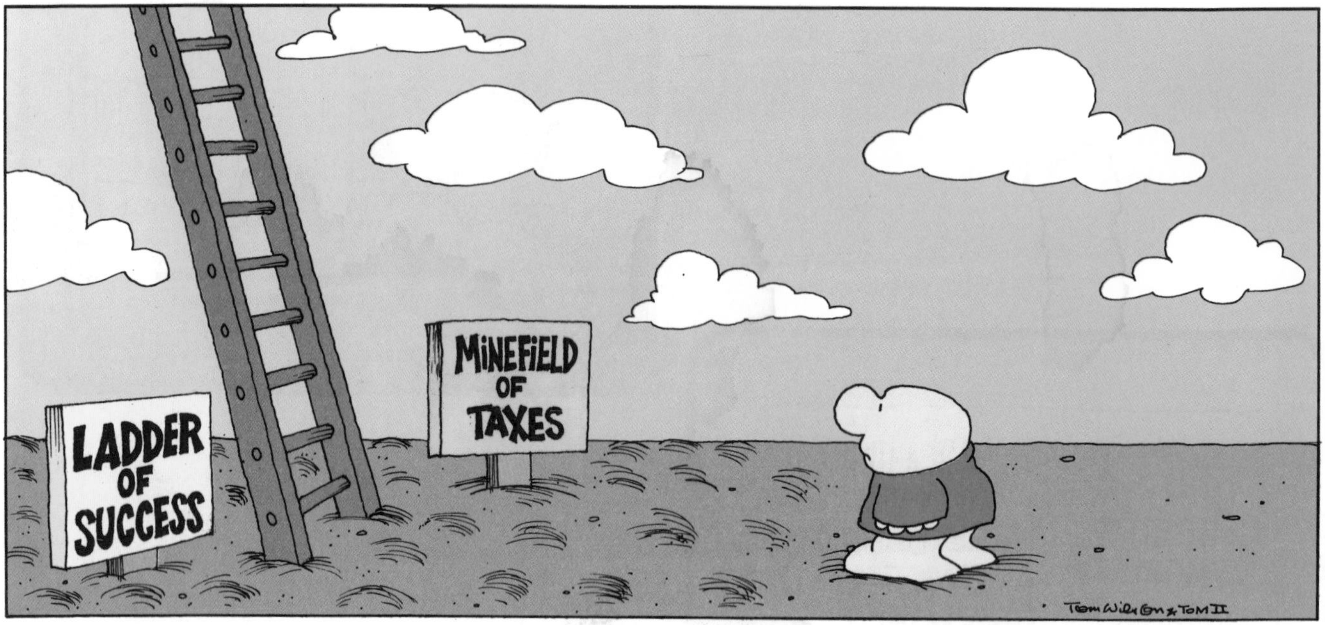
LADDER OF SUCCESS
MINEFIELD OF TAXES
Tom Wilson & Tom II

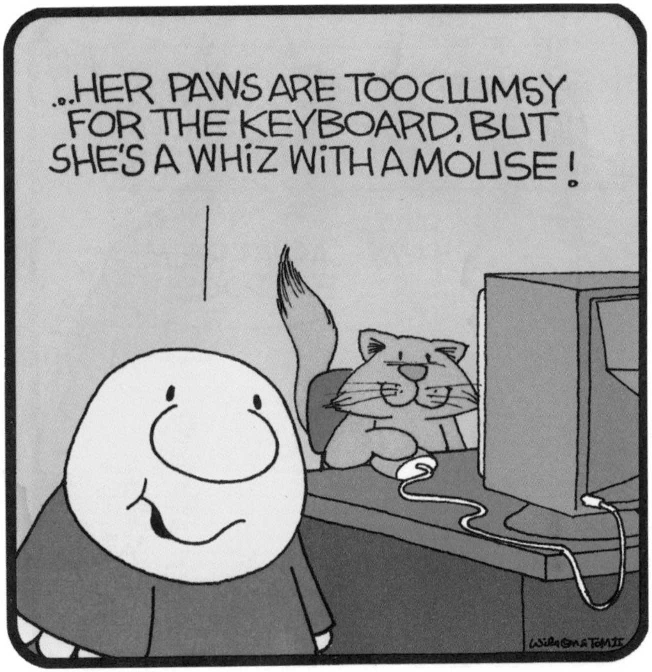
..HER PAWS ARE TOO CLUMSY FOR THE KEYBOARD, BUT SHE'S A WHIZ WITH A MOUSE!

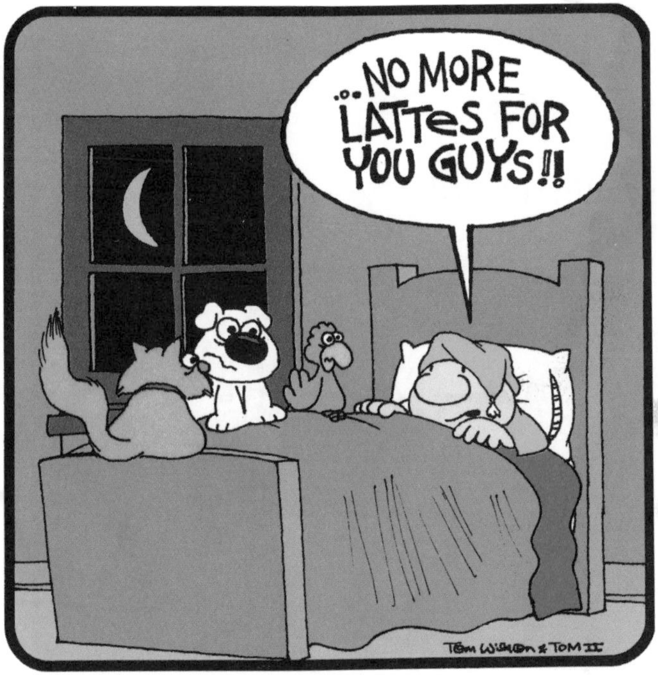
...NO MORE LATTES FOR YOU GUYS!!

BOW-WOW! ARF! GRRR WARF! YIP! YIP! GRF!!
..A CHAT ROOM FOR DOGS!?

WHAT TOM & JERRY FILM FESTIVAL?

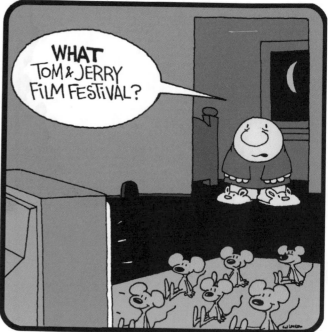

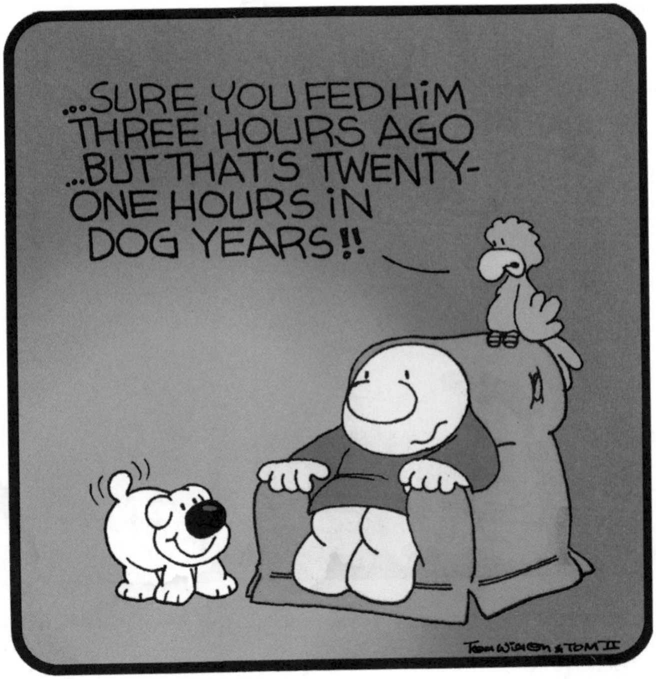
...SURE, YOU FED HiM THREE HOURS AGO ...BUT THAT'S TWENTY-ONE HOURS iN DOG YEARS!!
TOM WiLSON & TOM II

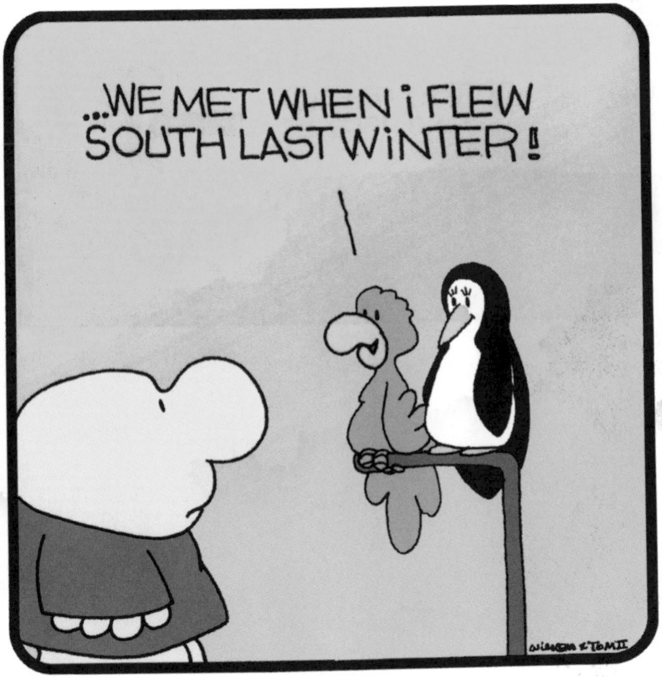
...WE MET WHEN i FLEW SOUTH LAST WiNTER!
WiLSON & TOM II

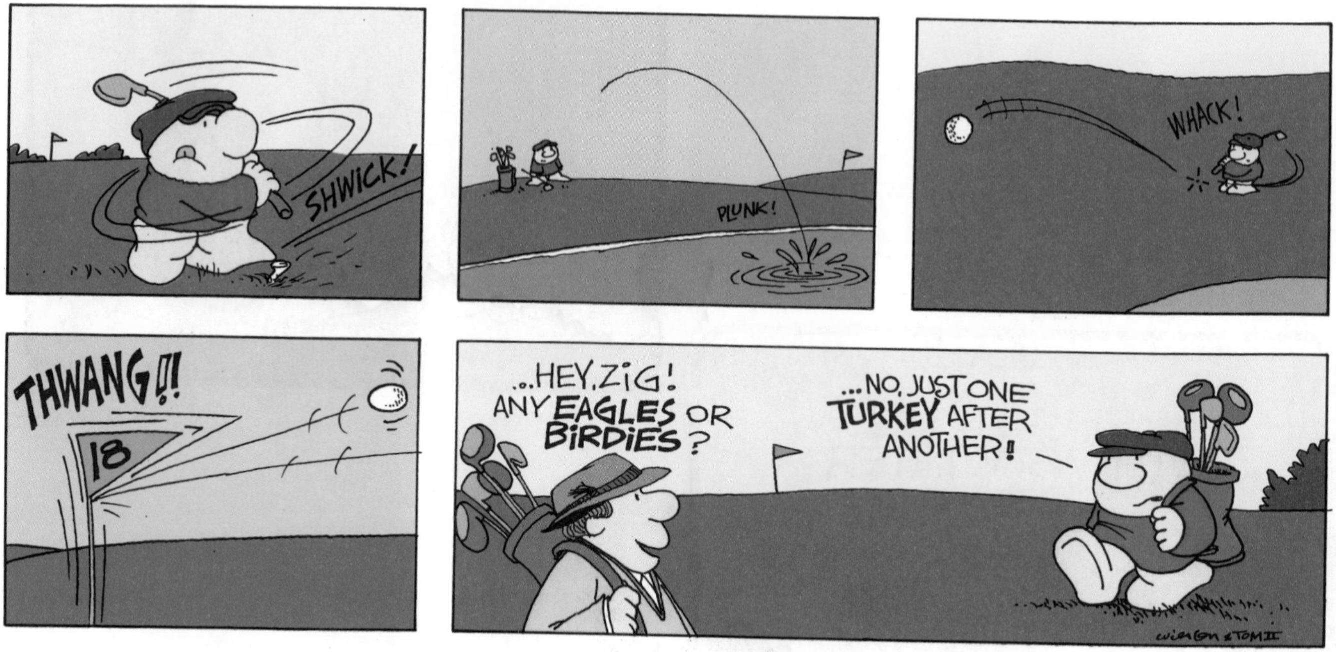
SHWICK!
PLUNK!
WHACK!
THWANG!?!
18
...HEY, ZIG! ANY EAGLES OR BIRDIES?
...NO, JUST ONE TURKEY AFTER ANOTHER!
WILSON & TOM II

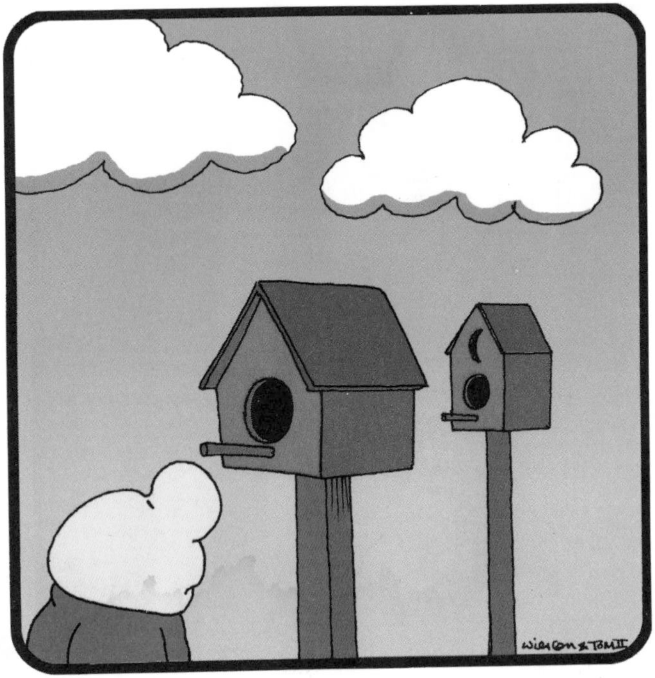
WILSON & TOM II

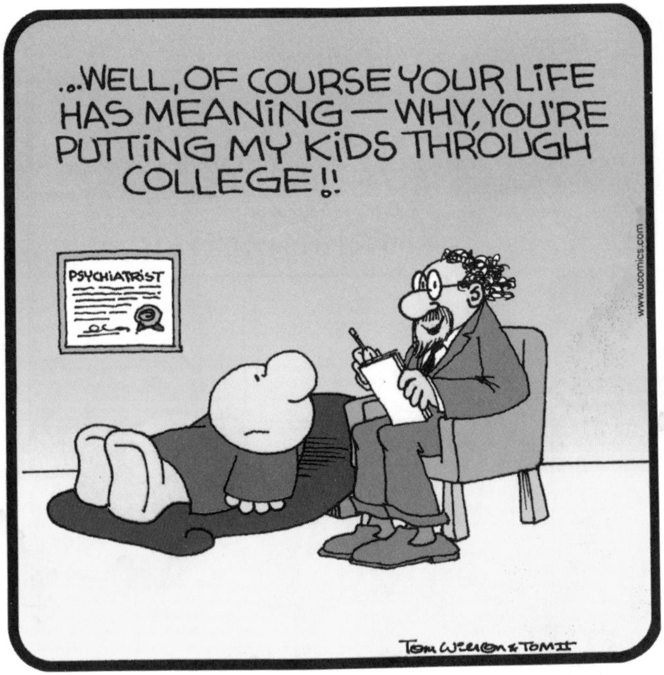
...WELL, OF COURSE YOUR LIFE HAS MEANING — WHY, YOU'RE PUTTING MY KIDS THROUGH COLLEGE!!
PSYCHIATRIST
www.ucomics.com
TOM WILSON & TOM II

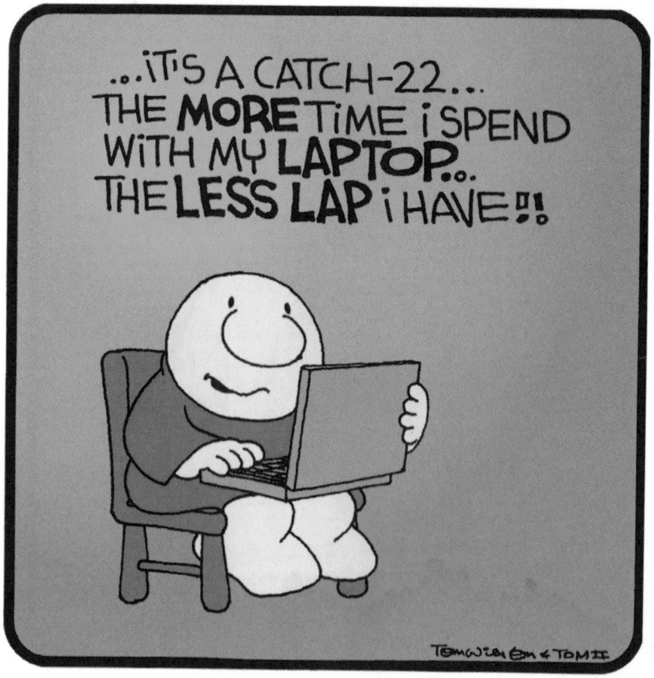
..iT'S A CATCH-22...
THE MORE TiME i SPEND
WiTH MY LAPTOP..
THE LESS LAP i HAVE!!

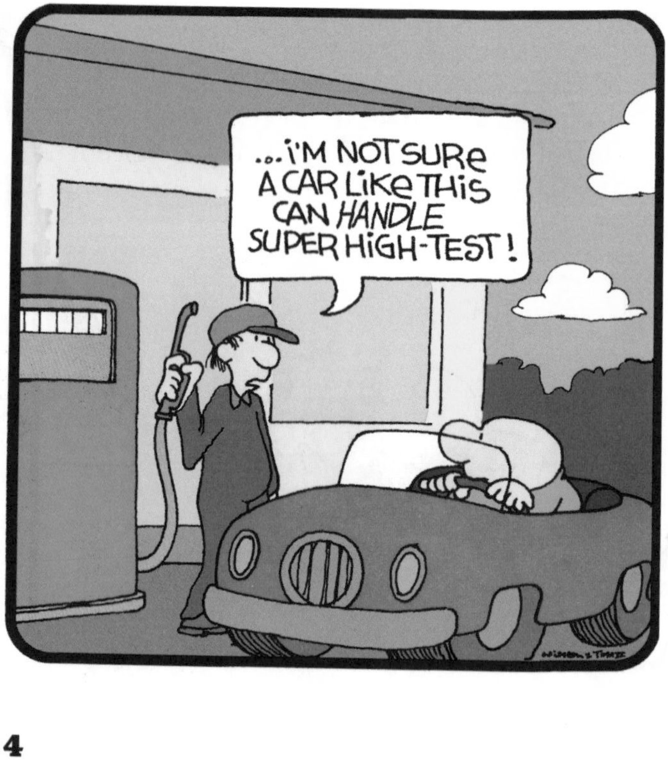
..i'M NOT SURe
A CAR LiKe THiS
CAN HANDLE
SUPER HiGH-TEST!

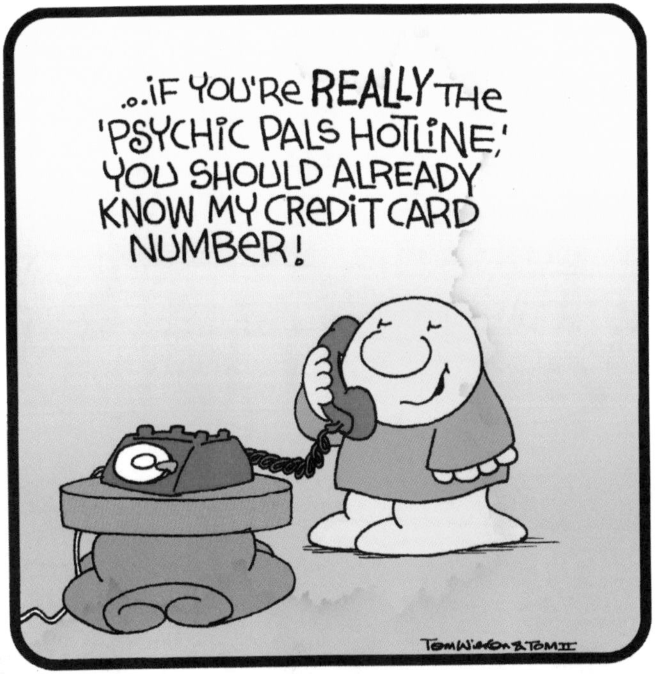
..IF YOU'RE REALLY THE 'PSYCHIC PALS HOTLINE,' YOU SHOULD ALREADY KNOW MY CREDIT CARD NUMBER!

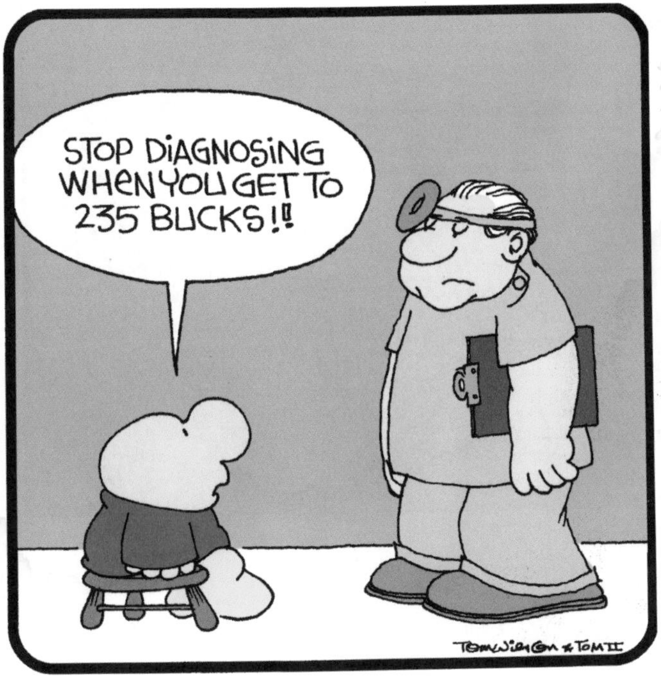
STOP DIAGNOSING WHEN YOU GET TO 235 BUCKS!!

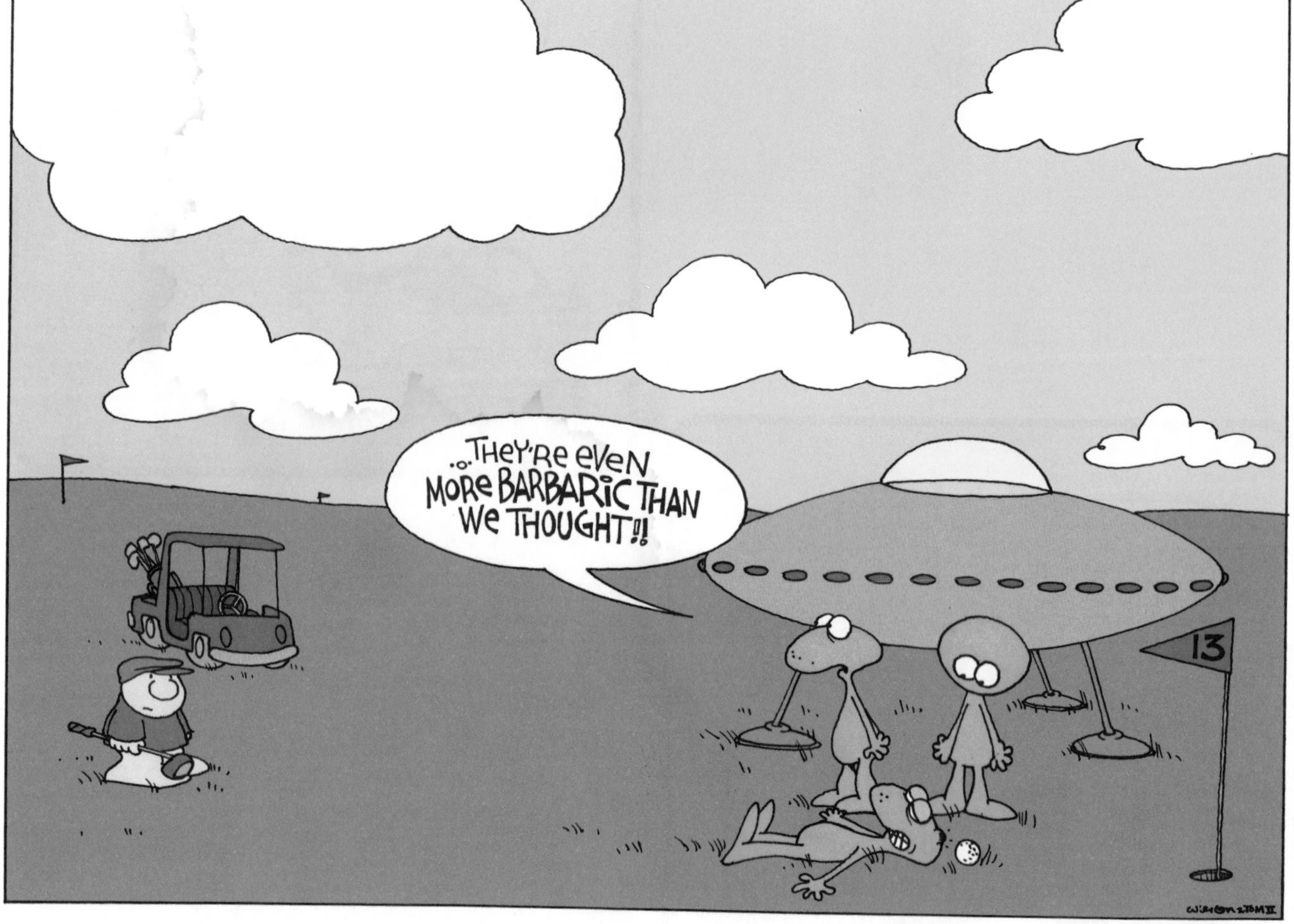
..THEY'RE EVEN MORE BARBARIC THAN WE THOUGHT!!
13

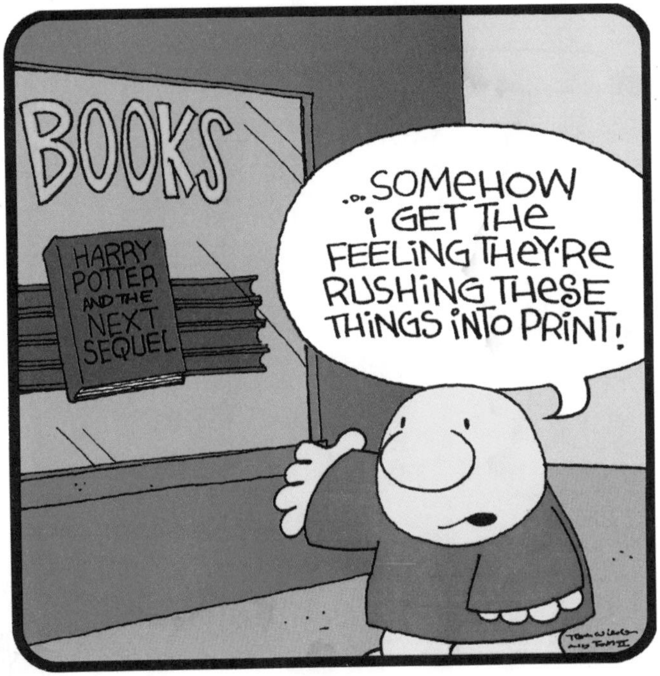
BOOKS
HARRY POTTER AND THE NEXT SEQUEL
...SOMEHOW I GET THE FEELING THEY'RE RUSHING THESE THINGS INTO PRINT!

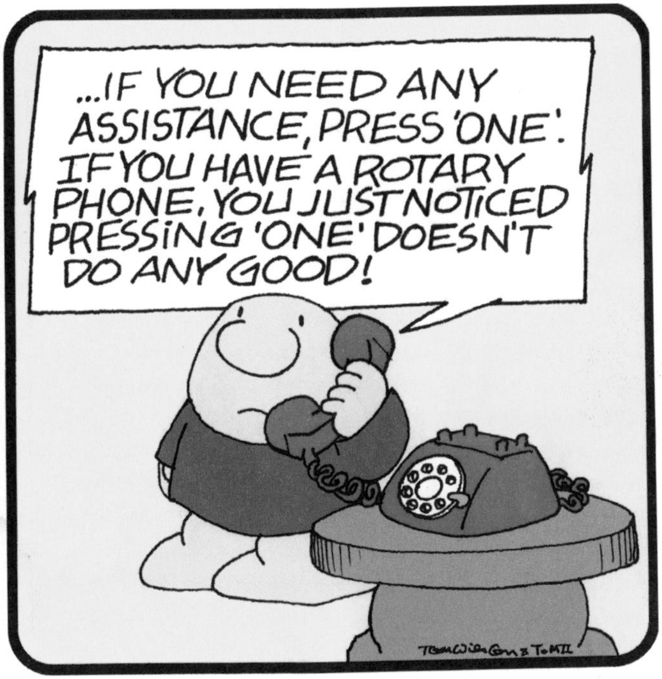
...IF YOU NEED ANY ASSISTANCE, PRESS 'ONE'. IF YOU HAVE A ROTARY PHONE, YOU JUST NOTICED PRESSING 'ONE' DOESN'T DO ANY GOOD!

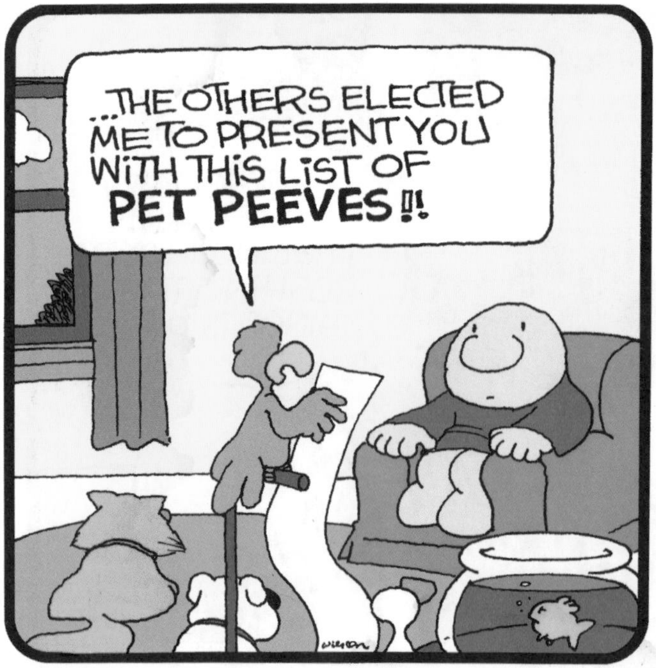
...THE OTHERS ELECTED ME TO PRESENT YOU WITH THIS LIST OF PET PEEVES!!

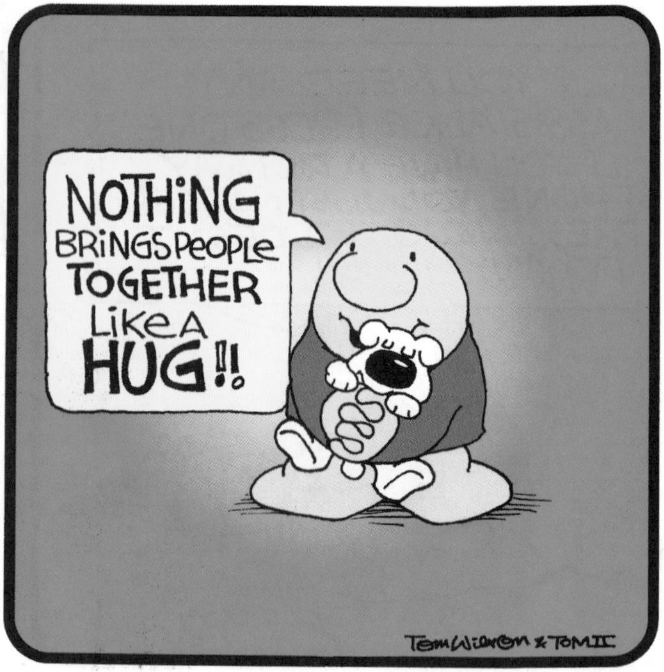
NOTHING BRINGS PEOPLE TOGETHER LIKE A HUG!!
Tom Wilson & TOM II

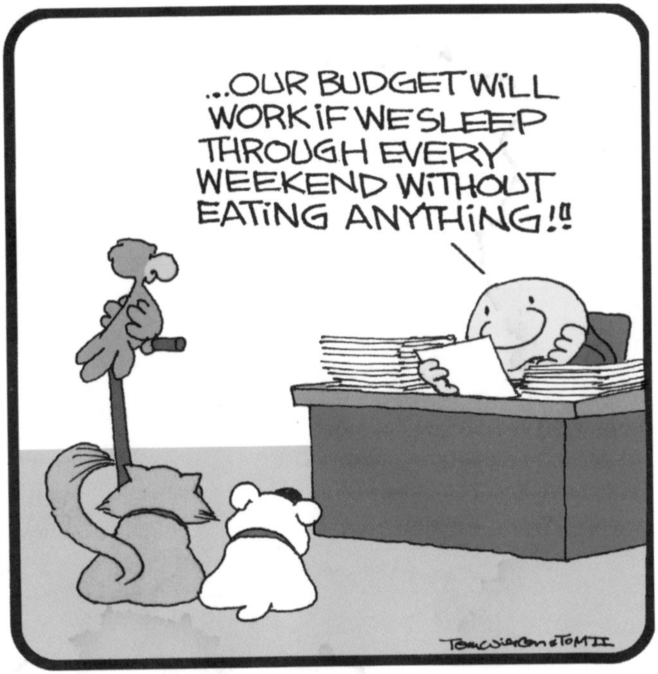
...OUR BUDGET WILL WORK IF WE SLEEP THROUGH EVERY WEEKEND WITHOUT EATING ANYTHING!!

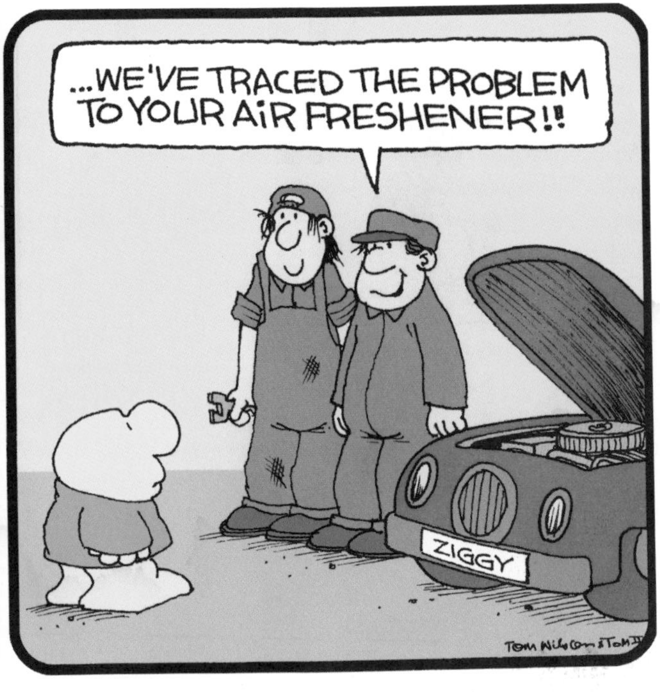
...WE'VE TRACED THE PROBLEM TO YOUR AIR FRESHENER!!
ZIGGY

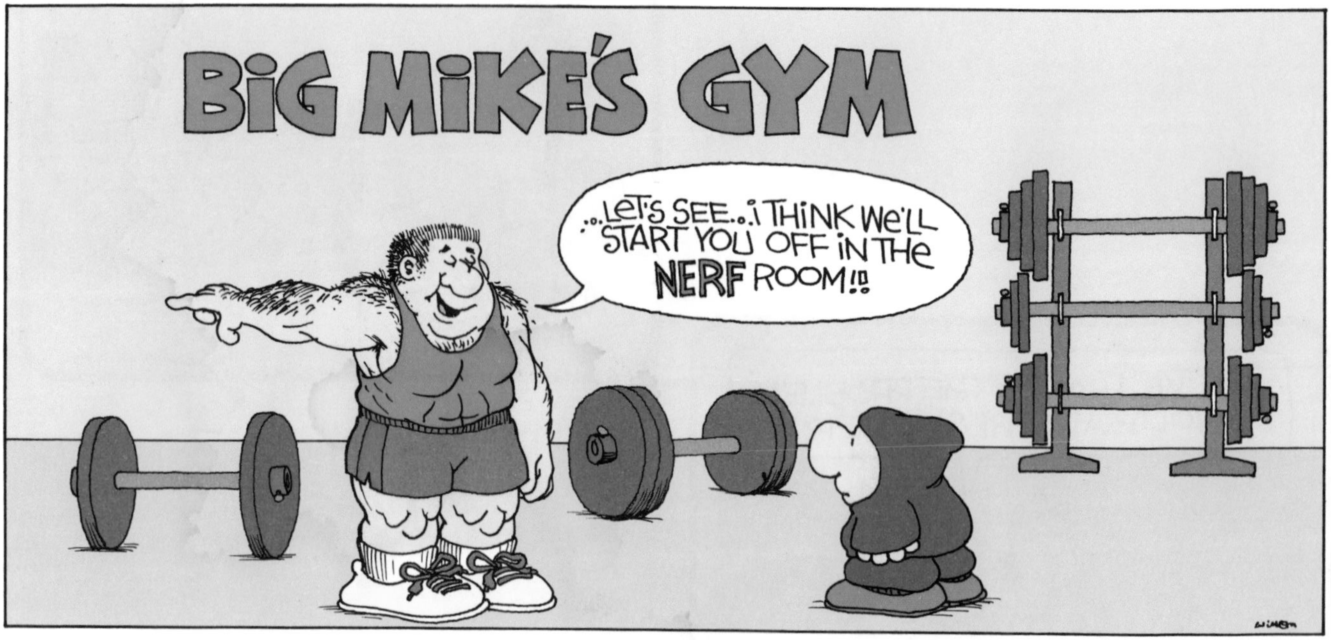
BiG MiKE'S GYM
..LET'S SEE..i THiNK WE'LL START YOU OFF iN THE NERF ROOM!!

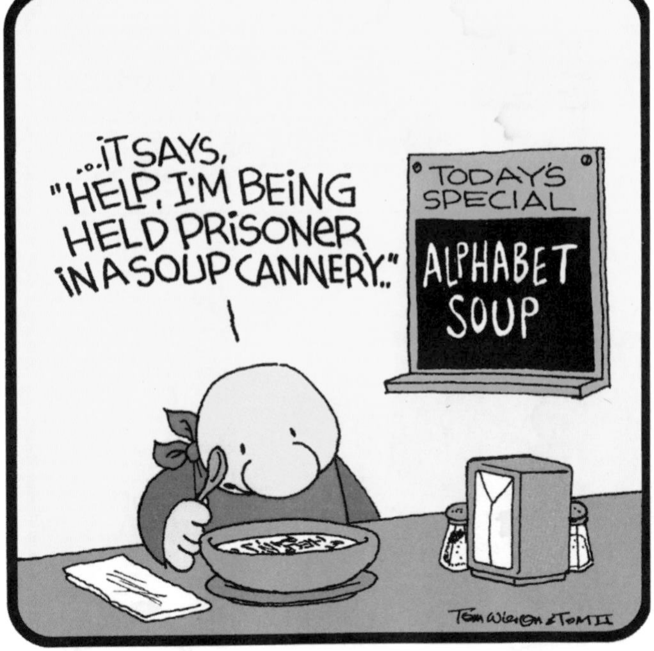
...IT SAYS, "HELP, I'M BEING HELD PRISONER IN A SOUP CANNERY.."
TODAY'S SPECIAL
ALPHABET SOUP

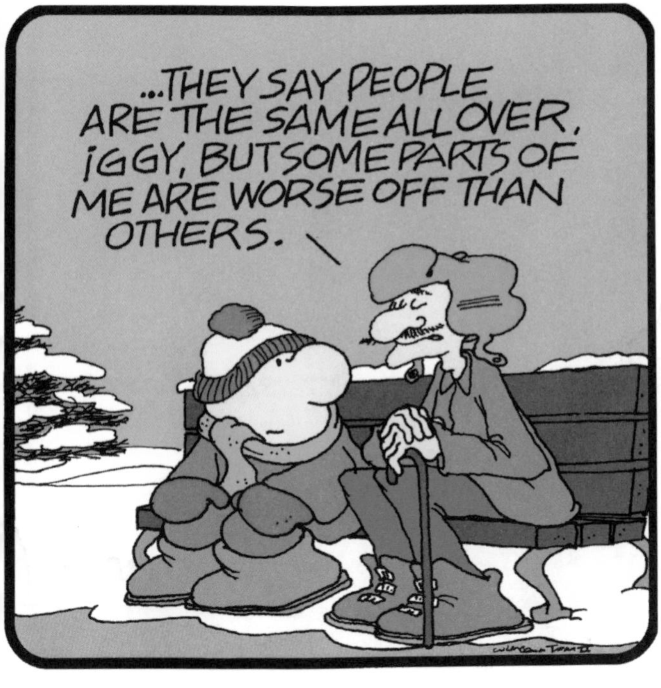
...THEY SAY PEOPLE ARE THE SAME ALL OVER, IGGY, BUT SOME PARTS OF ME ARE WORSE OFF THAN OTHERS.

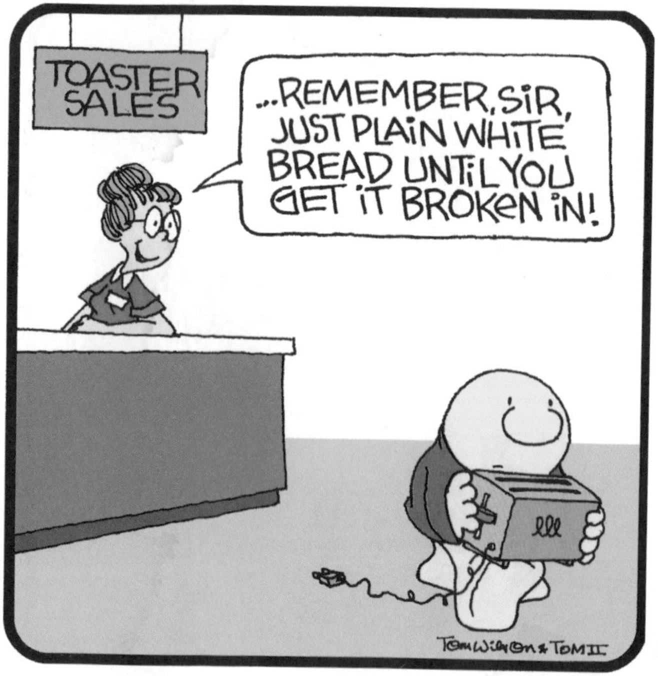
TOASTER SALES
...REMEMBER, SIR, JUST PLAIN WHITE BREAD UNTIL YOU GET IT BROKEN IN!
TOM WILSON & TOM II

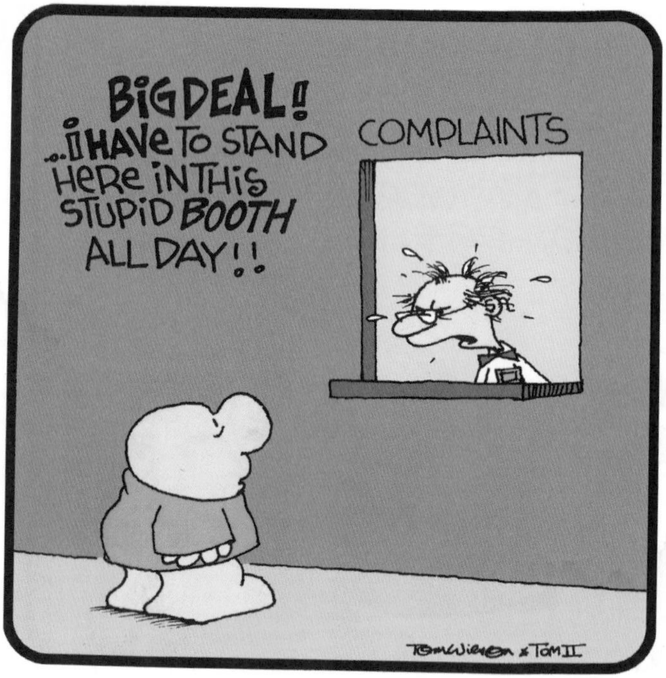
BIG DEAL! ...I HAVE TO STAND HERE IN THIS STUPID BOOTH ALL DAY!!
COMPLAINTS
TOM WILSON & TOM II

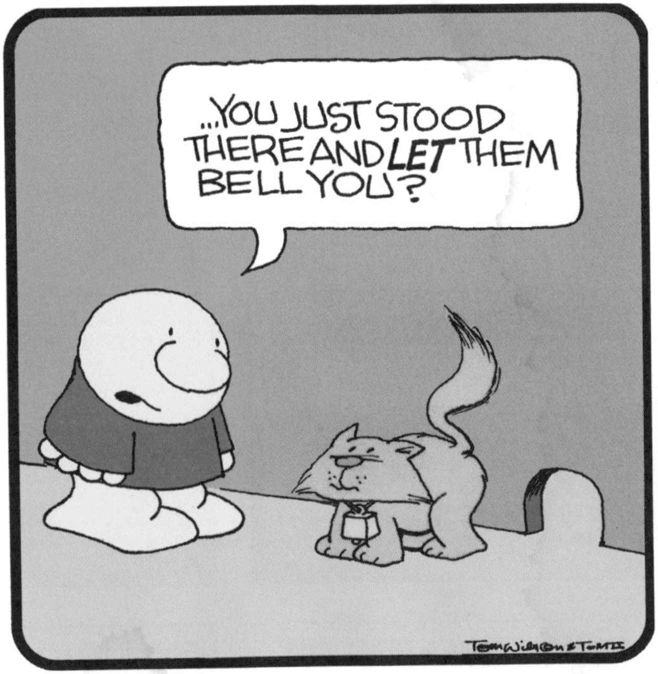
...YOU JUST STOOD THERE AND LET THEM BELL YOU?

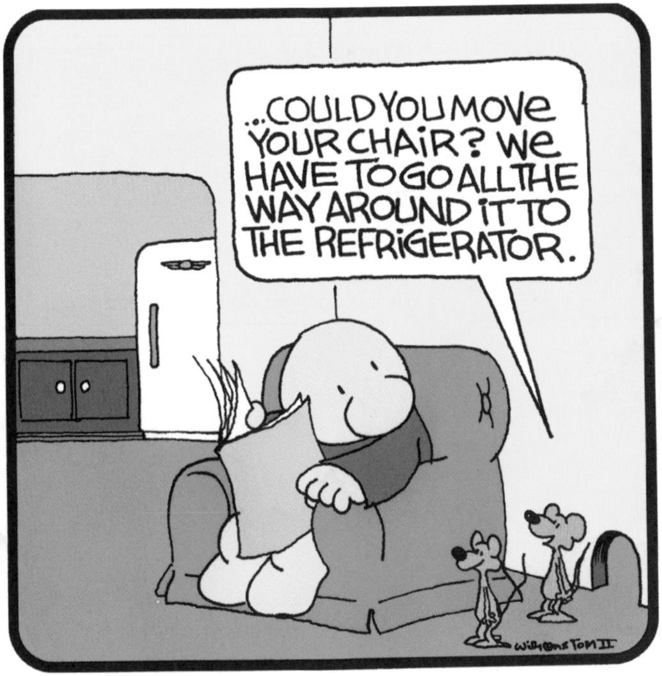
...COULD YOU MOVE YOUR CHAIR? WE HAVE TO GO ALL THE WAY AROUND IT TO THE REFRIGERATOR.

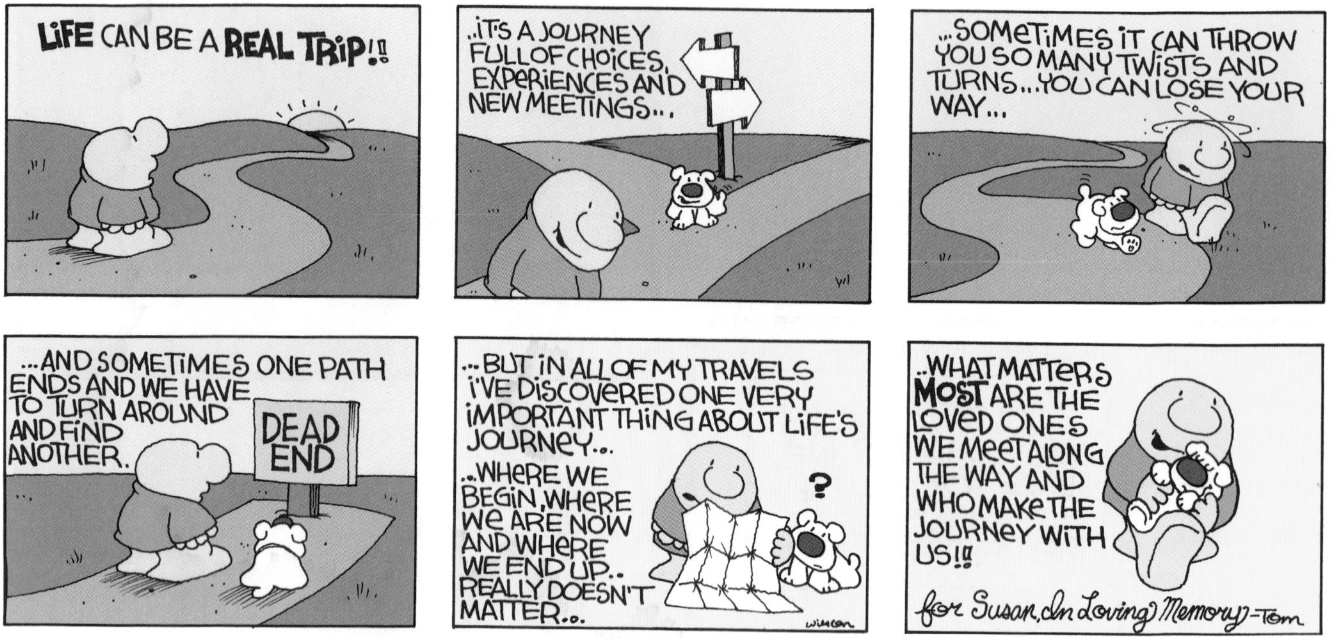
LIFE CAN BE A REAL TRIP!!
..IT'S A JOURNEY FULL OF CHOICES, EXPERIENCES AND NEW MEETINGS...
...SOMETIMES IT CAN THROW YOU SO MANY TWISTS AND TURNS...YOU CAN LOSE YOUR WAY...
...AND SOMETIMES ONE PATH ENDS AND WE HAVE TO TURN AROUND AND FIND ANOTHER.
DEAD END
...BUT IN ALL OF MY TRAVELS I'VE DISCOVERED ONE VERY IMPORTANT THING ABOUT LIFE'S JOURNEY...
...WHERE WE BEGIN, WHERE WE ARE NOW AND WHERE WE END UP.. REALLY DOESN'T MATTER...
?
..WHAT MATTERS MOST ARE THE LOVED ONES WE MEET ALONG THE WAY AND WHO MAKE THE JOURNEY WITH US!!
for Susan, In Loving Memory -Tom

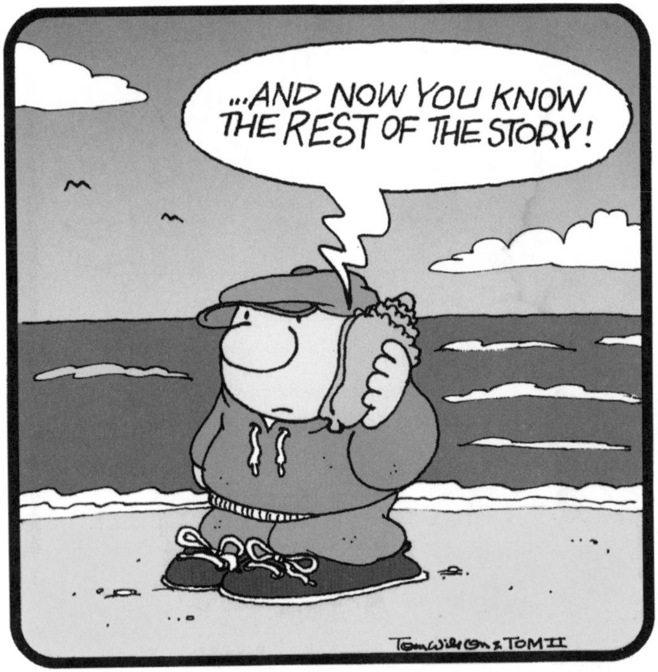
...AND NOW YOU KNOW THE REST OF THE STORY!
TOM WILSON & TOM II

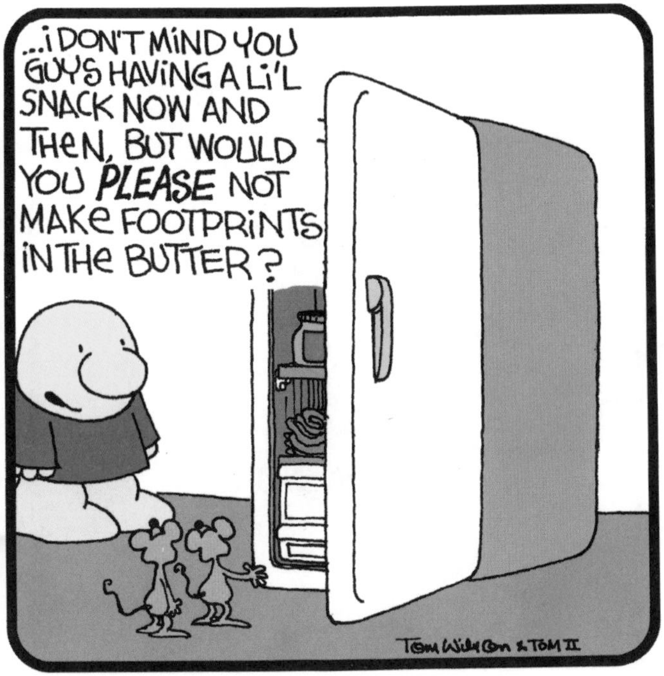
...I DON'T MIND YOU GUYS HAVING A LI'L SNACK NOW AND THEN, BUT WOULD YOU PLEASE NOT MAKE FOOTPRINTS IN THE BUTTER?
TOM WILSON & TOM II

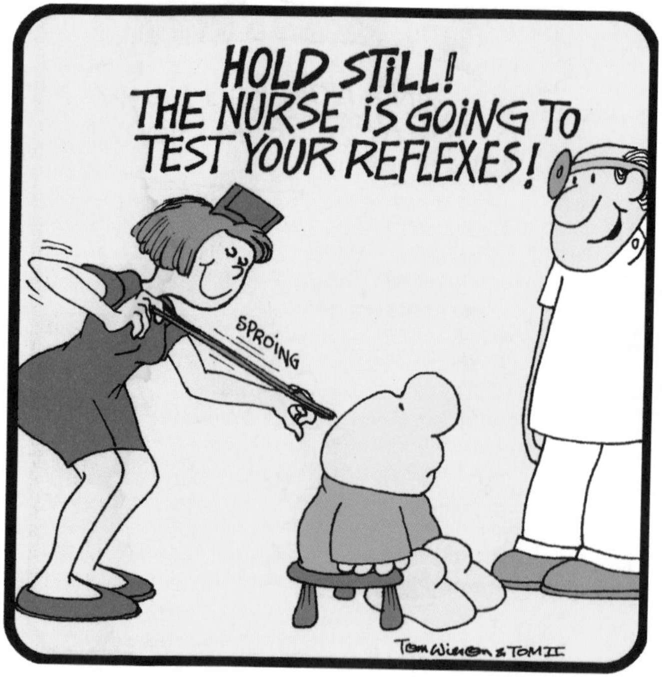
HOLD STILL! THE NURSE IS GOING TO TEST YOUR REFLEXES!
SPROING
TOM WILSON & TOM II

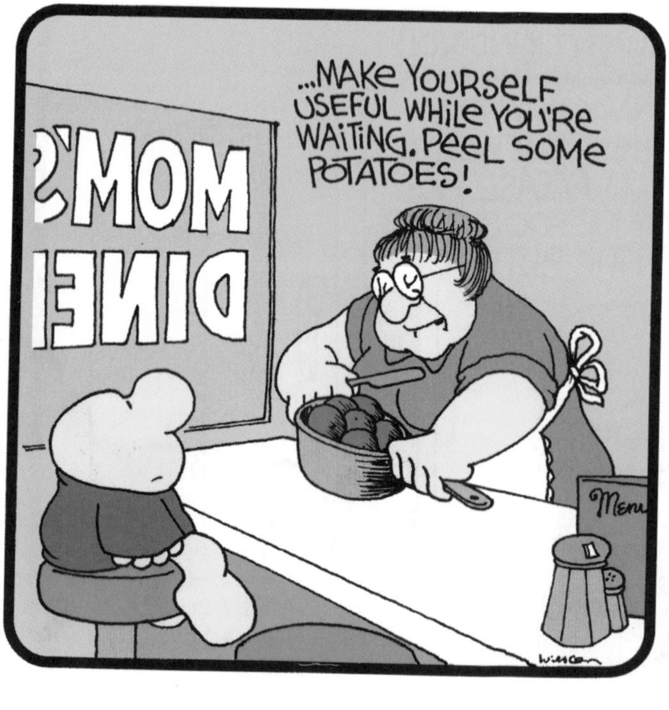
...MAKE YOURSELF USEFUL WHILE YOU'RE WAITING. PEEL SOME POTATOES!
Menu

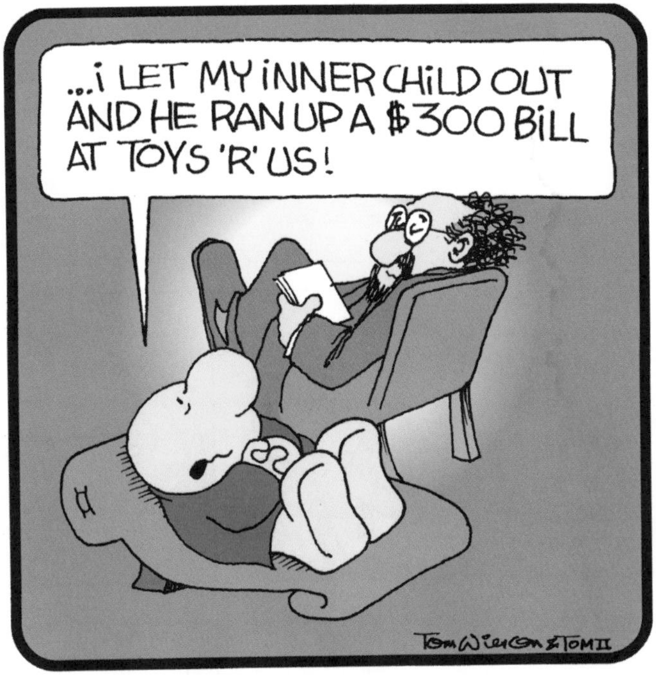
...i LET MY iNNER CHiLD OUT AND HE RAN UP A $300 BiLL AT TOYS 'R' US!
TOM WILSON & TOM II

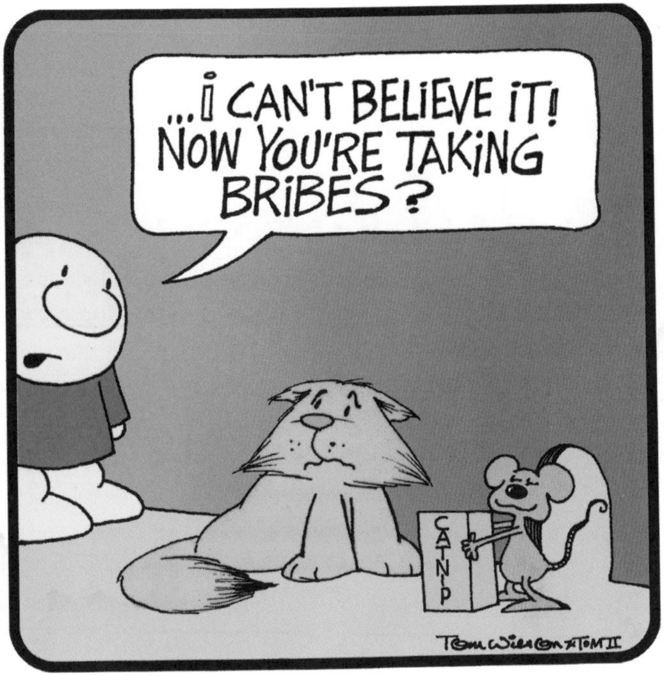
...i CAN'T BELiEVE iT! NOW YOU'RE TAKiNG BRiBES?
CATNIP
TOM WILSON & TOM II

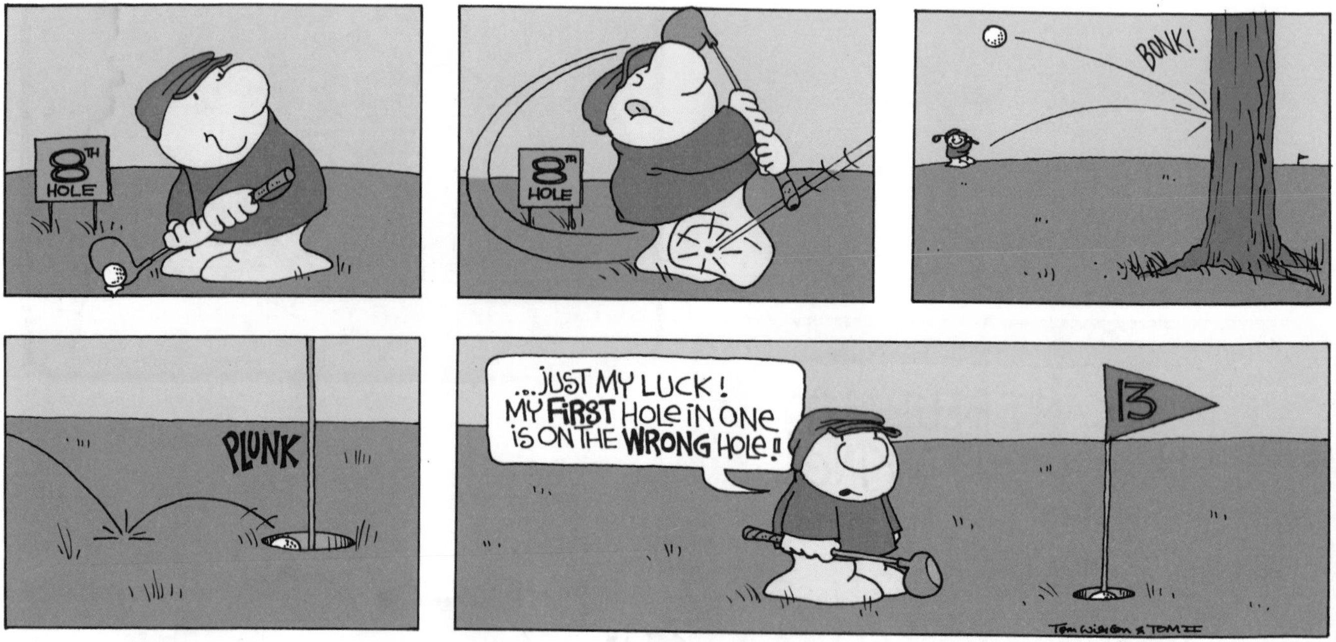
8TH HOLE
8TH HOLE
BONK!
PLUNK
...JUST MY LUCK! MY FIRST HOLE IN ONE IS ON THE WRONG HOLE!!
13
TOM WILSON & TOM II

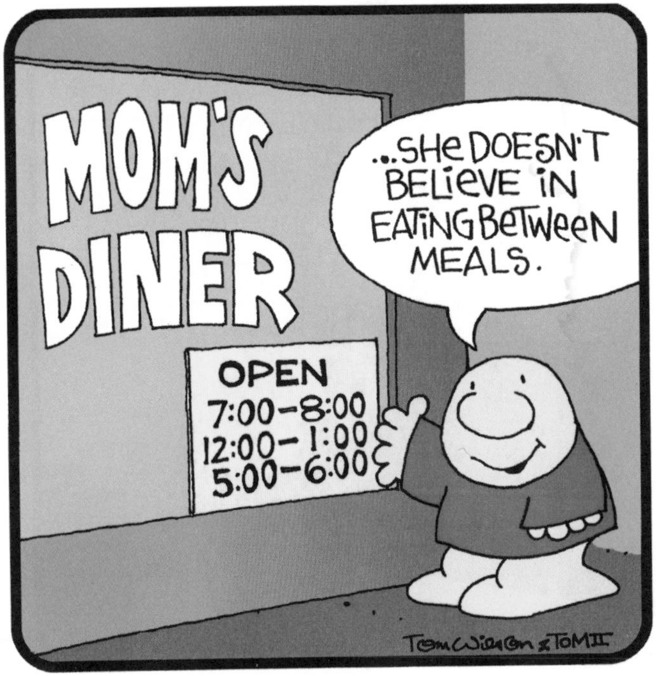
MOM'S DINER
OPEN
7:00-8:00
12:00-1:00
5:00-6:00
..SHE DOESN'T BELIEVE IN EATING BETWEEN MEALS.
TOM WILSON & TOM II

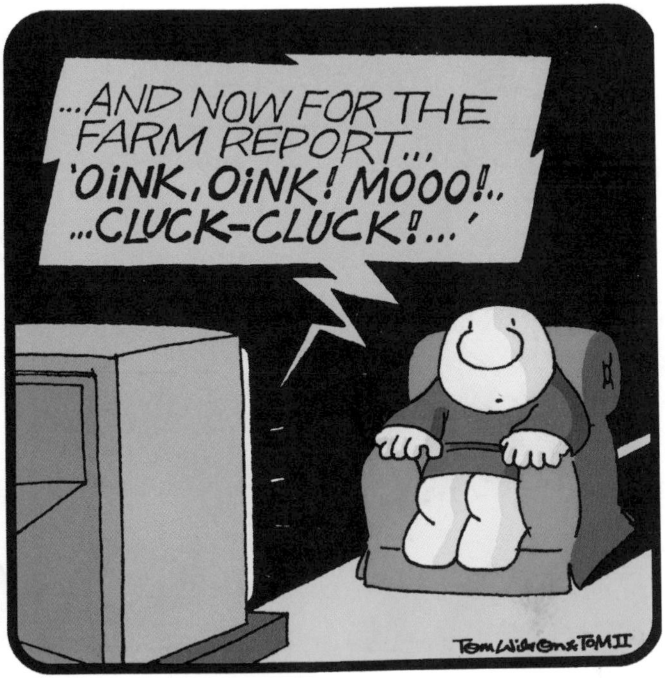
...AND NOW FOR THE FARM REPORT... 'OINK, OINK! MOOO!.. ...CLUCK-CLUCK!...'
TOM WILSON & TOM II

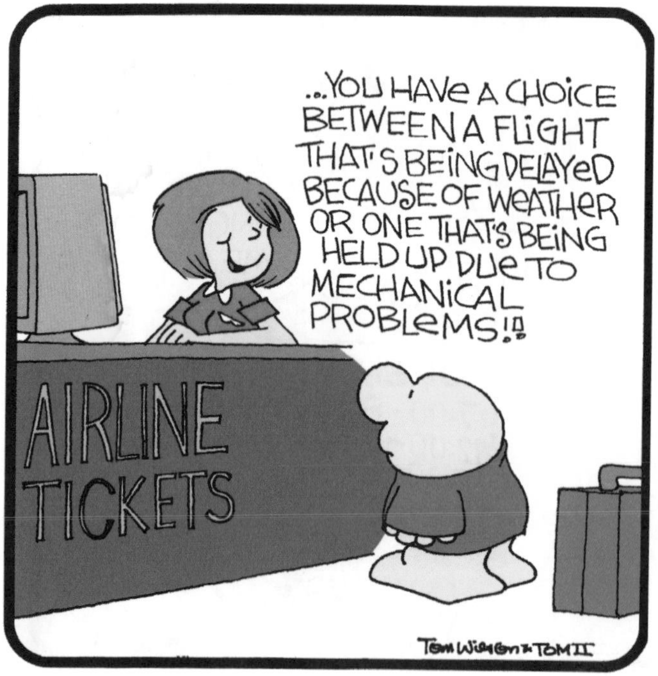
...YOU HAVE A CHOICE BETWEEN A FLIGHT THAT'S BEING DELAYED BECAUSE OF WEATHER OR ONE THAT'S BEING HELD UP DUE TO MECHANICAL PROBLEMS!!
AIRLINE TICKETS
Tom Wilson & Tom II

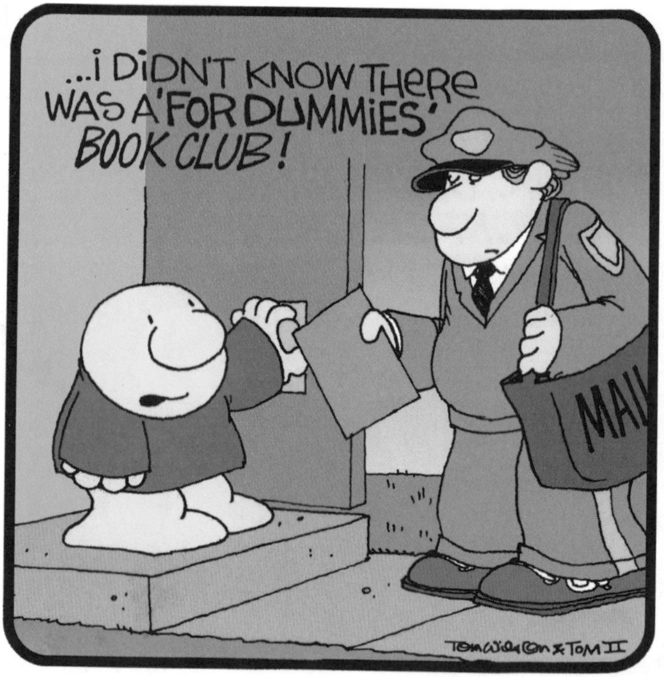
...I DIDN'T KNOW THERE WAS A 'FOR DUMMIES' BOOK CLUB!
Tom Wilson & Tom II

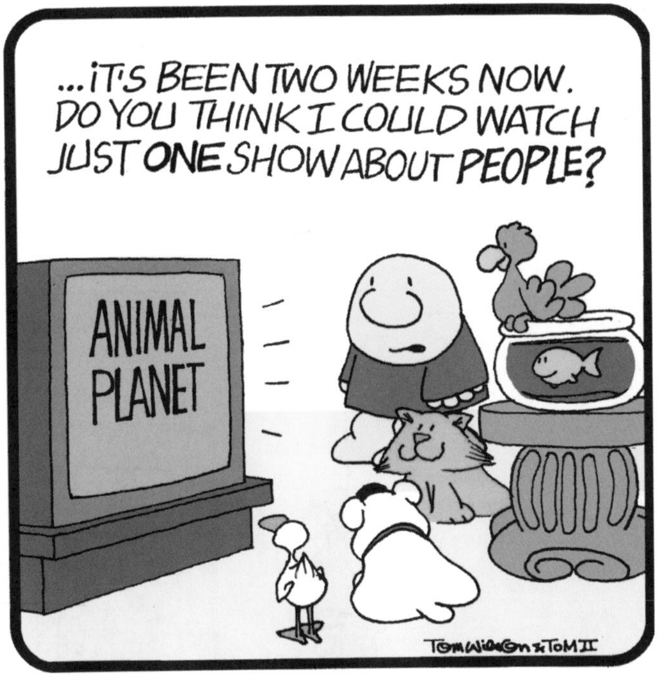
...IT'S BEEN TWO WEEKS NOW. DO YOU THINK I COULD WATCH JUST ONE SHOW ABOUT PEOPLE?
ANIMAL PLANET
TOM WILSON & TOM II

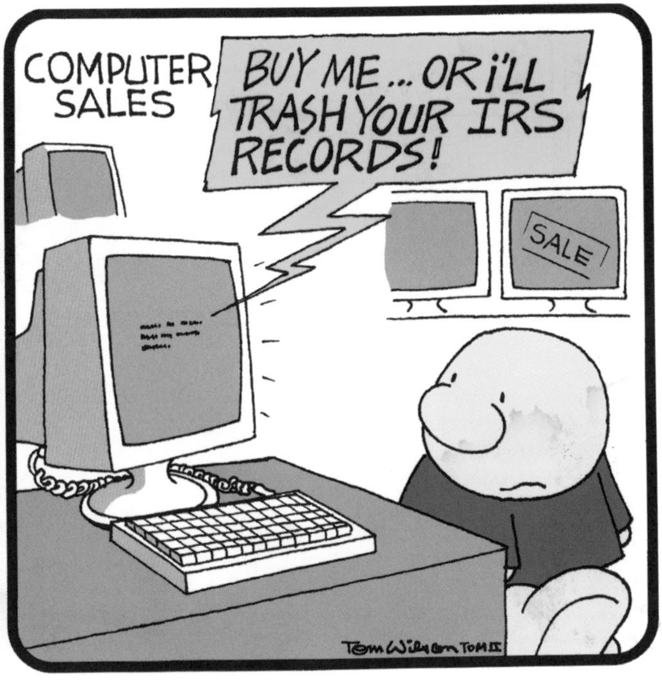
COMPUTER SALES
BUY ME... OR I'LL TRASH YOUR IRS RECORDS!
SALE
TOM WILSON TOM II

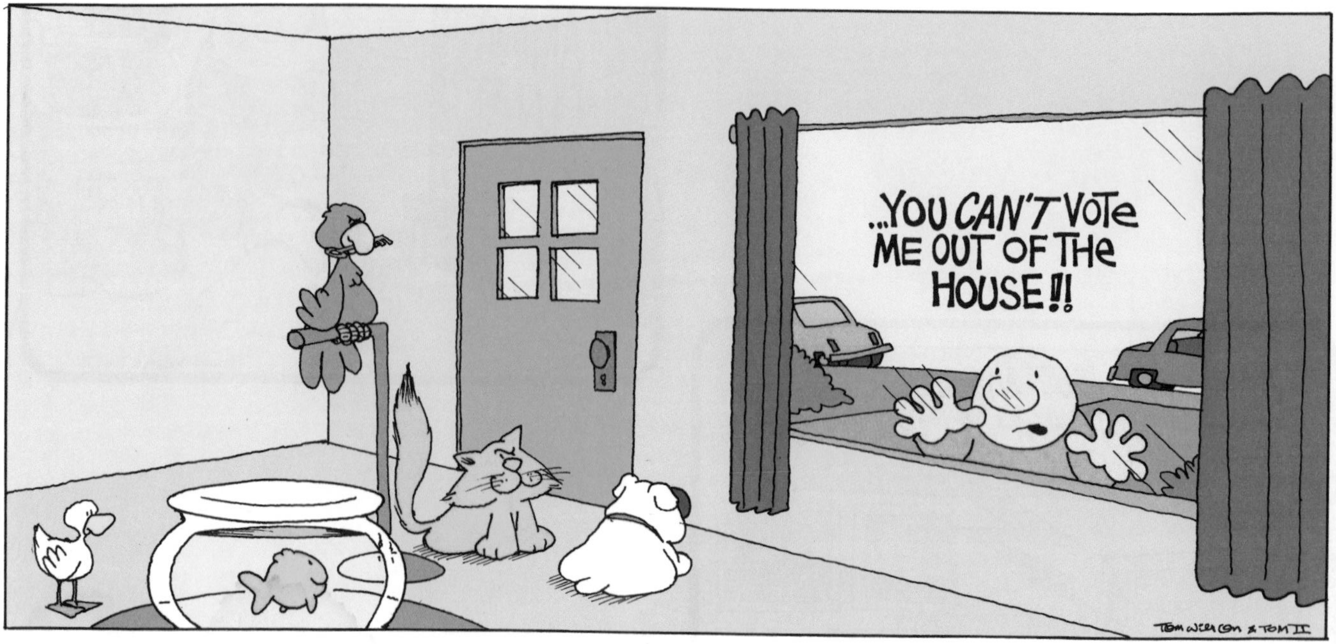
...YOU CAN'T VOTE ME OUT OF THE HOUSE!!
TOM WILSON & TOM II

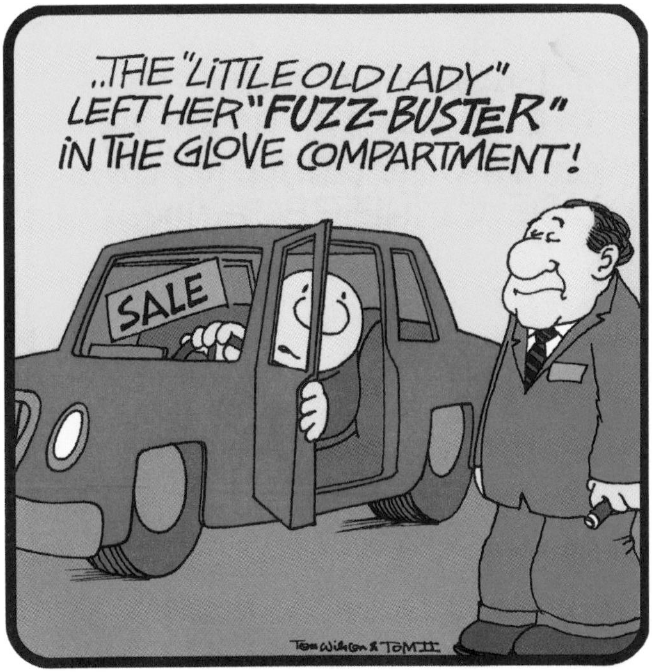
..THE "LITTLE OLD LADY" LEFT HER "FUZZ-BUSTER" IN THE GLOVE COMPARTMENT!
SALE
Tom Wilson & Tom II

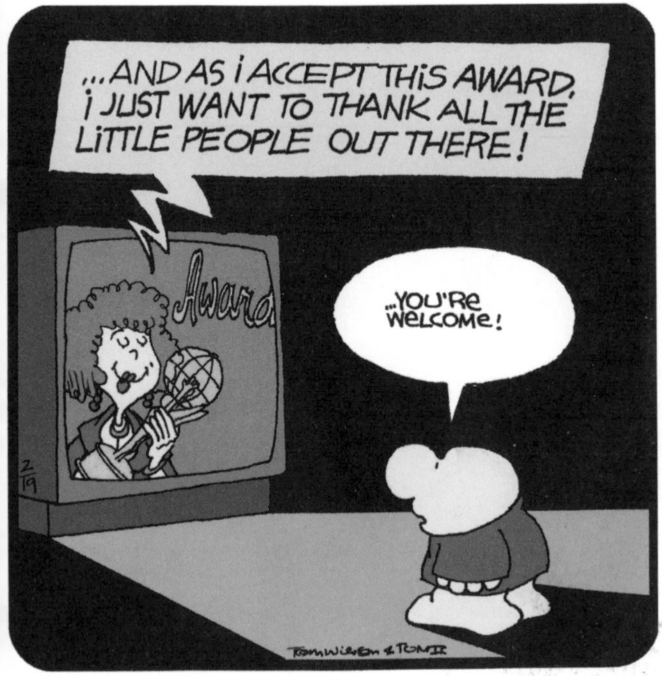
...AND AS I ACCEPT THIS AWARD, I JUST WANT TO THANK ALL THE LITTLE PEOPLE OUT THERE!
Award
...YOU'RE WELCOME!
2/19
Tom Wilson & Tom II

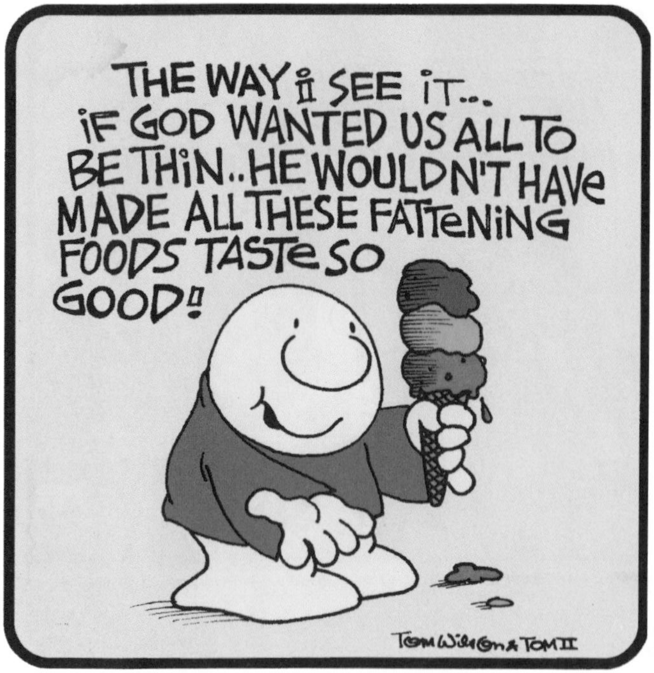
THE WAY I SEE IT...
IF GOD WANTED US ALL TO BE THIN..HE WOULDN'T HAVE MADE ALL THESE FATTENING FOODS TASTE SO GOOD!!
Tom Wilson & TOM II

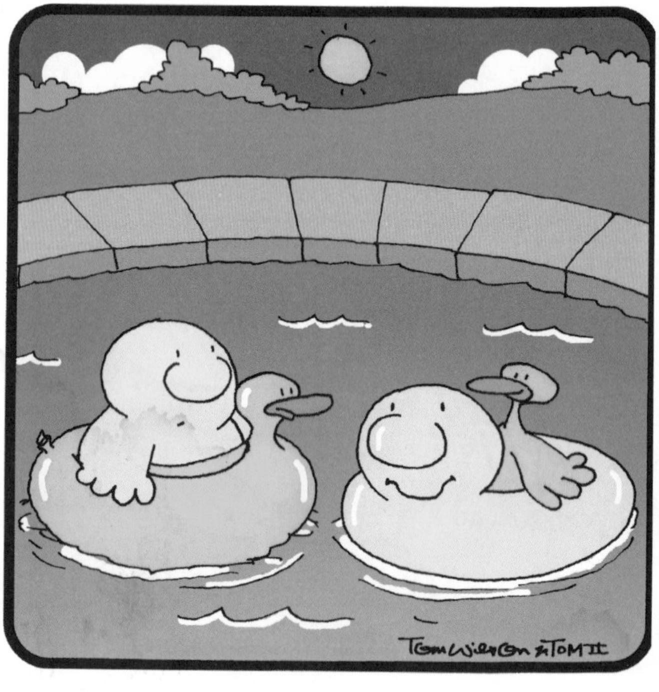
Tom Wilson & TOM II

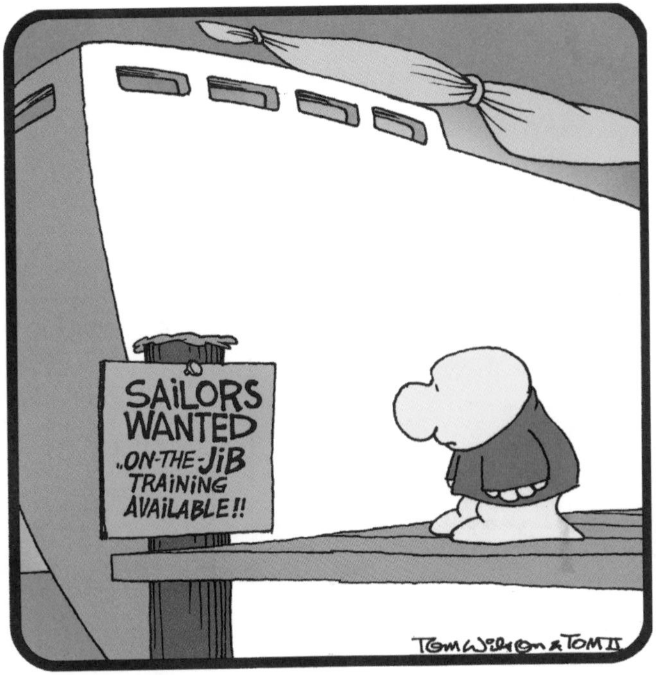
SAILORS WANTED
..ON-THE-JiB TRAINING AVAILABLE!!
TOM WILSON & TOM II

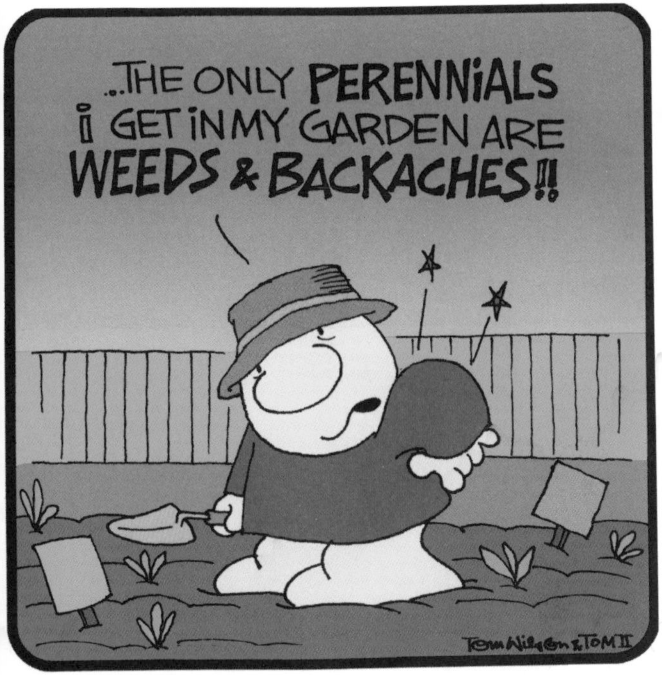
..THE ONLY PERENNIALS I GET IN MY GARDEN ARE WEEDS & BACKACHES!!
TOM WILSON & TOM II

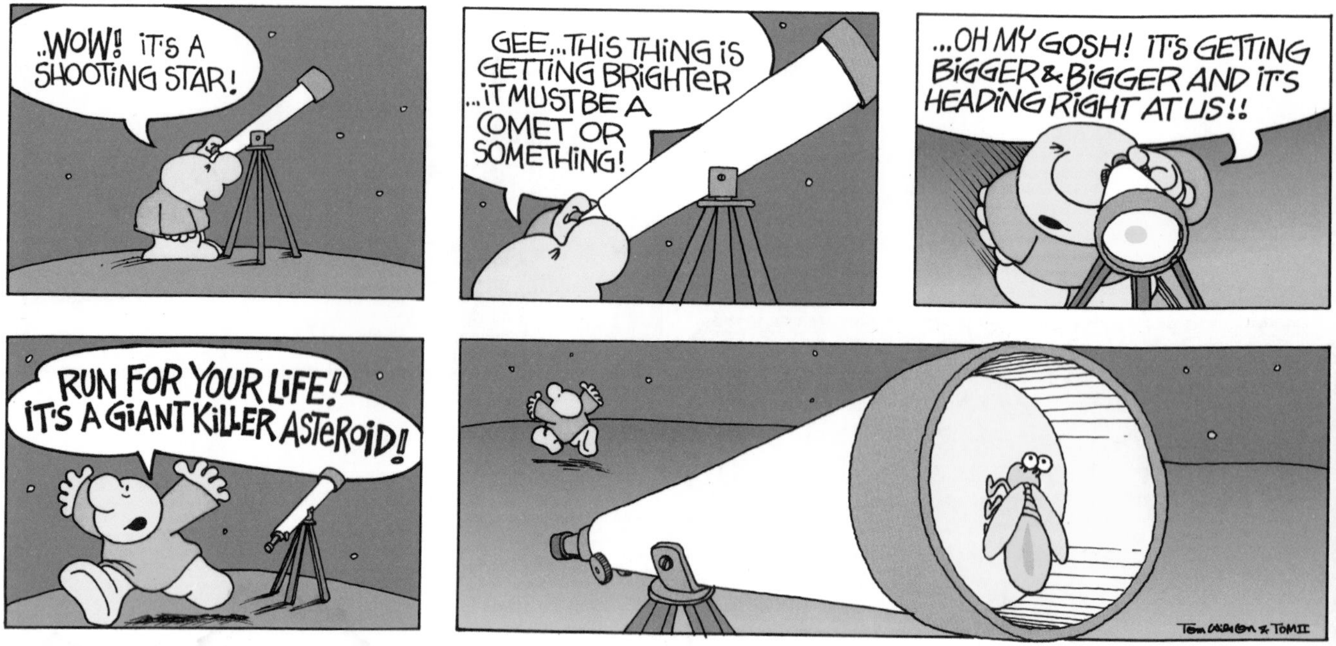
..WOW! IT'S A SHOOTING STAR!
GEE...THIS THING IS GETTING BRIGHTER ...IT MUST BE A COMET OR SOMETHING!
...OH MY GOSH! IT'S GETTING BIGGER & BIGGER AND IT'S HEADING RIGHT AT US!!
RUN FOR YOUR LIFE! IT'S A GIANT KILLER ASTEROID!

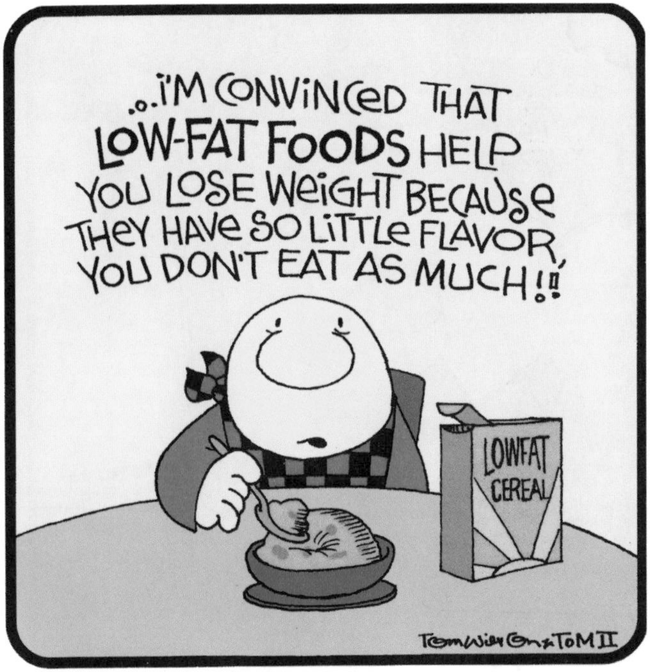
..i'M CONVINCED THAT LOW-FAT FOODS HELP YOU LOSE WEIGHT BECAUSE THEY HAVE SO LITTLE FLAVOR, YOU DON'T EAT AS MUCH!!
LOWFAT CEREAL
Tom Wilson & TOM II

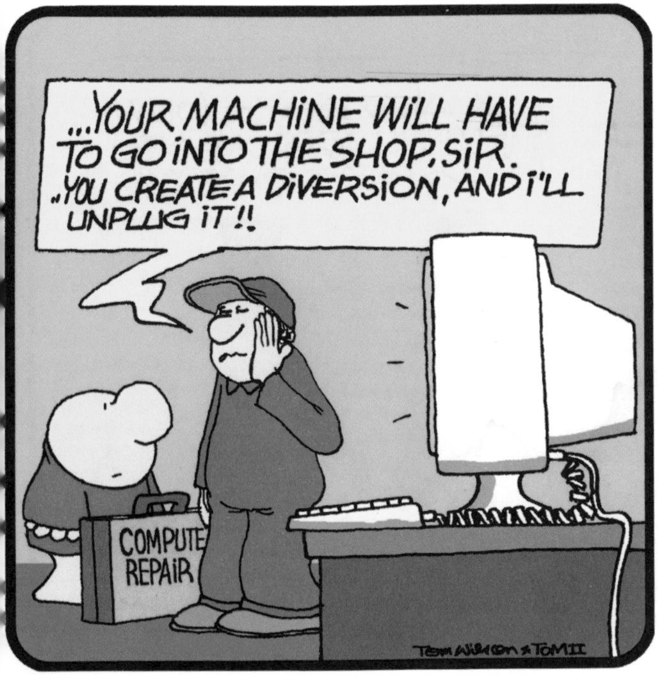
...YOUR MACHINE WILL HAVE TO GO INTO THE SHOP, SIR. ..YOU CREATE A DIVERSION, AND I'LL UNPLUG IT!!
COMPUTE REPAIR
Tom Wilson & TOM II

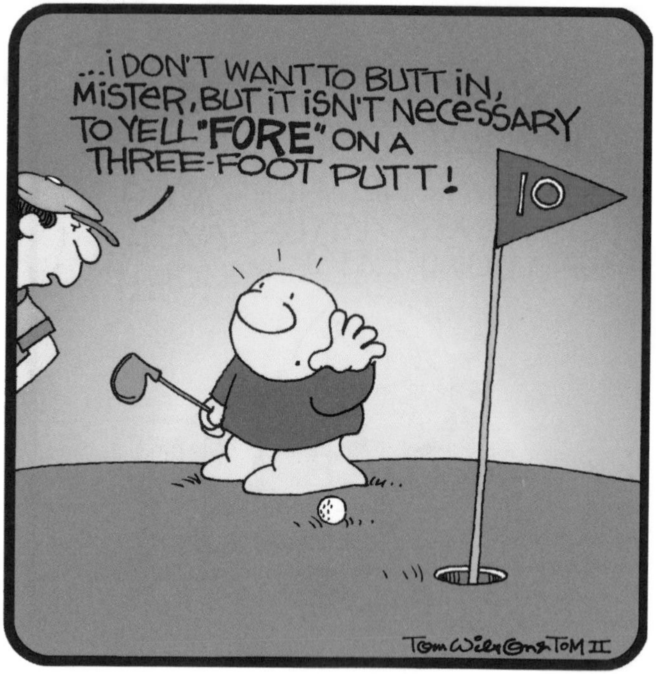
...I DON'T WANT TO BUTT IN, MISTER, BUT IT ISN'T NECESSARY TO YELL "FORE" ON A THREE-FOOT PUTT!
10
Tom Wilson & TOM II

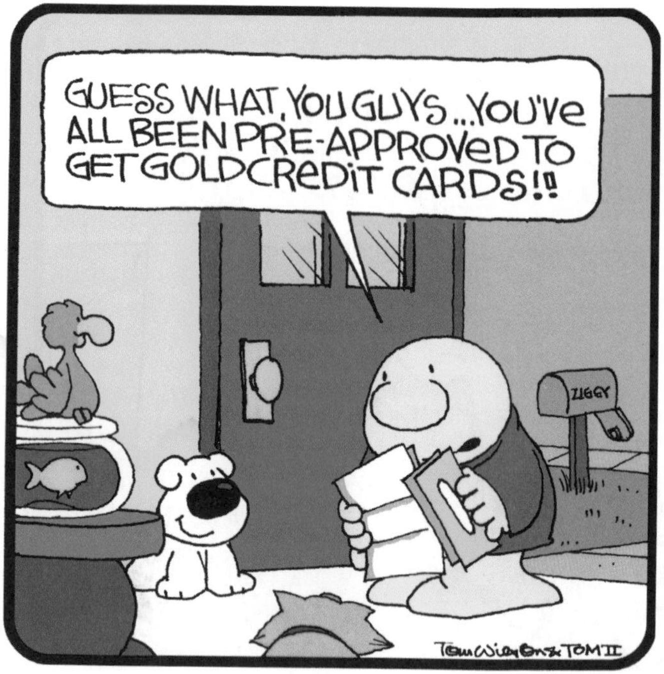
GUESS WHAT, YOU GUYS...YOU'VE ALL BEEN PRE-APPROVED TO GET GOLD CREDIT CARDS!!
ZIGGY
Tom Wilson & TOM II

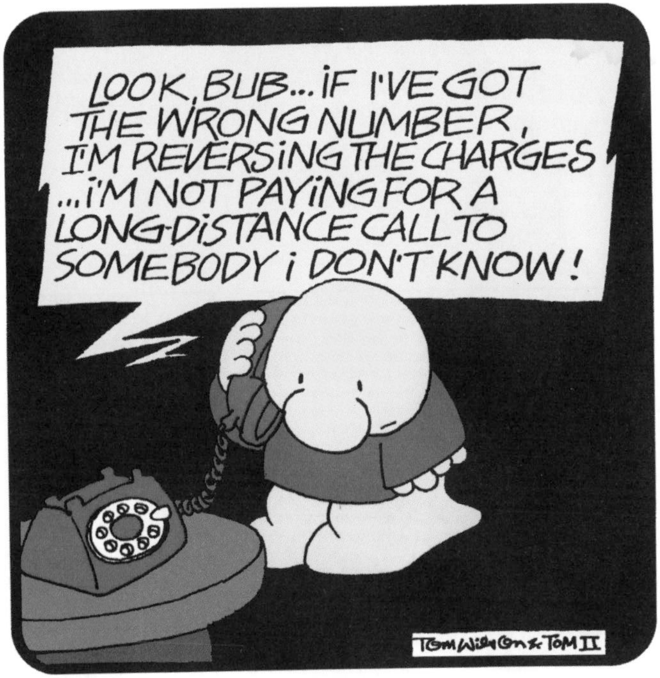
LOOK, BUB... IF I'VE GOT THE WRONG NUMBER, I'M REVERSING THE CHARGES ...I'M NOT PAYING FOR A LONG-DISTANCE CALL TO SOMEBODY I DON'T KNOW!
TOM WILSON & TOM II

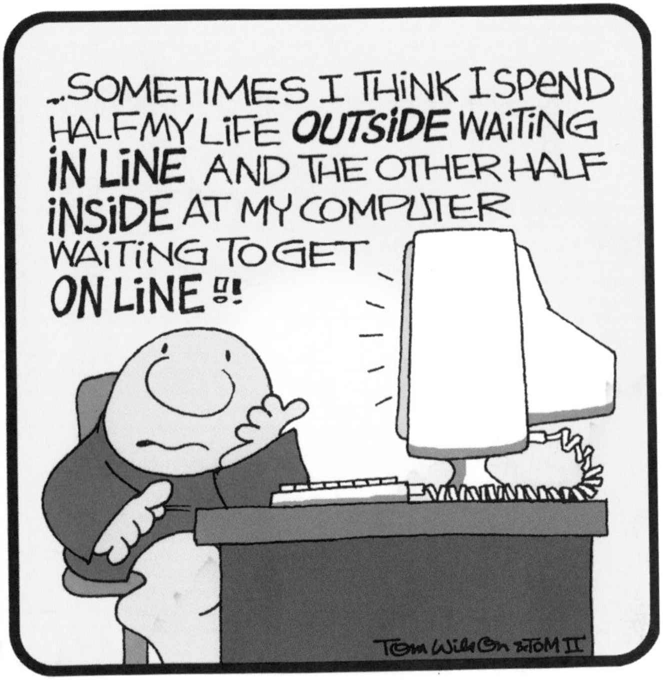
...SOMETIMES I THINK I SPEND HALF MY LIFE OUTSIDE WAITING IN LINE AND THE OTHER HALF INSIDE AT MY COMPUTER WAITING TO GET ON LINE!!
TOM WILSON & TOM II

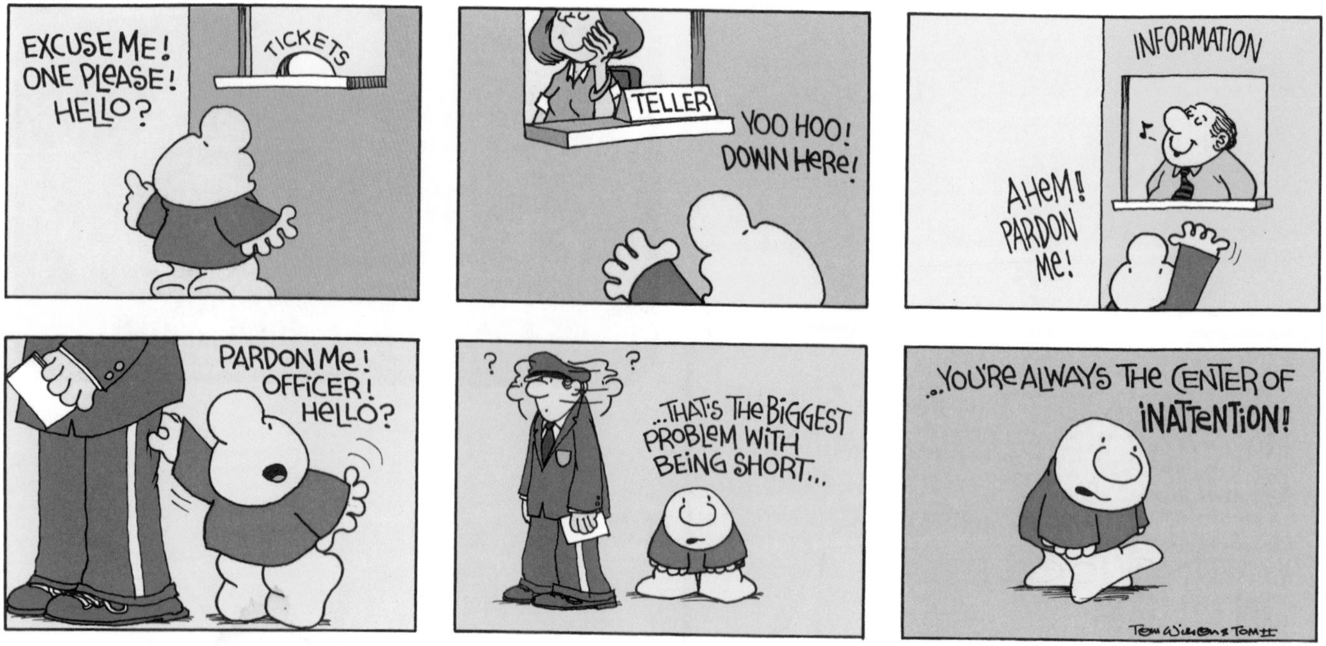
EXCUSE ME! ONE PLEASE! HELLO?
TICKETS
TELLER
YOO HOO! DOWN HERE!
INFORMATION
AHEM!! PARDON ME!
PARDON ME! OFFICER! HELLO?
?
?
...THAT'S THE BIGGEST PROBLEM WITH BEING SHORT...
...YOU'RE ALWAYS THE CENTER OF INATTENTION!

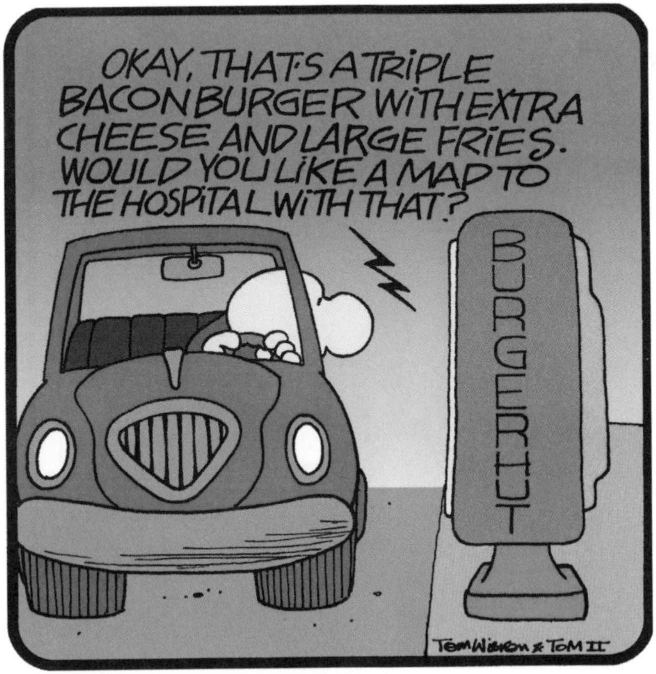
OKAY, THAT'S A TRIPLE BACON BURGER WITH EXTRA CHEESE AND LARGE FRIES. WOULD YOU LIKE A MAP TO THE HOSPITAL WITH THAT?
BURGER HUT
TOM WILSON & TOM II

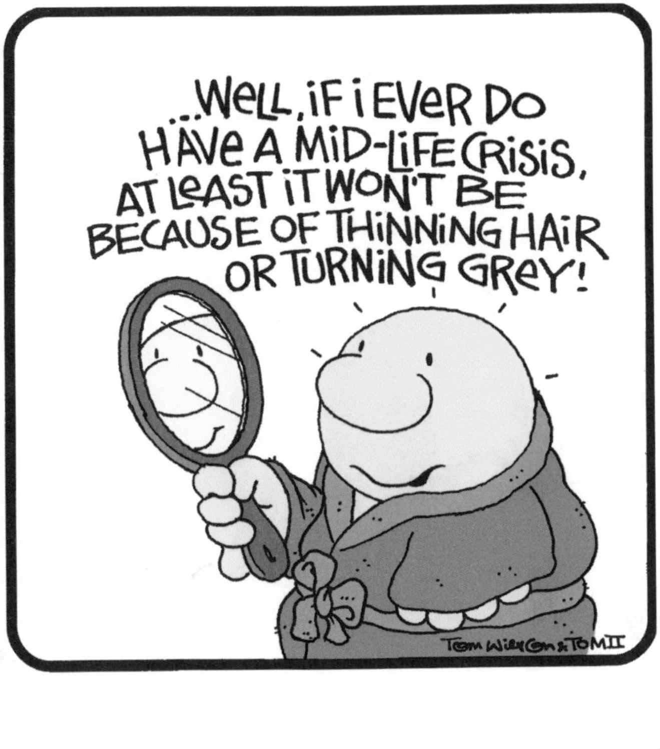
...WELL, IF I EVER DO HAVE A MID-LIFE CRISIS, AT LEAST IT WON'T BE BECAUSE OF THINNING HAIR OR TURNING GREY!
TOM WILSON & TOM II

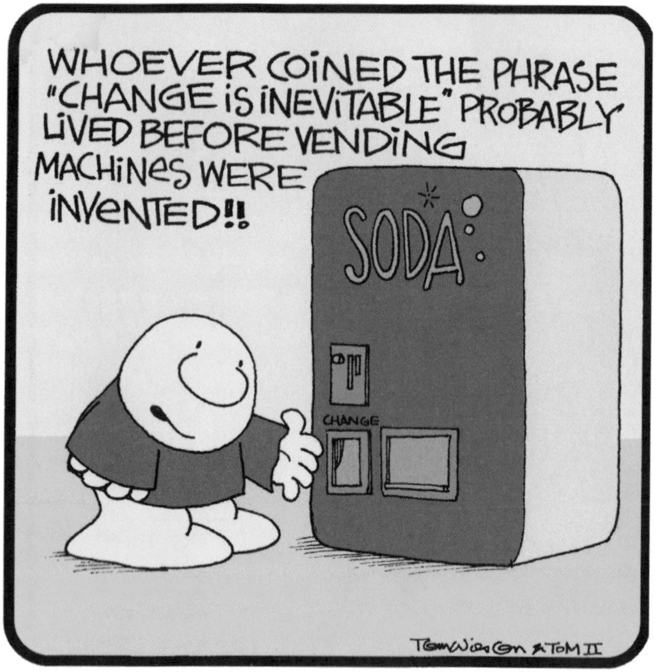
WHOEVER COINED THE PHRASE "CHANGE IS INEVITABLE" PROBABLY LIVED BEFORE VENDING MACHINES WERE INVENTED!!
SODA
CHANGE
TOM WILSON & TOM II

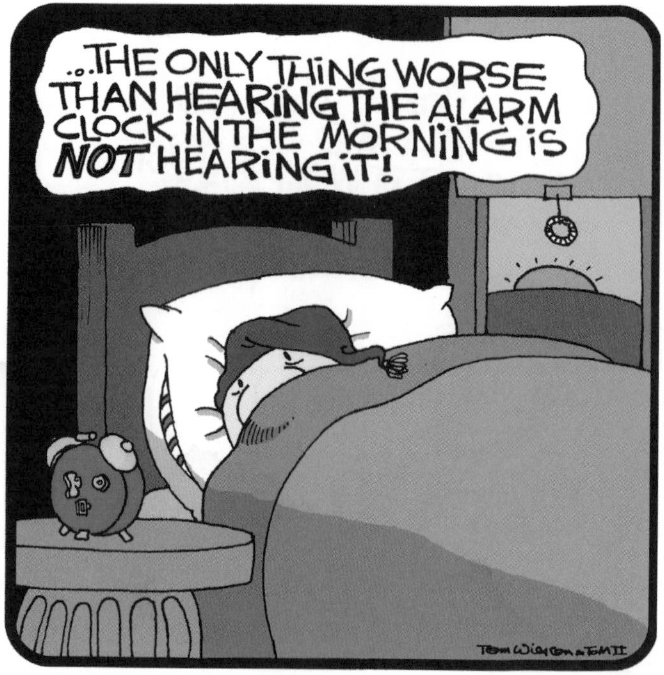
...THE ONLY THING WORSE THAN HEARING THE ALARM CLOCK IN THE MORNING IS *NOT* HEARING IT!
TOM WILSON & TOM II

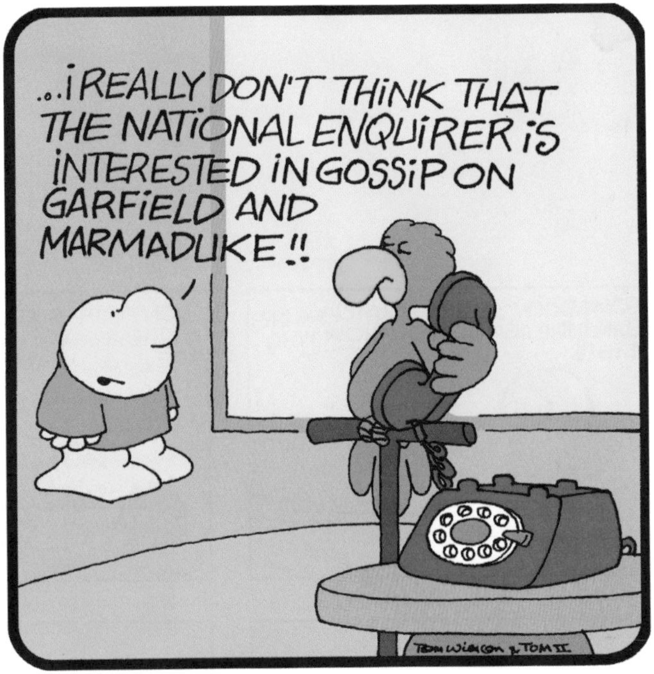
...I REALLY DON'T THINK THAT THE NATIONAL ENQUIRER IS INTERESTED IN GOSSIP ON GARFIELD AND MARMADUKE!!
Tom Wilson & TOM II

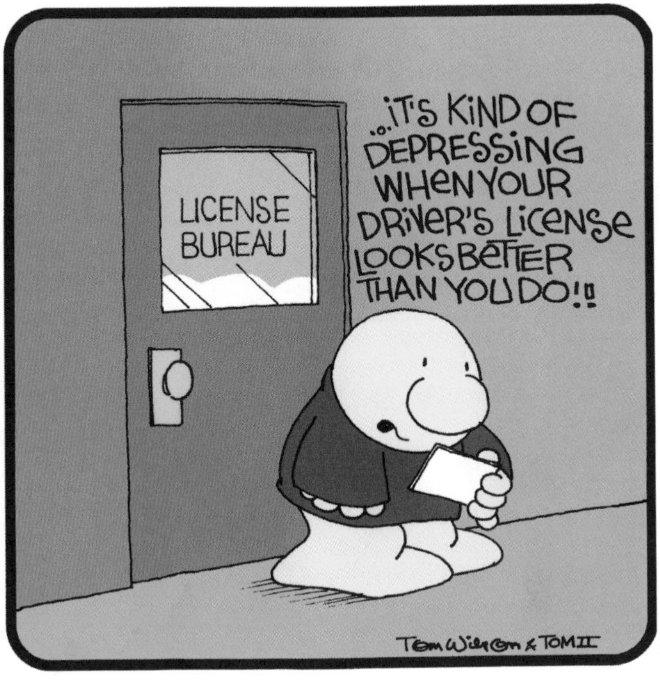
LICENSE BUREAU
...IT'S KIND OF DEPRESSING WHEN YOUR DRIVER'S LICENSE LOOKS BETTER THAN YOU DO!!
Tom Wilson & TOM II

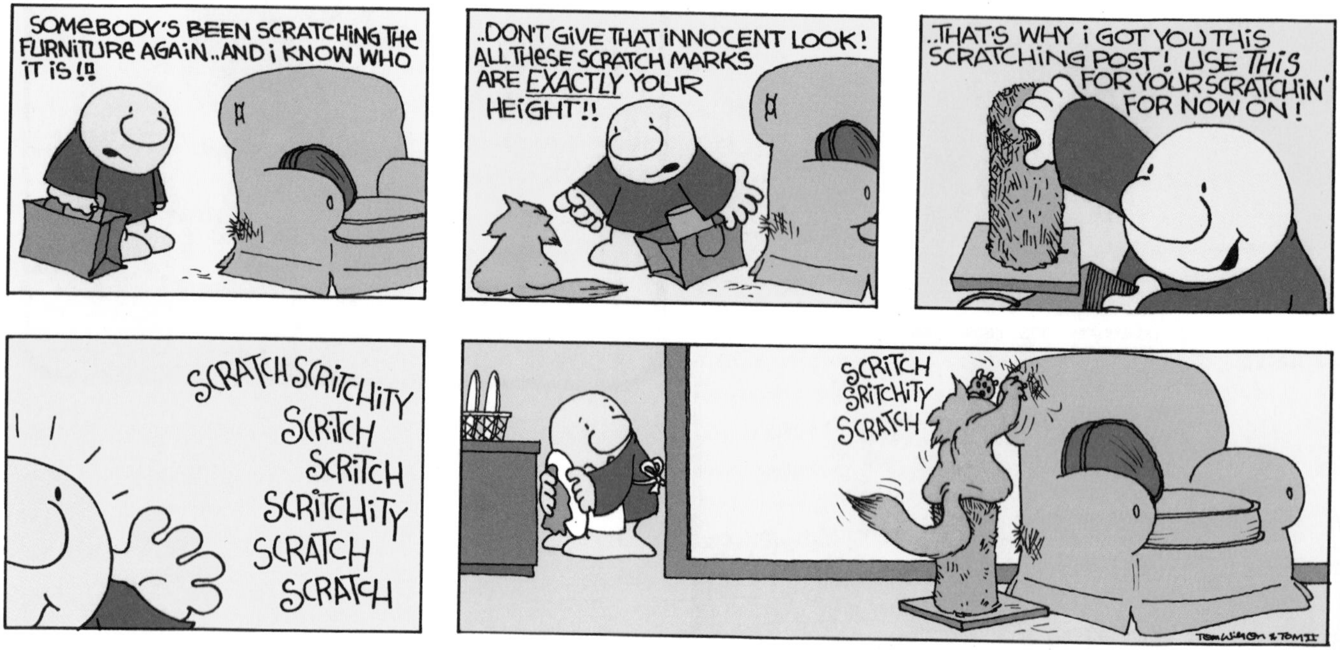
SOMEBODY'S BEEN SCRATCHING THE FURNITURE AGAIN..AND i KNOW WHO iT iS !!
..DON'T GiVE THAT iNNOCENT LOOK! ALL THESE SCRATCH MARKS ARE EXACTLY YOUR HEiGHT!!
..THAT'S WHY i GOT YOU THiS SCRATCHiNG POST! USE THiS FOR YOUR SCRATCHiN' FOR NOW ON!
SCRATCH SCRiTCHiTY SCRiTCH SCRiTCH SCRiTCHiTY SCRATCH SCRATCH
SCRiTCH SRiTCHiTY SCRATCH

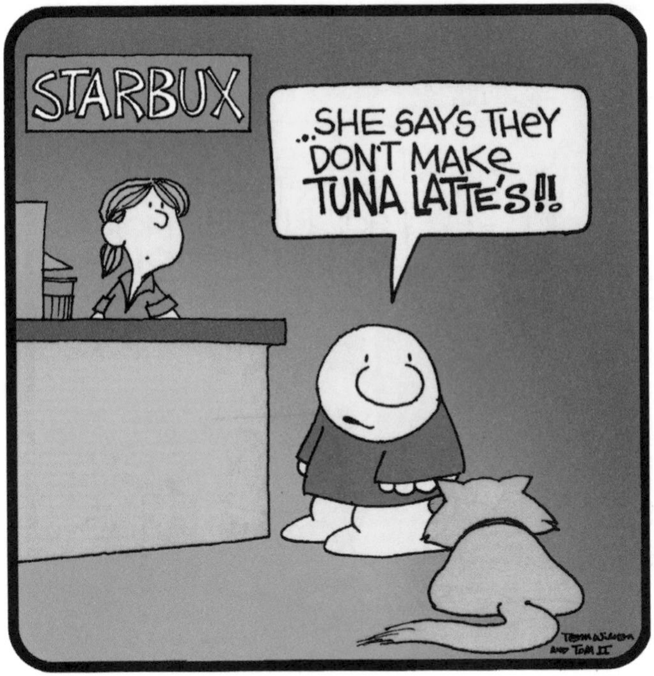
STARBUX
..SHE SAYS THEY DON'T MAKE TUNA LATTE'S!!

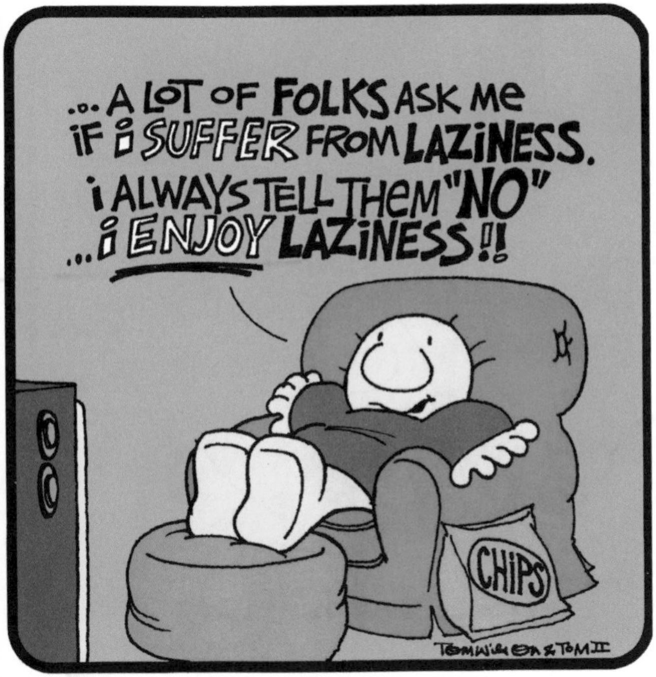
...A LOT OF FOLKS ASK ME IF I SUFFER FROM LAZINESS. I ALWAYS TELL THEM "NO" ...I ENJOY LAZINESS!!
CHIPS

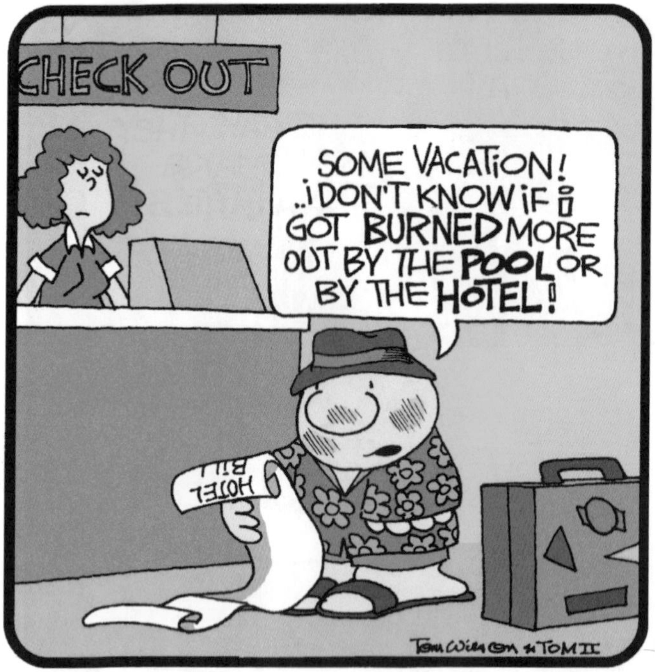
CHECK OUT
SOME VACATION! ..I DON'T KNOW IF I GOT BURNED MORE OUT BY THE POOL OR BY THE HOTEL!
HOTEL BILL
Tom Wilson &TOM II

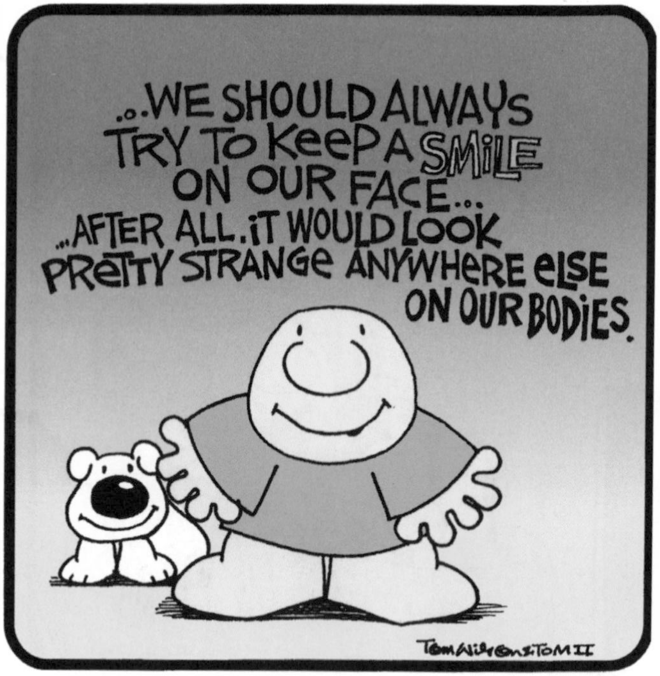
..WE SHOULD ALWAYS TRY TO KEEP A SMILE ON OUR FACE... ...AFTER ALL, IT WOULD LOOK PRETTY STRANGE ANYWHERE ELSE ON OUR BODIES.
Tom Wilson & TOM II

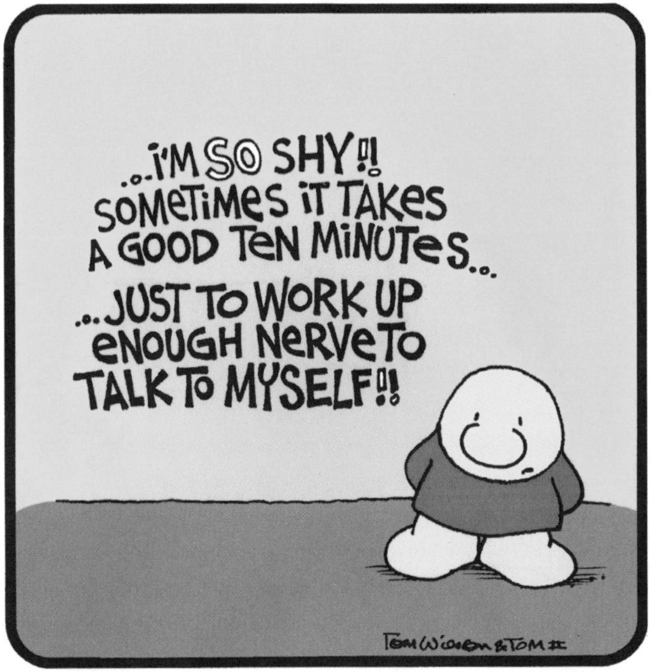
..I'M SO SHY!!
SOMETIMES IT TAKES A GOOD TEN MINUTES...
...JUST TO WORK UP ENOUGH NERVE TO TALK TO MYSELF!!
TOM WILSON & TOM II

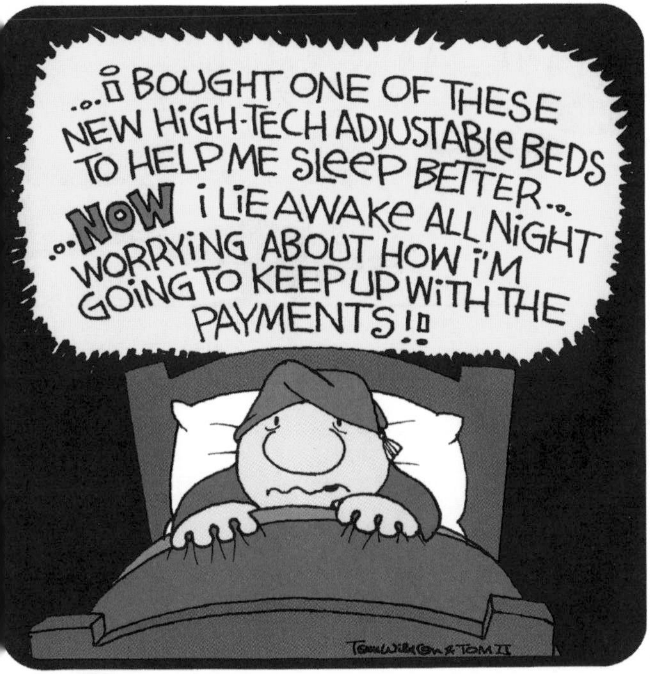
...I BOUGHT ONE OF THESE NEW HIGH-TECH ADJUSTABLE BEDS TO HELP ME SLEEP BETTER...
...NOW I LIE AWAKE ALL NIGHT WORRYING ABOUT HOW I'M GOING TO KEEP UP WITH THE PAYMENTS!!
TOM WILSON & TOM II

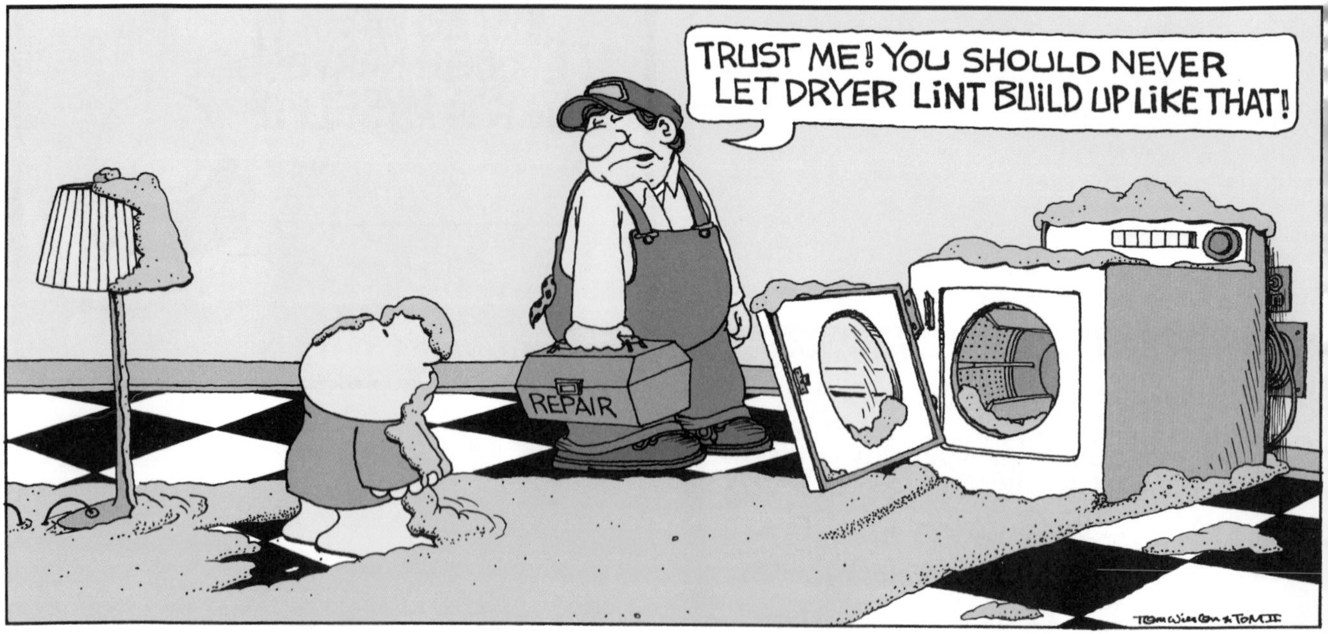
TRUST ME! YOU SHOULD NEVER LET DRYER LINT BUILD UP LIKE THAT!
REPAIR

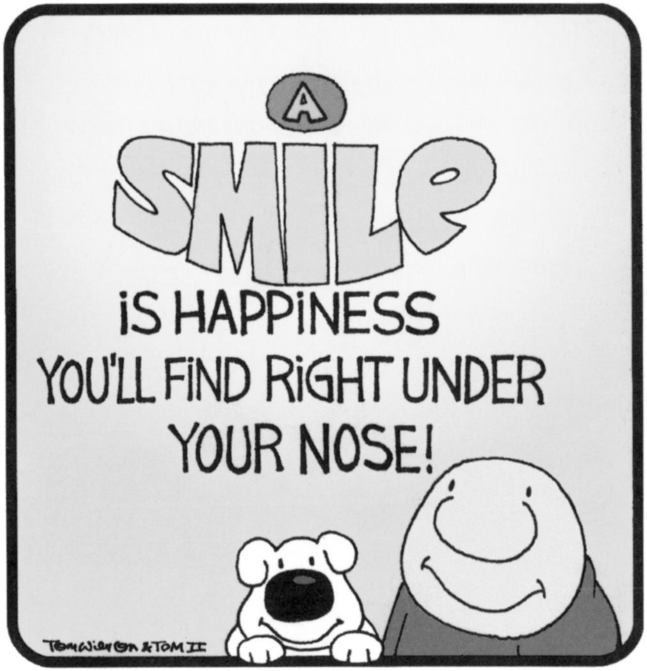
A
SMILE
IS HAPPINESS
YOU'LL FIND RIGHT UNDER
YOUR NOSE!
Tom Wilson & TOM II

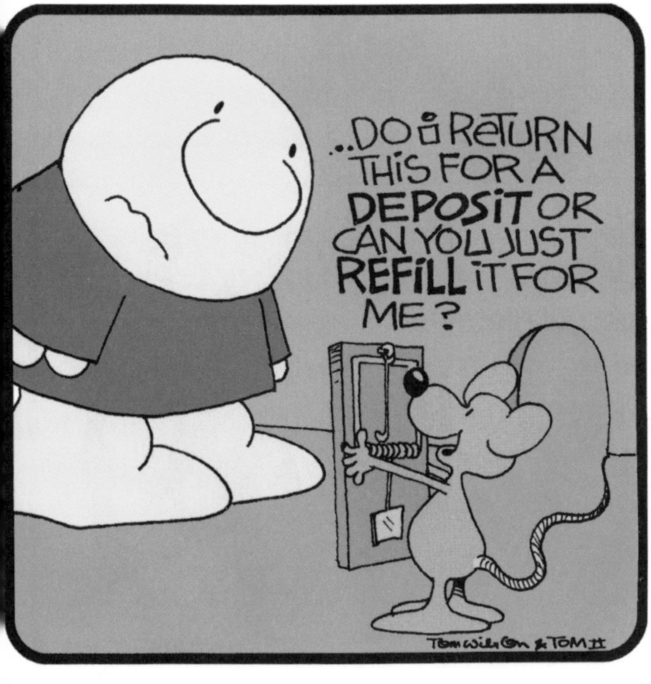
...DO I RETURN THIS FOR A DEPOSIT OR CAN YOU JUST REFILL IT FOR ME?
Tom Wilson & TOM II

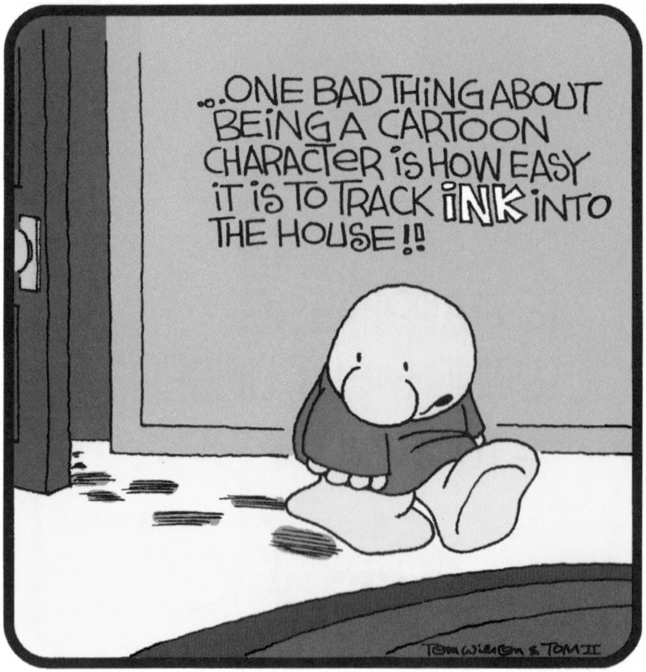
..ONE BAD THING ABOUT BEING A CARTOON CHARACTER IS HOW EASY IT IS TO TRACK INK INTO THE HOUSE!!
TOM WILSON & TOM II

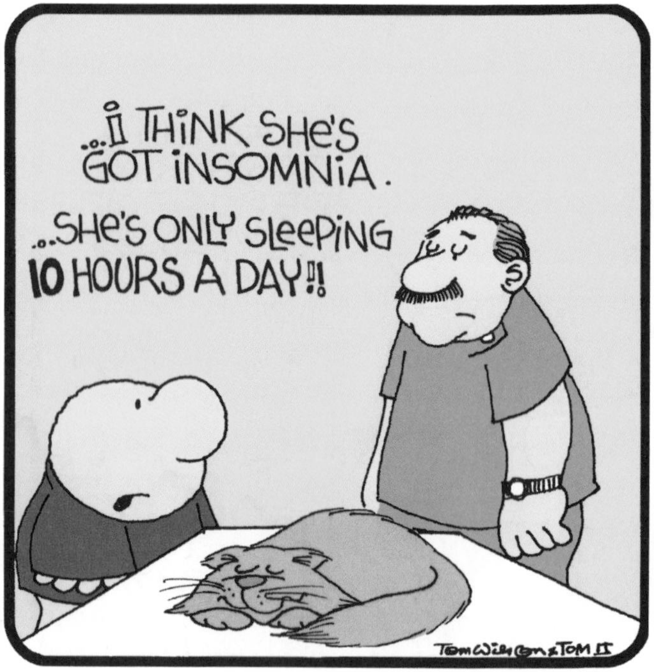
..I THINK SHE'S GOT INSOMNIA.
..SHE'S ONLY SLEEPING 10 HOURS A DAY!!
TOM WILSON & TOM II

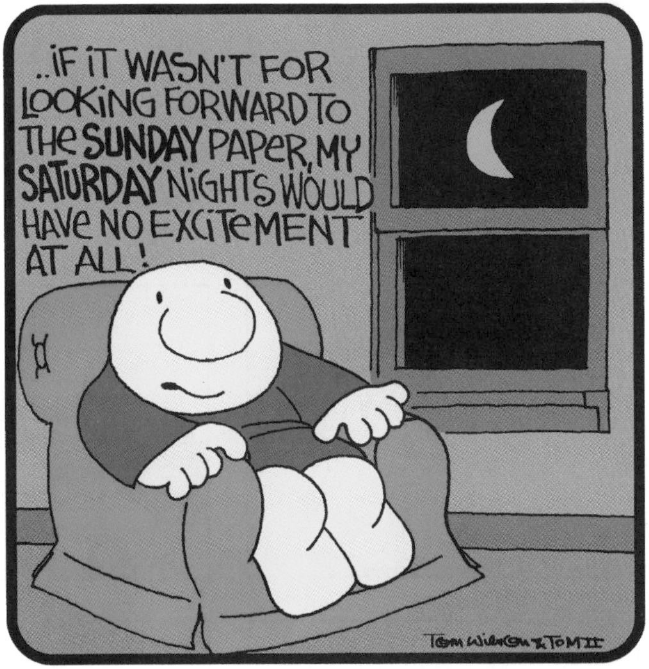
..IF IT WASN'T FOR LOOKING FORWARD TO THE SUNDAY PAPER, MY SATURDAY NIGHTS WOULD HAVE NO EXCITEMENT AT ALL!
TOM WILSON & TOM II

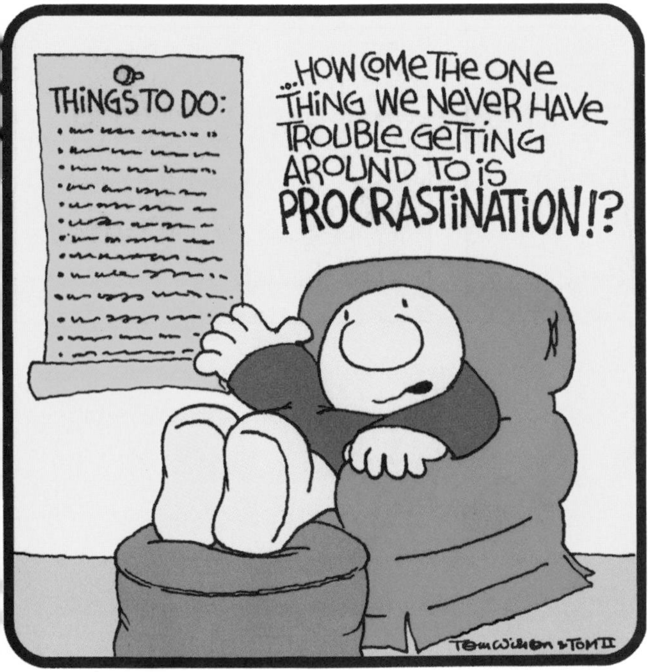
THINGS TO DO:
..HOW COME THE ONE THING WE NEVER HAVE TROUBLE GETTING AROUND TO IS PROCRASTINATION!?
TOM WILSON & TOM II

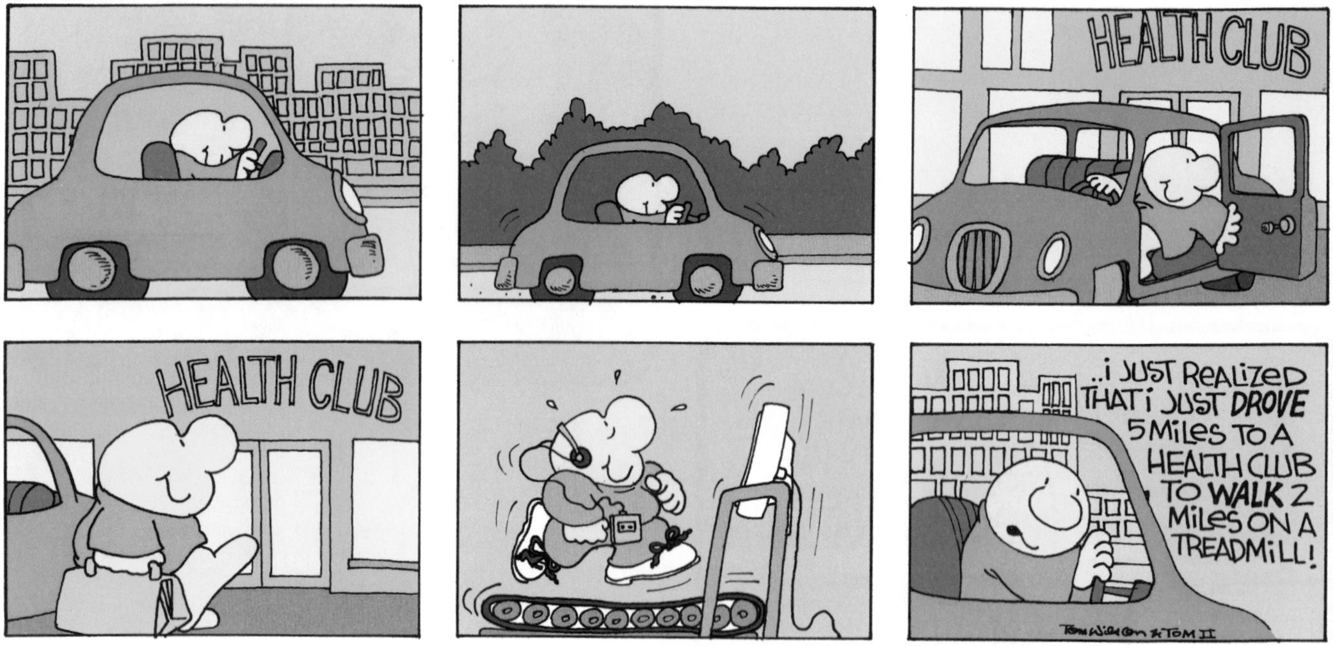
HEALTH CLUB
HEALTH CLUB
..i JUST REALIZED THAT i JUST DROVE 5 MILES TO A HEALTH CLUB TO WALK 2 MILES ON A TREADMILL!
TOM WILSON & TOM II

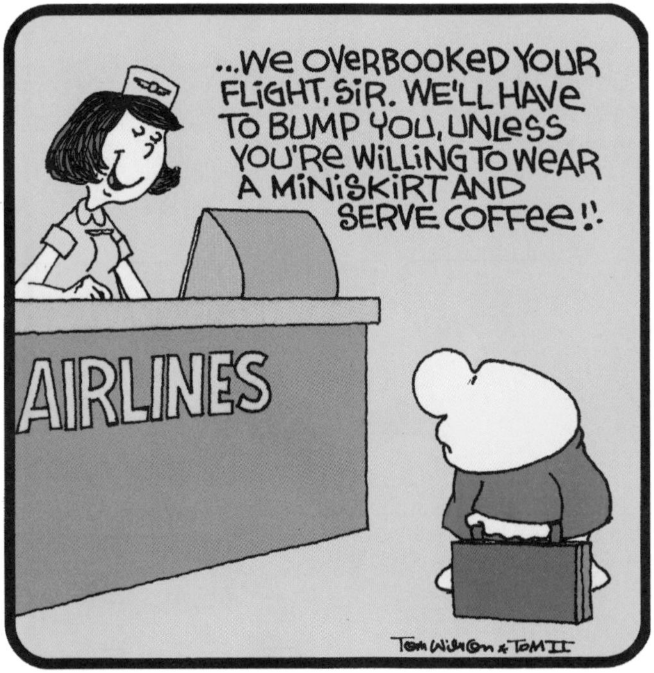
...WE OVERBOOKED YOUR FLIGHT, SIR. WE'LL HAVE TO BUMP YOU, UNLESS YOU'RE WILLING TO WEAR A MINISKIRT AND SERVE COFFEE!!
AIRLINES
TOM WILSON & TOM II

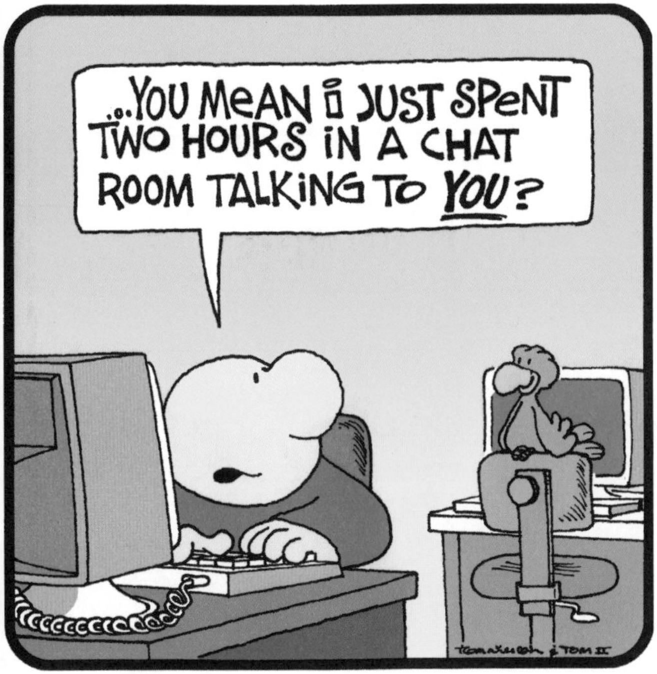
...YOU MEAN I JUST SPENT TWO HOURS IN A CHAT ROOM TALKING TO YOU?
TOM WILSON & TOM II

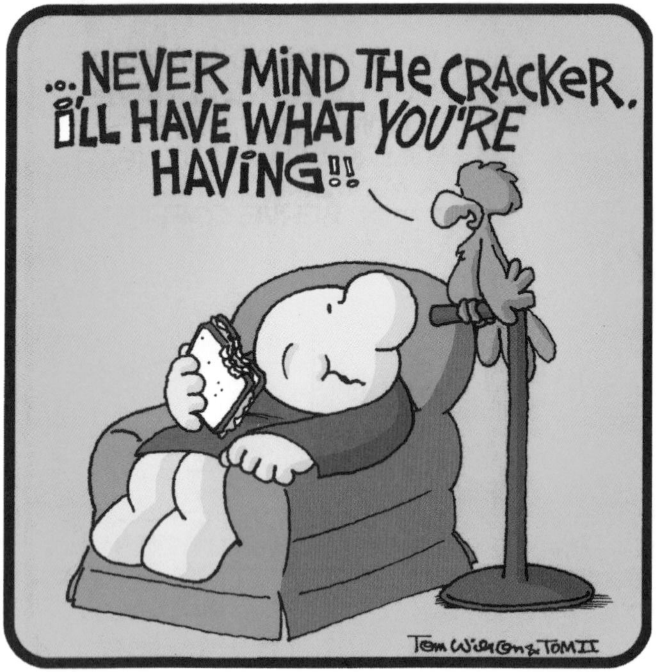
...NEVER MIND THE CRACKER. I'LL HAVE WHAT YOU'RE HAVING!!
Tom Wilson & TOM II

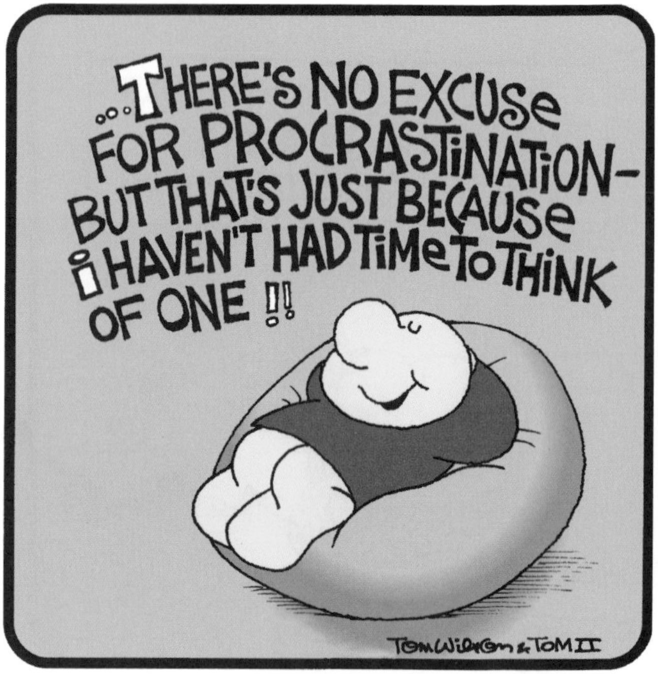
...THERE'S NO EXCUSE FOR PROCRASTINATION- BUT THAT'S JUST BECAUSE I HAVEN'T HAD TIME TO THINK OF ONE !!
Tom Wilson & TOM II

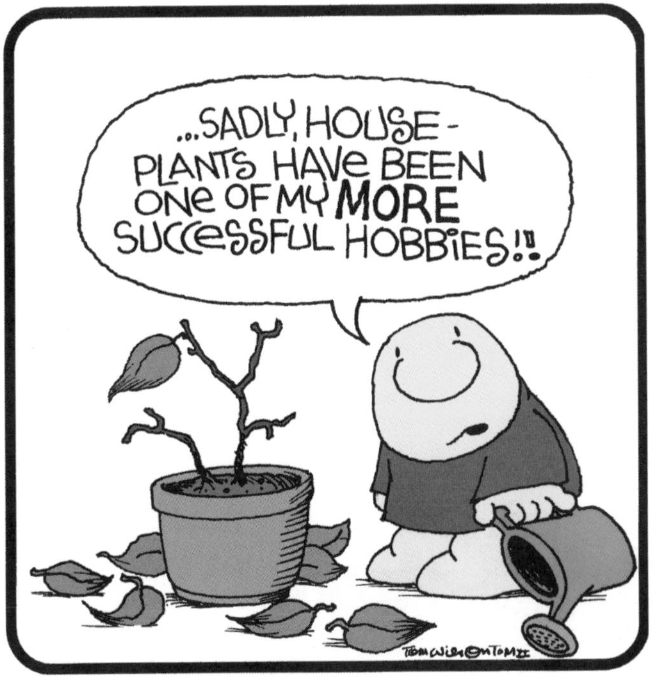
...SADLY, HOUSE-PLANTS HAVE BEEN ONE OF MY MORE SUCCESSFUL HOBBIES!!
TOM WILSON TOM II

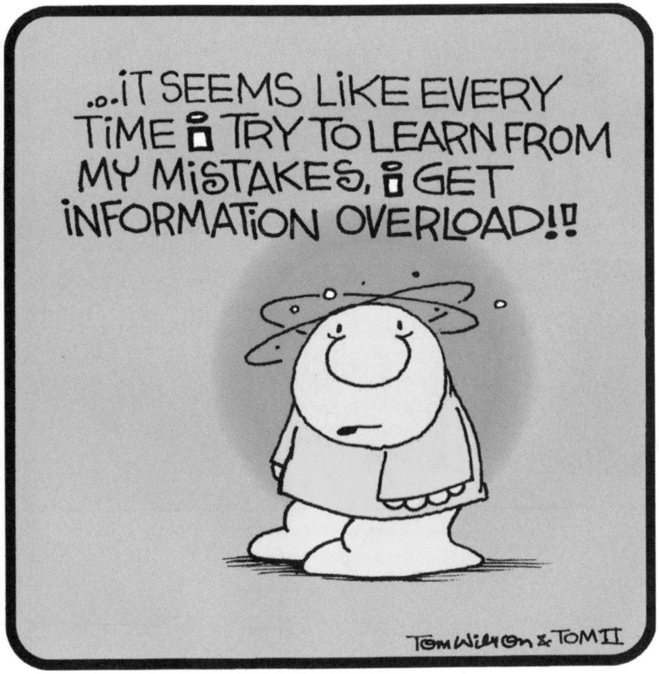
...IT SEEMS LIKE EVERY TIME I TRY TO LEARN FROM MY MISTAKES, I GET INFORMATION OVERLOAD!!
TOM WILSON & TOM II

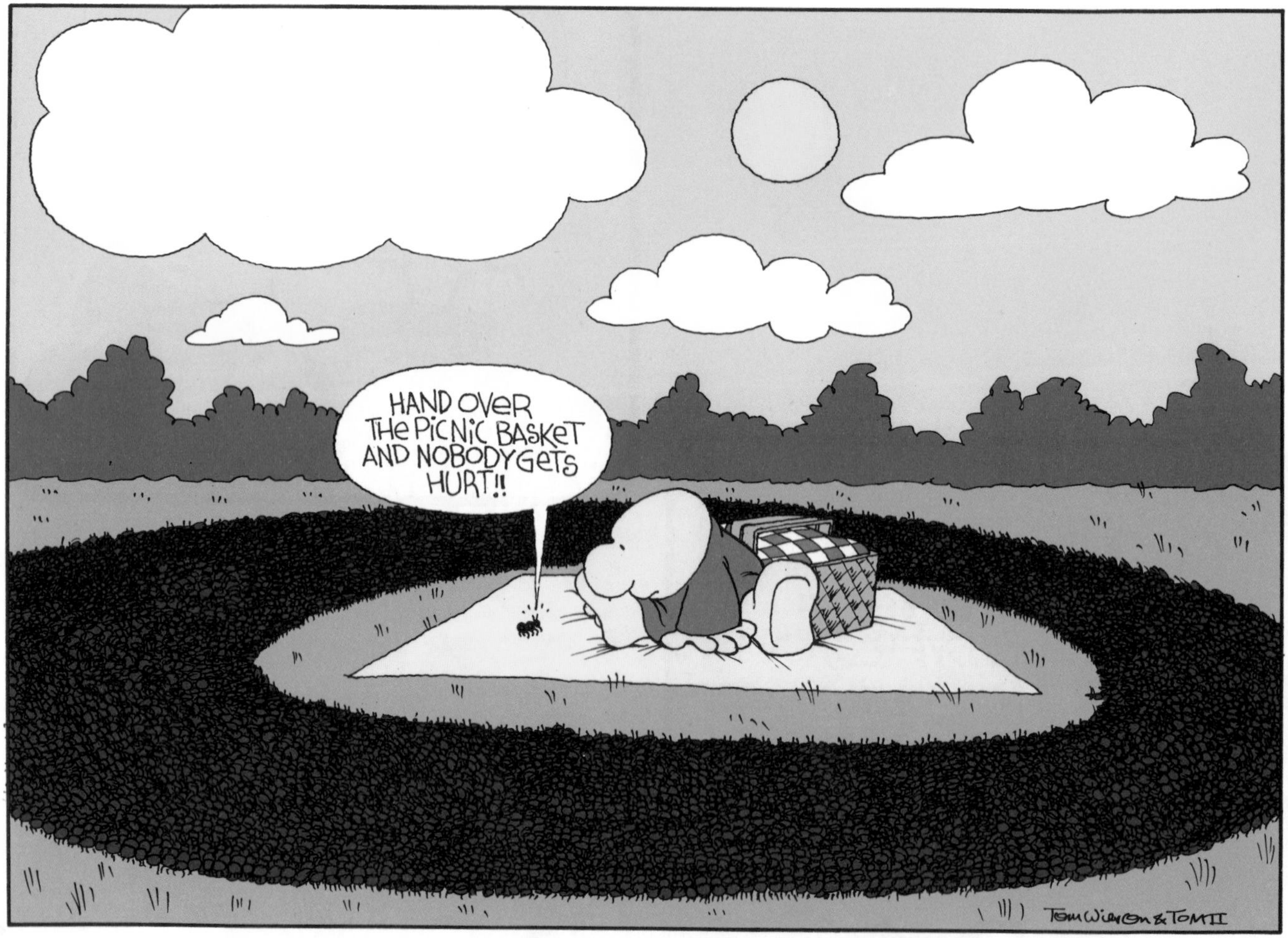
HAND OVER THE PICNIC BASKET AND NOBODY GETS HURT!!
TOM WILSON & TOM II

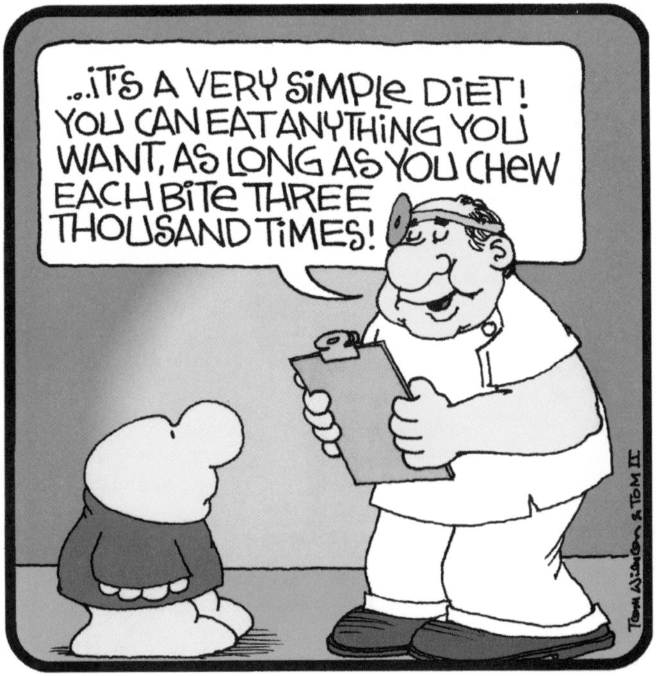
..IT'S A VERY SIMPLE DIET! YOU CAN EAT ANYTHING YOU WANT, AS LONG AS YOU CHEW EACH BITE THREE THOUSAND TIMES!
Tom Wilson & Tom II

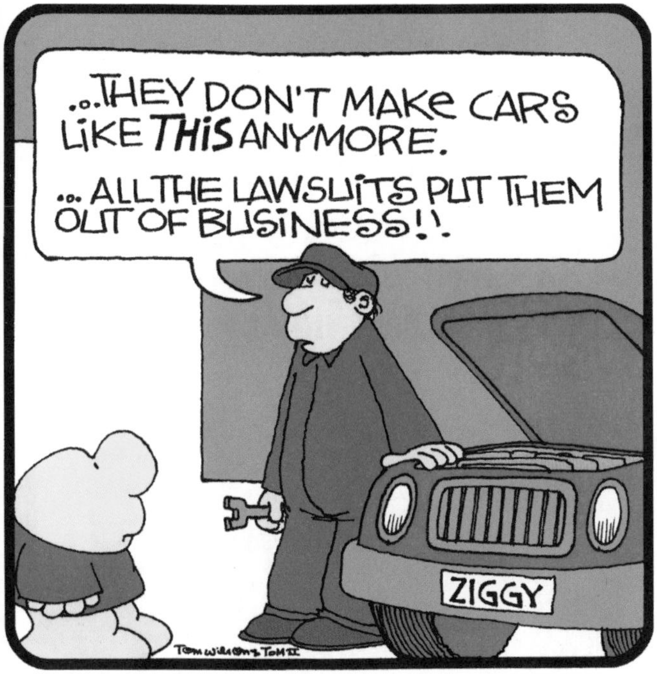
...THEY DON'T MAKE CARS LIKE THIS ANYMORE.
... ALL THE LAWSUITS PUT THEM OUT OF BUSINESS!!
ZIGGY
Tom Wilson & Tom II

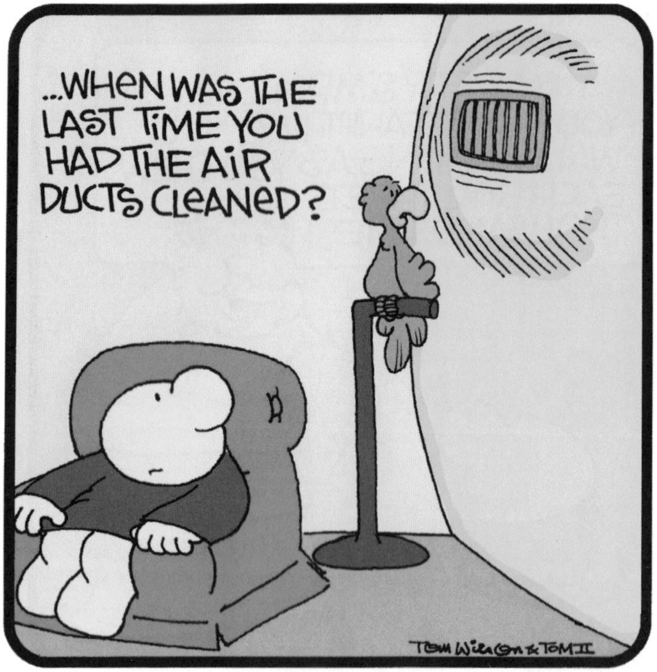
...WHEN WAS THE LAST TIME YOU HAD THE AIR DUCTS CLEANED?
TOM WILSON & TOM II

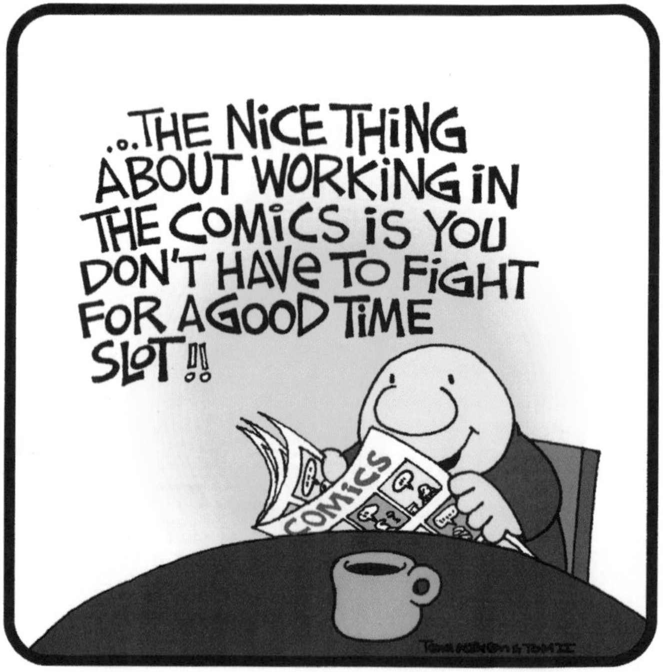
...THE NICE THING ABOUT WORKING IN THE COMICS IS YOU DON'T HAVE TO FIGHT FOR A GOOD TIME SLOT!!
COMICS

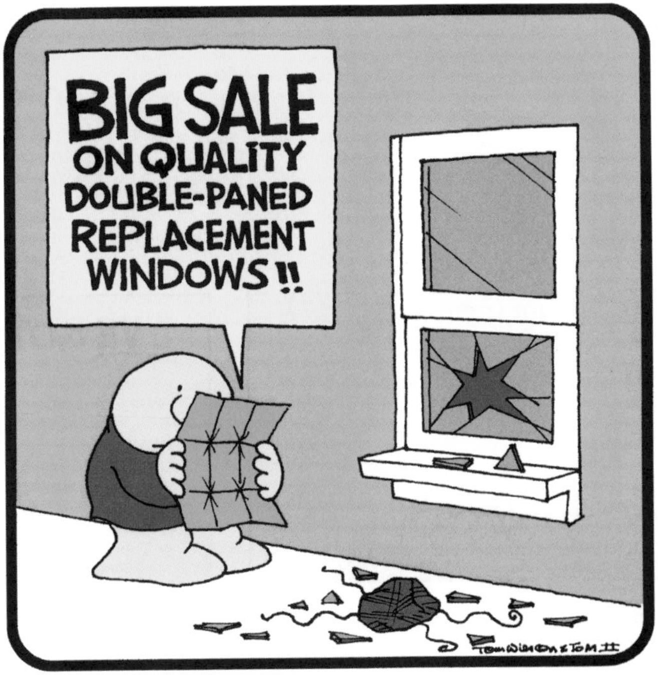
BIG SALE ON QUALITY DOUBLE-PANED REPLACEMENT WINDOWS!!
TOM WILSON & TOM II

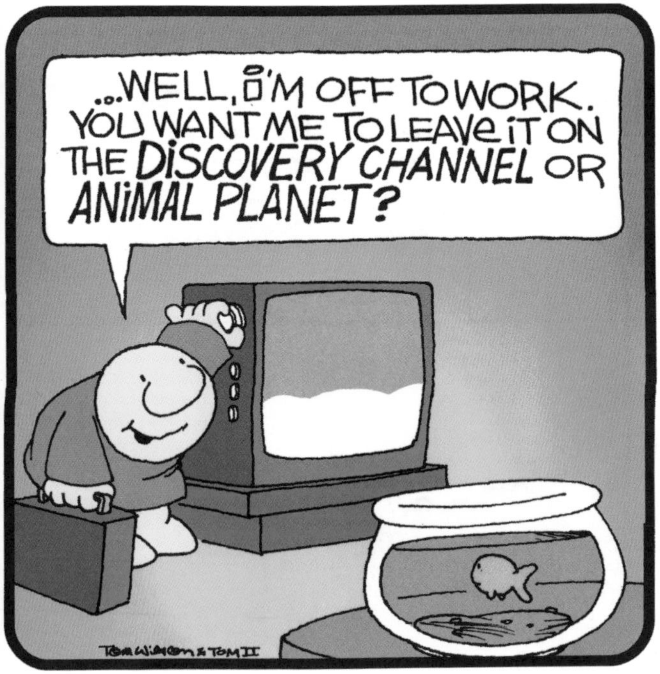
...WELL, I'M OFF TO WORK. YOU WANT ME TO LEAVE IT ON THE *DISCOVERY CHANNEL* OR *ANIMAL PLANET*?
TOM WILSON & TOM II

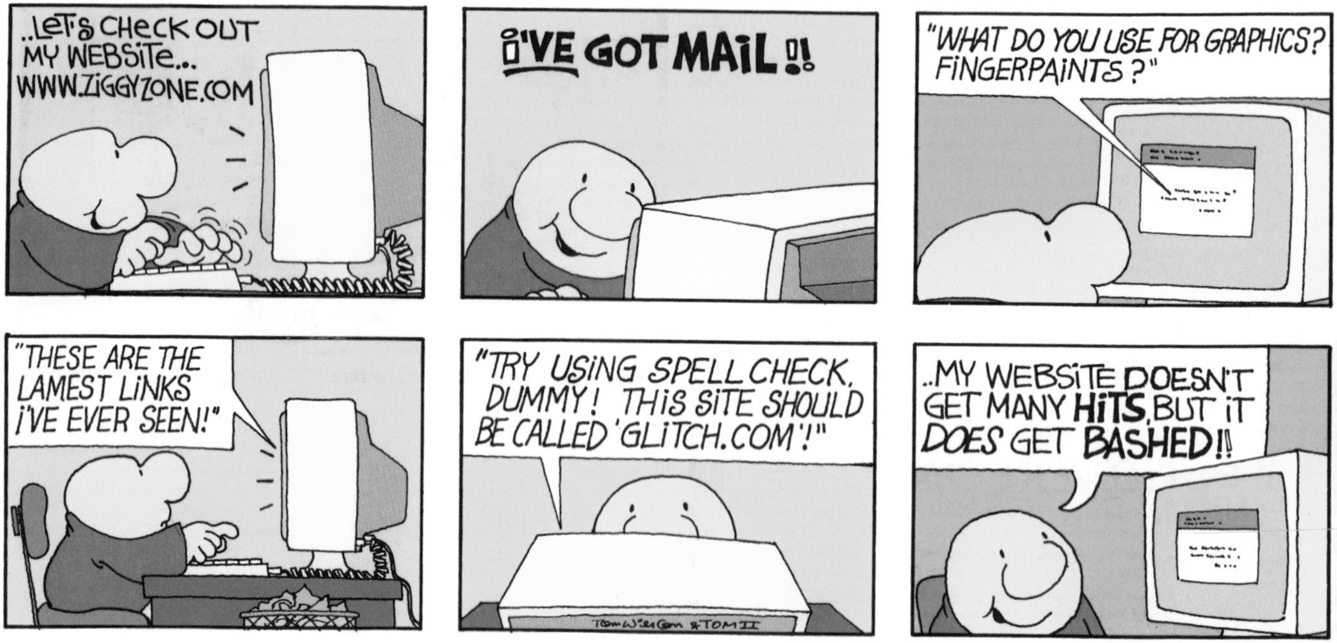
..LET'S CHECK OUT MY WEBSITE... WWW.ZIGGYZONE.COM
I'VE GOT MAIL!!
"WHAT DO YOU USE FOR GRAPHICS? FINGERPAINTS?"
"THESE ARE THE LAMEST LINKS I'VE EVER SEEN!"
"TRY USING SPELL CHECK, DUMMY! THIS SITE SHOULD BE CALLED 'GLITCH.COM'!"
TOM WILSON & TOM II
..MY WEBSITE DOESN'T GET MANY HITS, BUT IT DOES GET BASHED!!

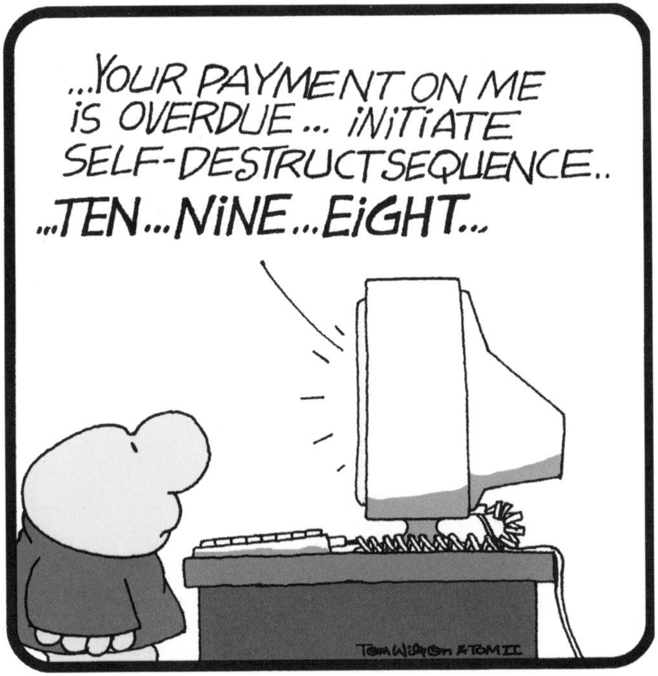
...YOUR PAYMENT ON ME IS OVERDUE ... INITIATE SELF-DESTRUCT SEQUENCE..
...TEN...NINE...EIGHT...
Tom Wilson & TOM II

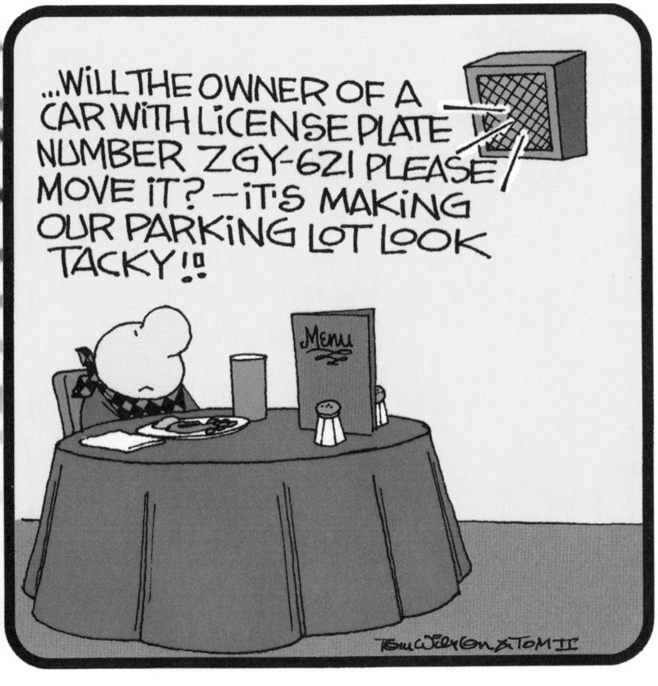
...WILL THE OWNER OF A CAR WITH LICENSE PLATE NUMBER ZGY-621 PLEASE MOVE IT? —IT'S MAKING OUR PARKING LOT LOOK TACKY!!
Menu
Tom Wilson & TOM II

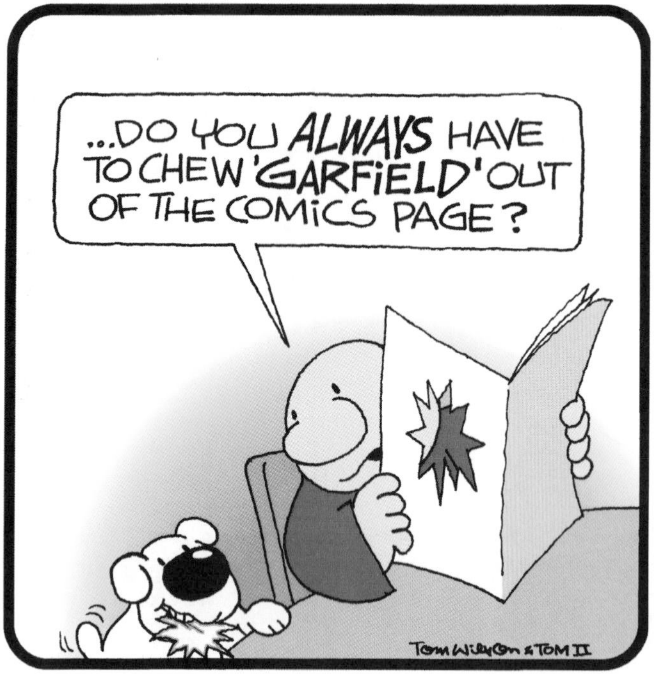
...DO YOU ALWAYS HAVE TO CHEW 'GARFIELD' OUT OF THE COMICS PAGE?
TOM WILSON & TOM II

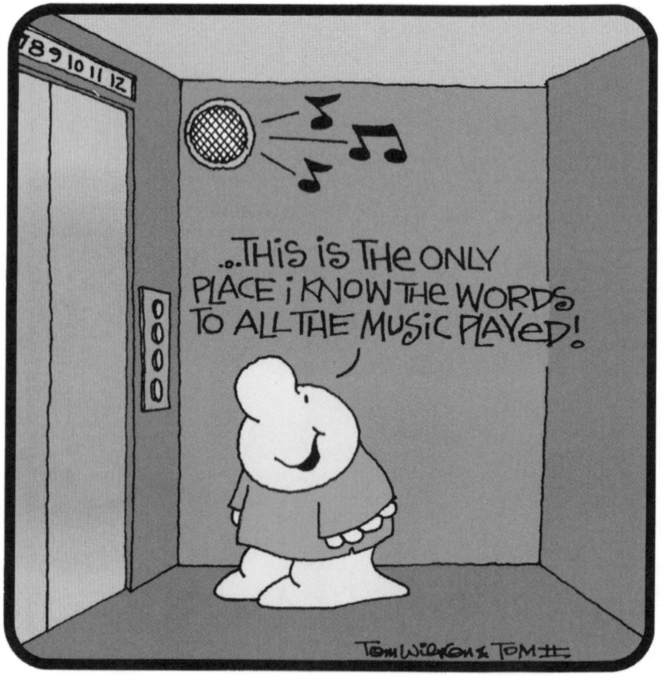
7 8 9 10 11 12
...THIS IS THE ONLY PLACE I KNOW THE WORDS TO ALL THE MUSIC PLAYED!
TOM WILSON & TOM II

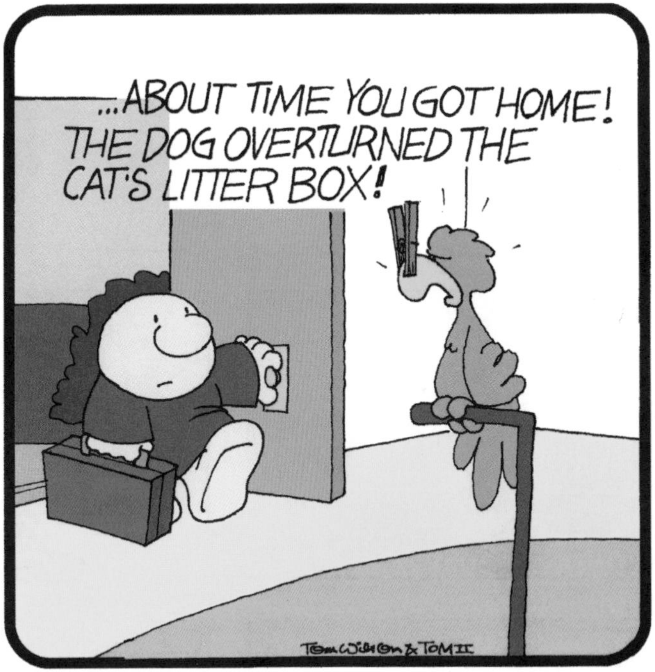
...ABOUT TIME YOU GOT HOME! THE DOG OVERTURNED THE CAT'S LITTER BOX!
TOM WILSON & TOM II

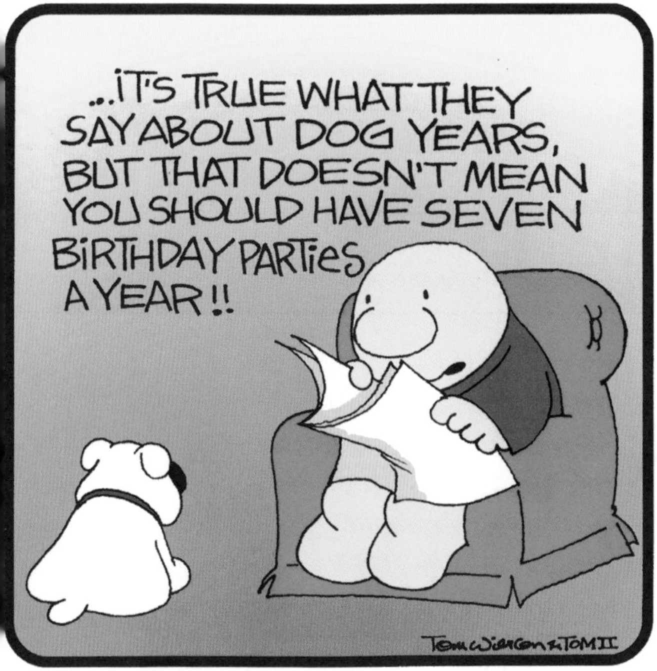
...IT'S TRUE WHAT THEY SAY ABOUT DOG YEARS, BUT THAT DOESN'T MEAN YOU SHOULD HAVE SEVEN BIRTHDAY PARTIES A YEAR!!
TOM WILSON & TOM II

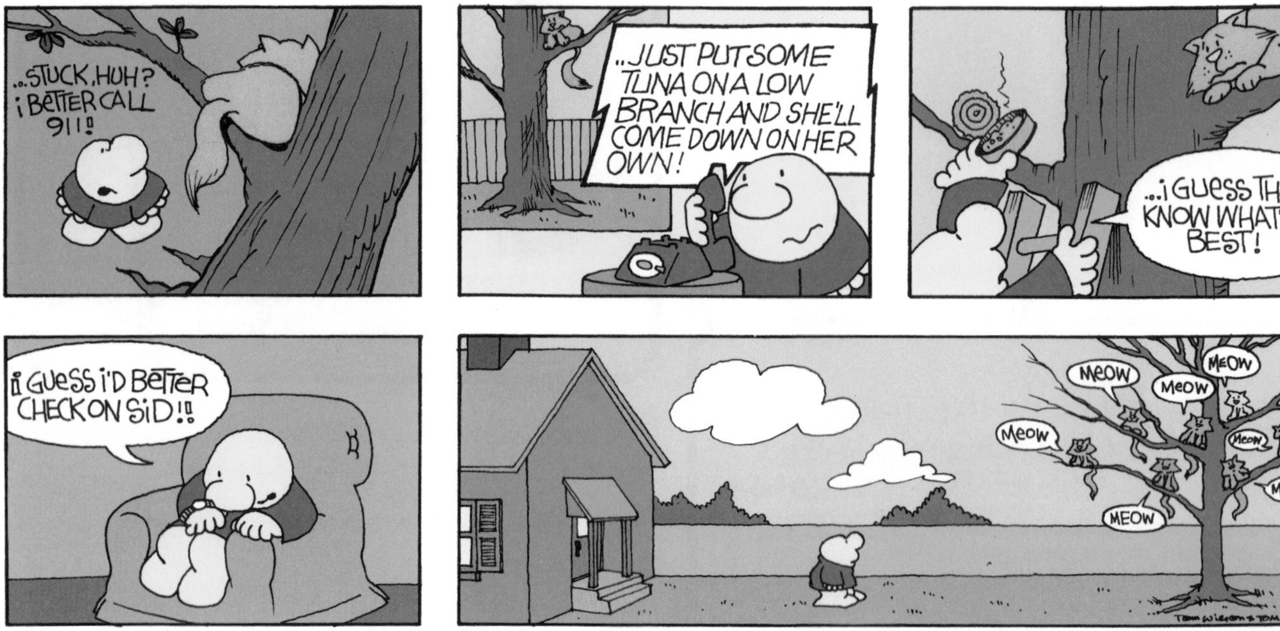
..STUCK, HUH? i BETTER CALL 911!!
..JUST PUT SOME TUNA ON A LOW BRANCH AND SHE'LL COME DOWN ON HER OWN!
..i GUESS THEY KNOW WHAT'S BEST!
i GUESS i'D BETTER CHECK ON SiD!!
MEOW
MEOW
MEOW
MEOW
MEOW
MEOW
MEOW
TOM WILSON & TOM II

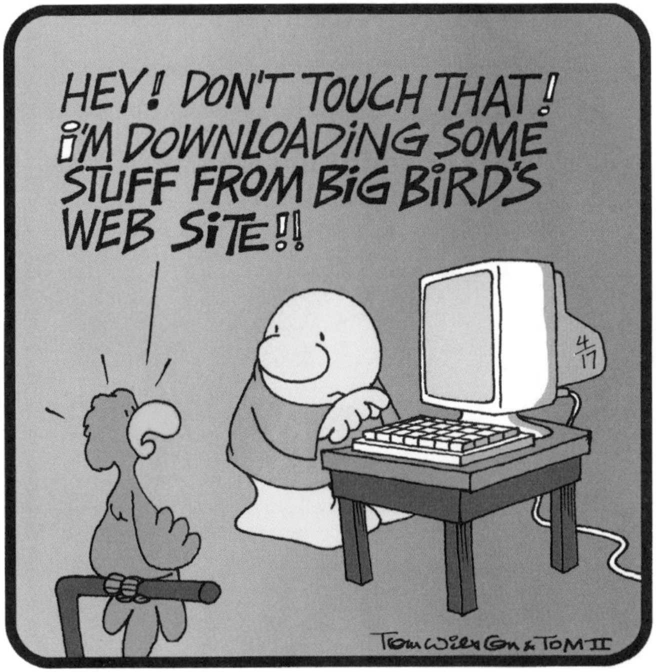
HEY! DON'T TOUCH THAT! I'M DOWNLOADING SOME STUFF FROM BIG BIRD'S WEB SITE!!
4/17
TOM WILSON & TOM II

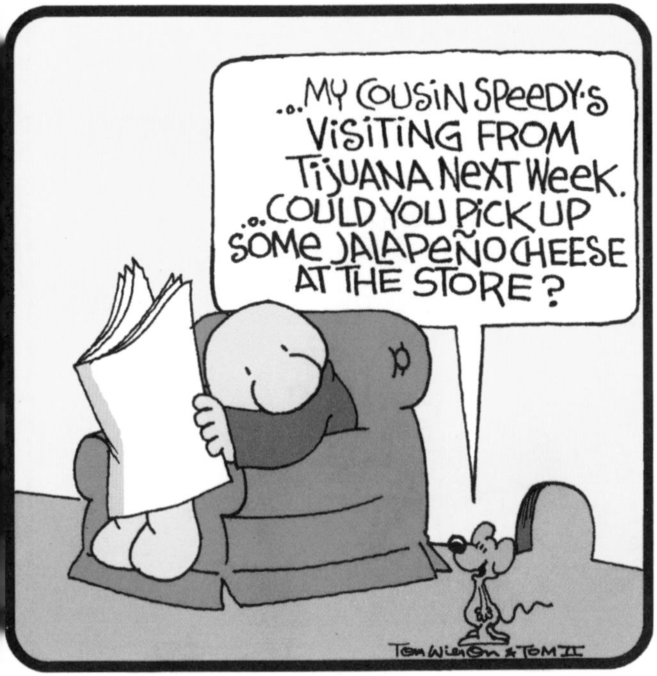
...MY COUSIN SPEEDY'S VISITING FROM TIJUANA NEXT WEEK. ...COULD YOU PICK UP SOME JALAPEÑO CHEESE AT THE STORE?
TOM WILSON & TOM II

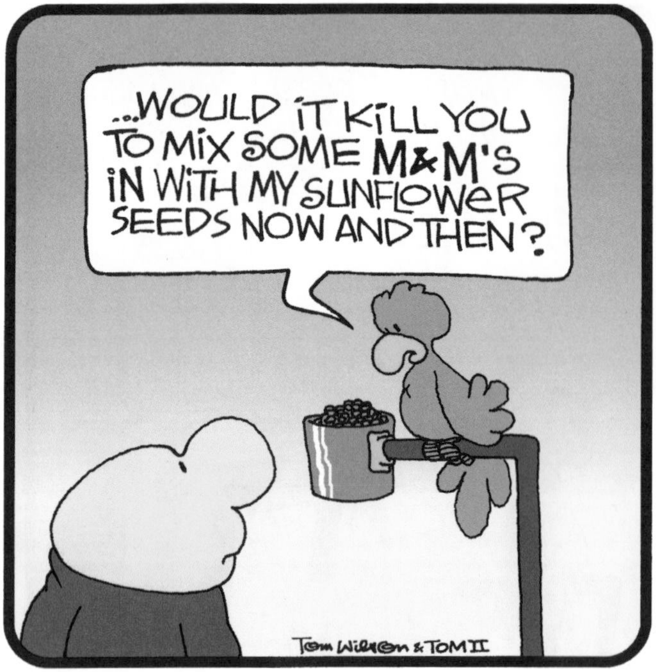
...WOULD IT KILL YOU TO MIX SOME M&M'S IN WITH MY SUNFLOWER SEEDS NOW AND THEN?
Tom Wilson & TOM II

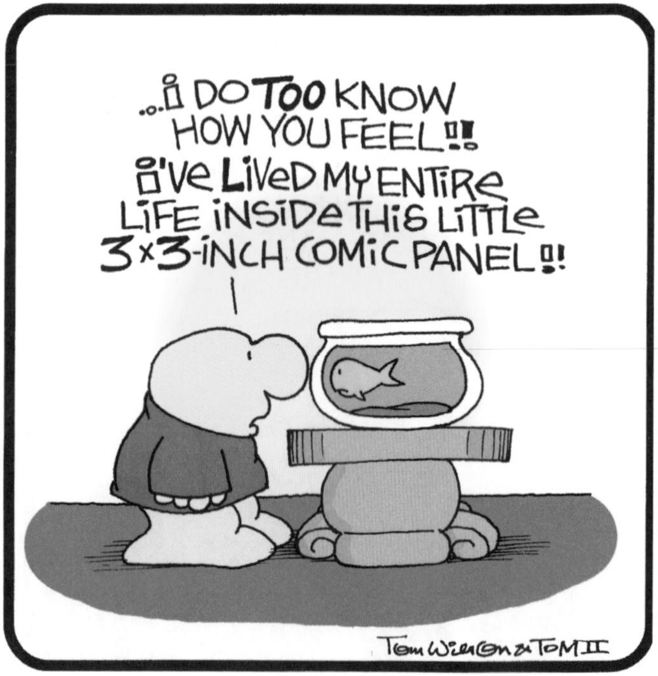
...I DO TOO KNOW HOW YOU FEEL!! I'VE LIVED MY ENTIRE LIFE INSIDE THIS LITTLE 3x3-INCH COMIC PANEL!!
Tom Wilson & TOM II

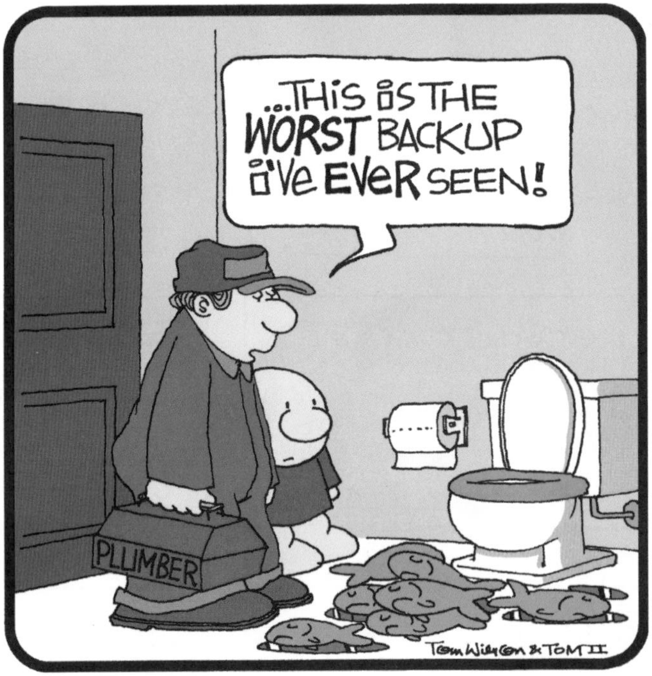
...THIS IS THE WORST BACKUP I'VE EVER SEEN!
PLUMBER
Tom Wilson & Tom II

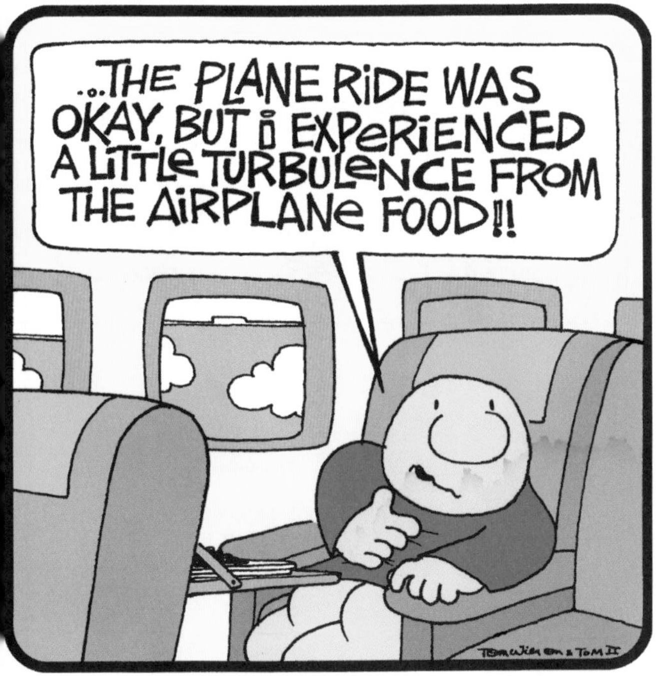
...THE PLANE RIDE WAS OKAY, BUT I EXPERIENCED A LITTLE TURBULENCE FROM THE AIRPLANE FOOD!!
Tom Wilson & Tom II

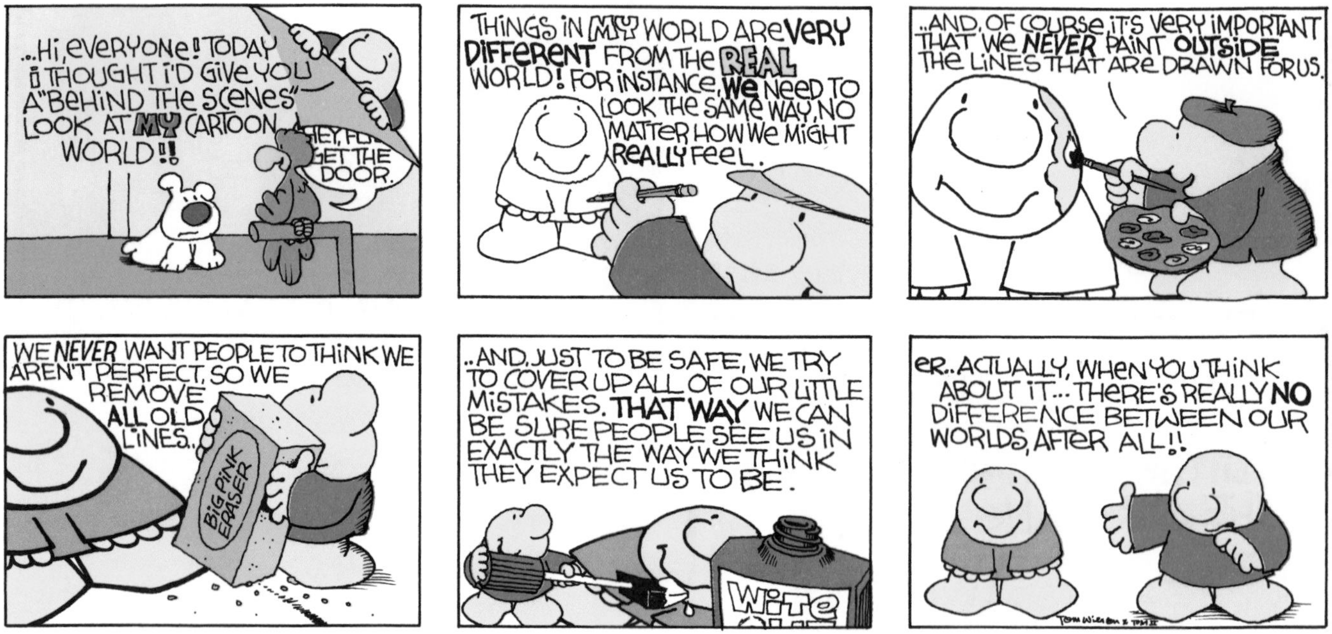
..Hi, EVERYONE! TODAY I THOUGHT I'D GIVE YOU A "BEHIND THE SCENES" LOOK AT MY CARTOON WORLD!!
HEY, FL GET THE DOOR.
THINGS IN MY WORLD ARE VERY DIFFERENT FROM THE REAL WORLD! FOR INSTANCE, WE NEED TO LOOK THE SAME WAY, NO MATTER HOW WE MIGHT REALLY FEEL.
..AND, OF COURSE IT'S VERY IMPORTANT THAT WE NEVER PAINT OUTSIDE THE LINES THAT ARE DRAWN FOR US.
WE NEVER WANT PEOPLE TO THINK WE AREN'T PERFECT, SO WE REMOVE ALL OLD LINES..
BIG PINK ERASER
..AND, JUST TO BE SAFE, WE TRY TO COVER UP ALL OF OUR LITTLE MISTAKES. THAT WAY WE CAN BE SURE PEOPLE SEE US IN EXACTLY THE WAY WE THINK THEY EXPECT US TO BE.
WITE
ER.. ACTUALLY, WHEN YOU THINK ABOUT IT... THERE'S REALLY NO DIFFERENCE BETWEEN OUR WORLDS, AFTER ALL!!

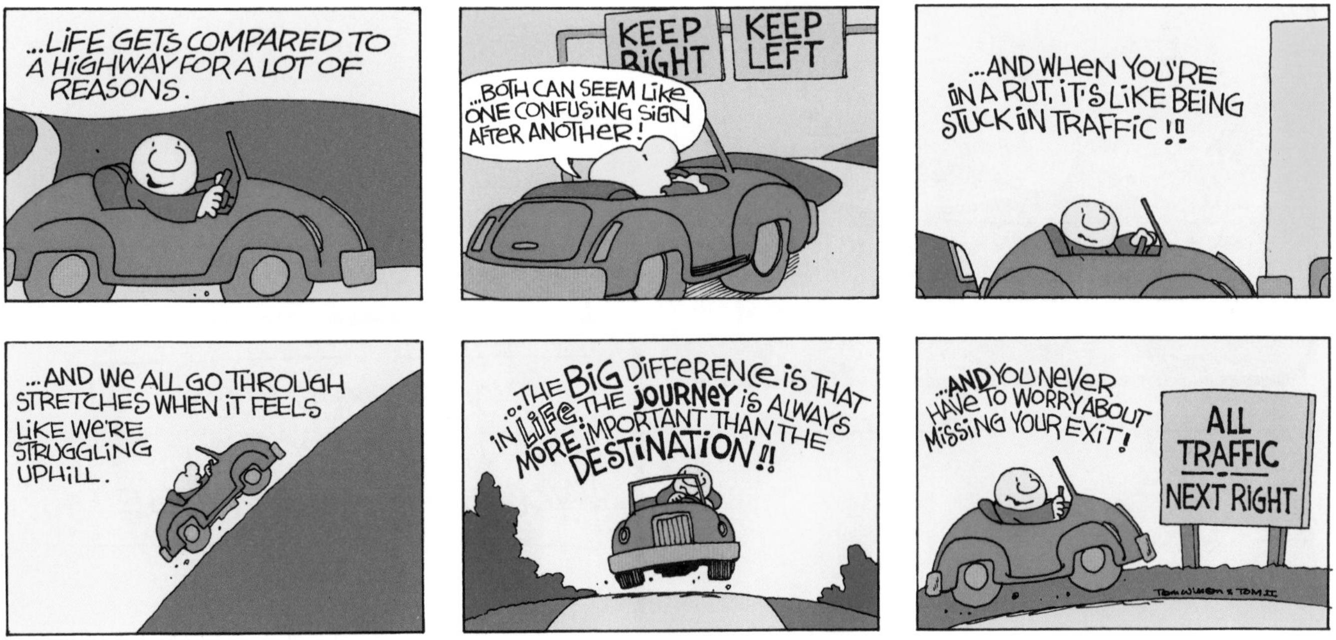
...LIFE GETS COMPARED TO A HIGHWAY FOR A LOT OF REASONS.
KEEP RIGHT
KEEP LEFT
...BOTH CAN SEEM LIKE ONE CONFUSING SIGN AFTER ANOTHER!
...AND WHEN YOU'RE IN A RUT, IT'S LIKE BEING STUCK IN TRAFFIC!!
...AND WE ALL GO THROUGH STRETCHES WHEN IT FEELS LIKE WE'RE STRUGGLING UPHILL.
...THE BIG DIFFERENCE IS THAT IN LIFE, THE JOURNEY IS ALWAYS MORE IMPORTANT THAN THE DESTINATION!!
...AND YOU NEVER HAVE TO WORRY ABOUT MISSING YOUR EXIT!
ALL TRAFFIC
NEXT RIGHT

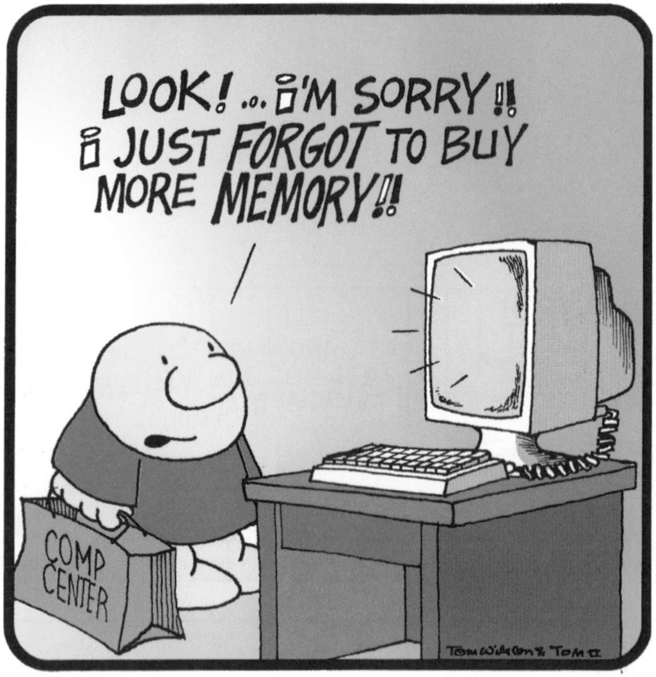
LOOK! ... I'M SORRY!!
I JUST FORGOT TO BUY
MORE MEMORY!!
COMP
CENTER

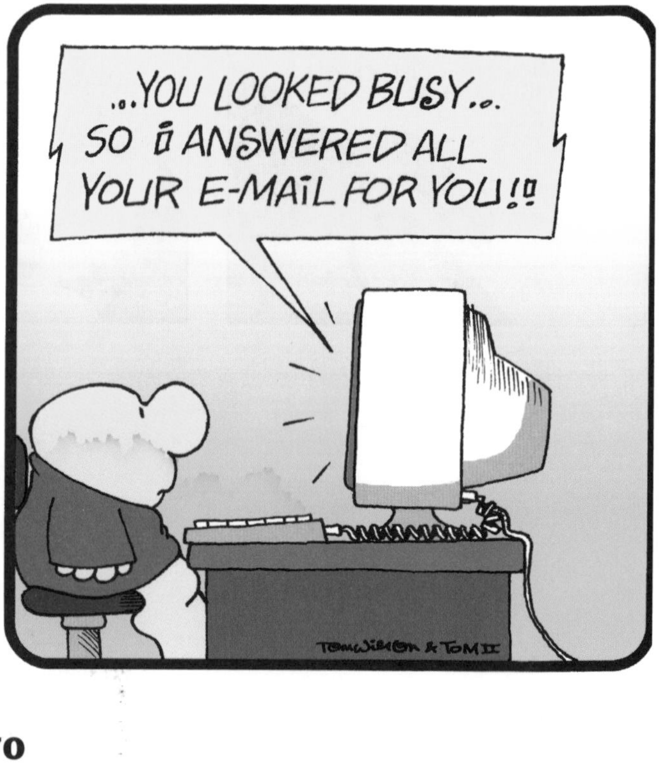
...YOU LOOKED BUSY...
SO I ANSWERED ALL
YOUR E-MAIL FOR YOU!!

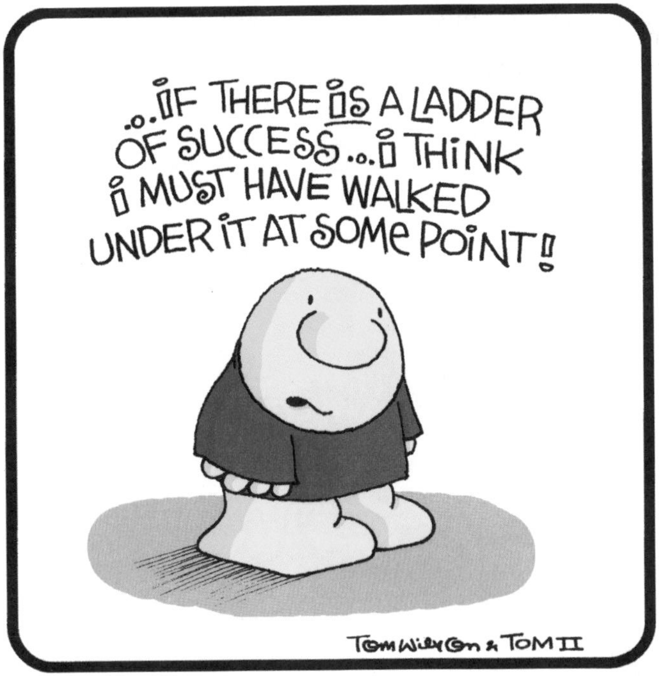
..o..IF THERE IS A LADDER OF SUCCESS ..o.. I THINK I MUST HAVE WALKED UNDER IT AT SOME POINT!
TOM WILSON & TOM II

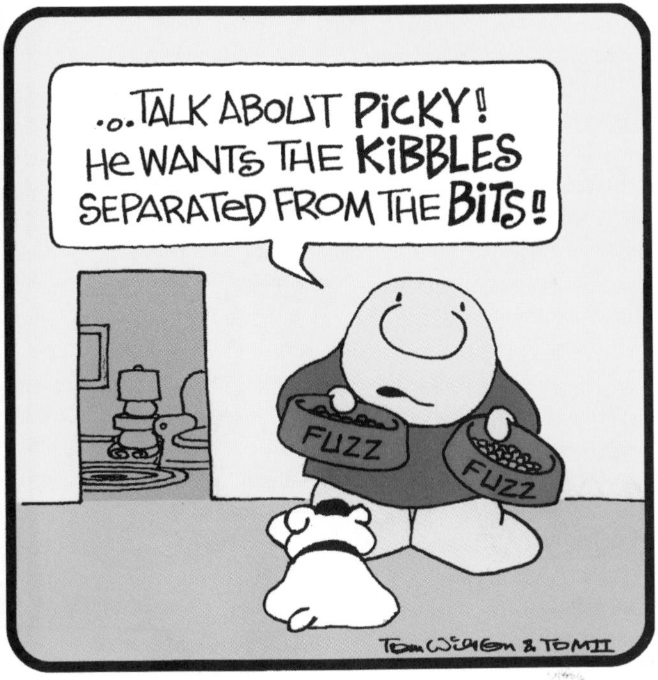
..o..TALK ABOUT PICKY! He WANTS THE KIBBLES SEPARATED FROM THE BITS!
FUZZ
FUZZ
TOM WILSON & TOM II

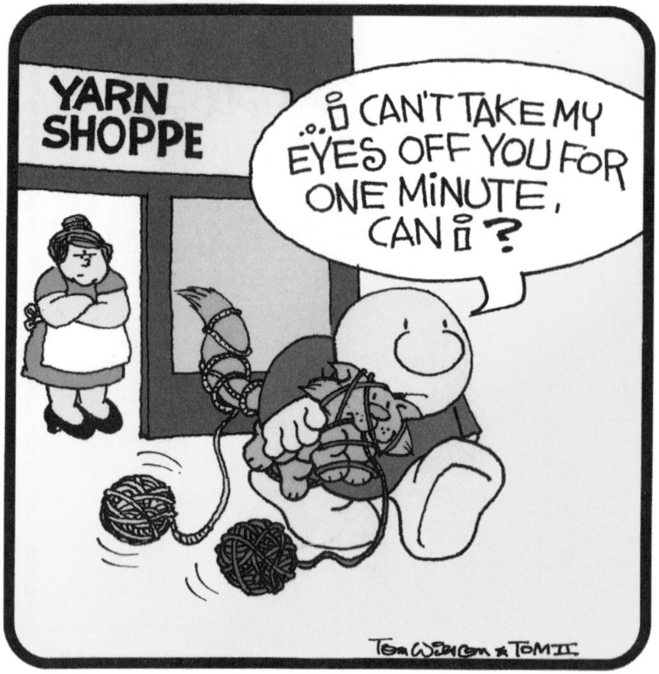
YARN SHOPPE
..I CAN'T TAKE MY EYES OFF YOU FOR ONE MINUTE, CAN I?
Tom Wilson & TOM II

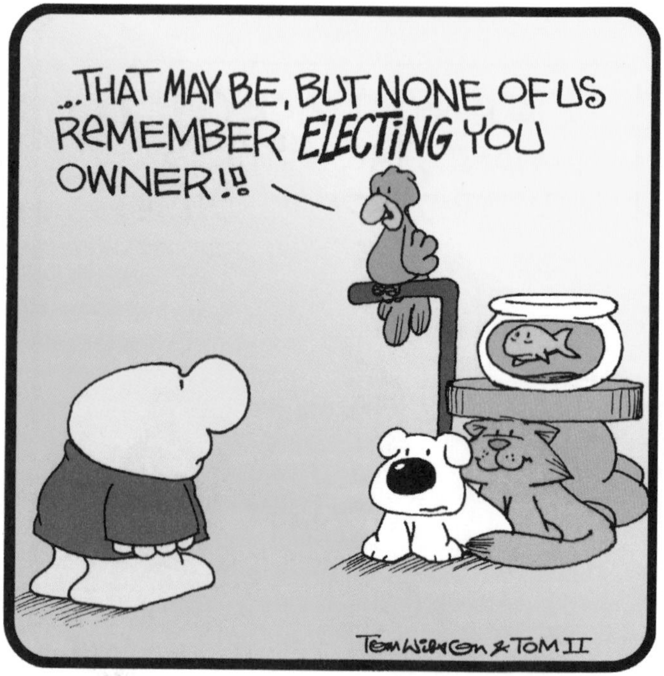
..THAT MAY BE, BUT NONE OF US REMEMBER ELECTING YOU OWNER!!
Tom Wilson & TOM II

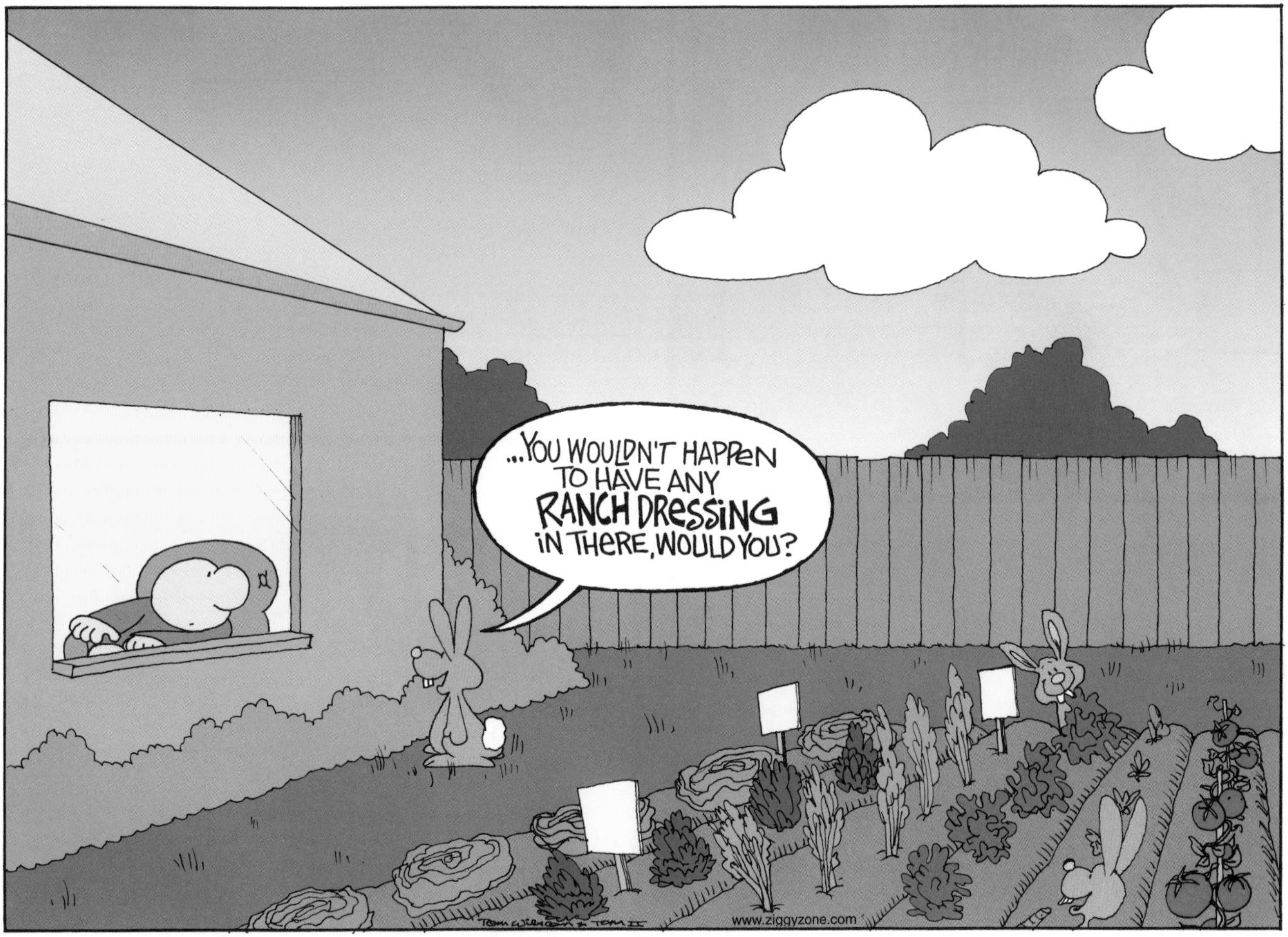
...YOU WOULDN'T HAPPEN TO HAVE ANY RANCH DRESSING IN THERE, WOULD YOU?
www.ziggyzone.com

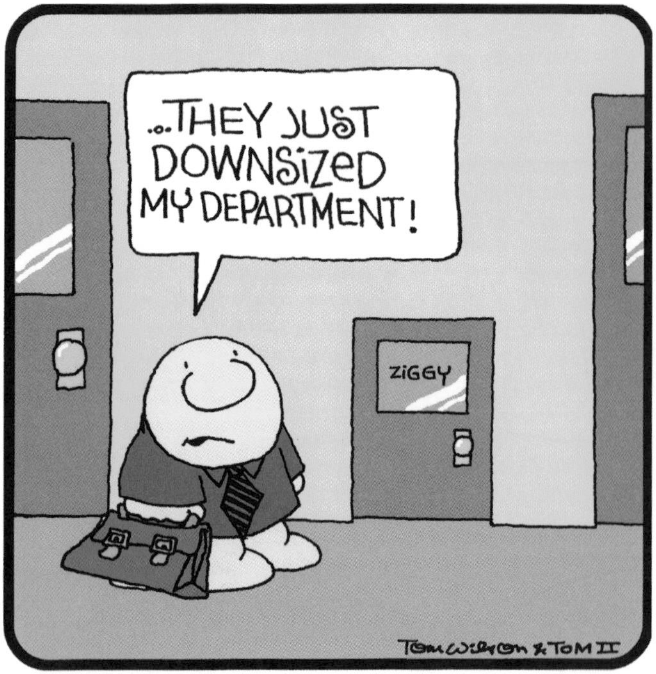
..o..THEY JUST DOWNSIZED MY DEPARTMENT!
ZIGGY
Tom Wilson & TOM II

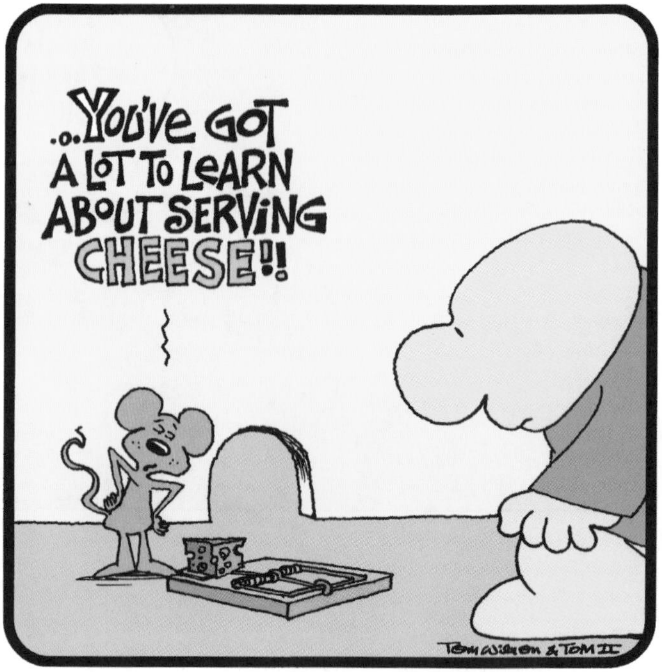
..o..YOU'VE GOT A LOT TO LEARN ABOUT SERVING CHEESE!!
Tom Wilson & TOM II

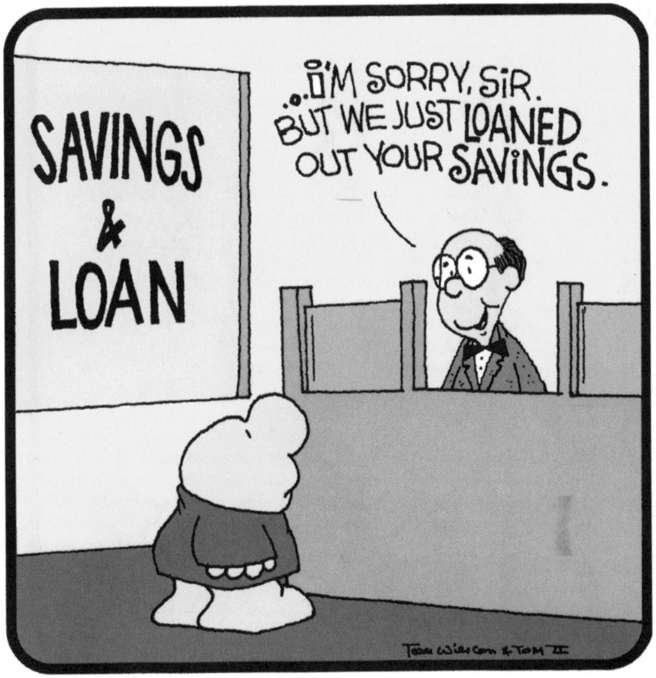
SAVINGS & LOAN
..o..I'M SORRY, SIR. BUT WE JUST LOANED OUT YOUR SAVINGS.
TOM WILSON & TOM II

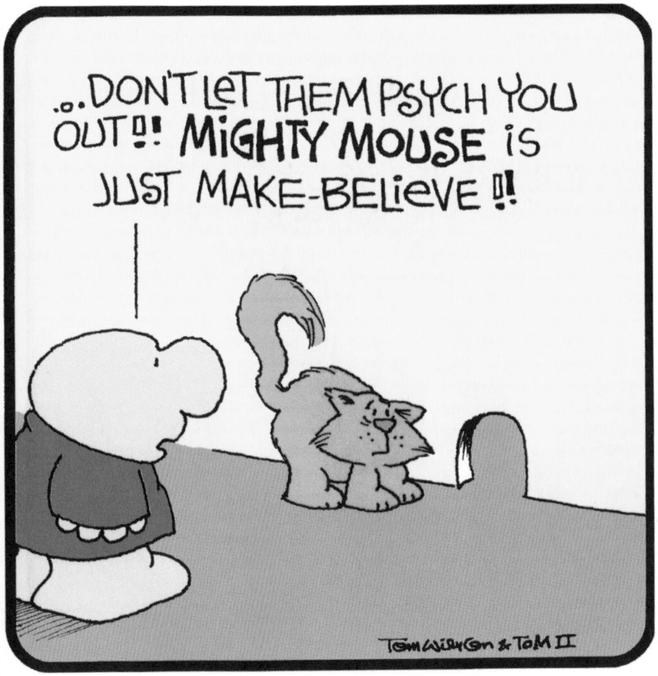
..o..DON'T LET THEM PSYCH YOU OUT!! MIGHTY MOUSE IS JUST MAKE-BELIEVE!!
TOM WILSON & TOM II

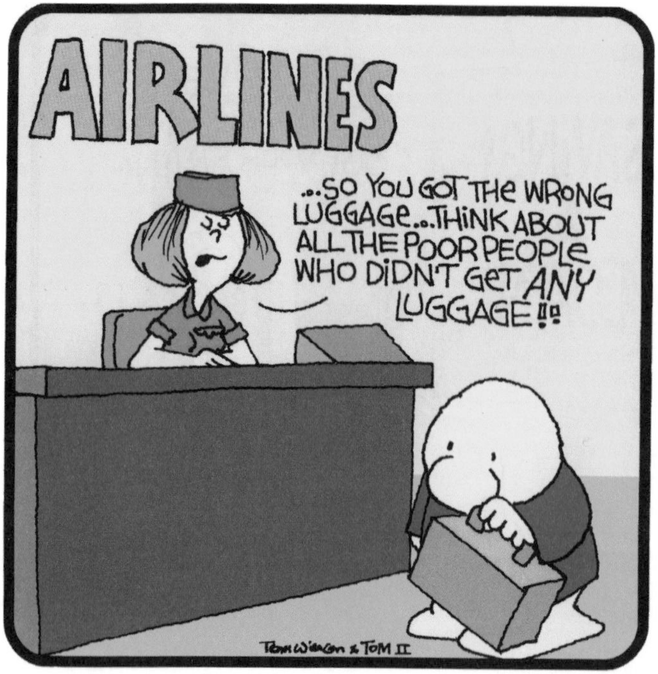
AIRLINES
..SO YOU GOT THE WRONG LUGGAGE...THINK ABOUT ALL THE POOR PEOPLE WHO DIDN'T GET ANY LUGGAGE!!
TOM WILSON & TOM II

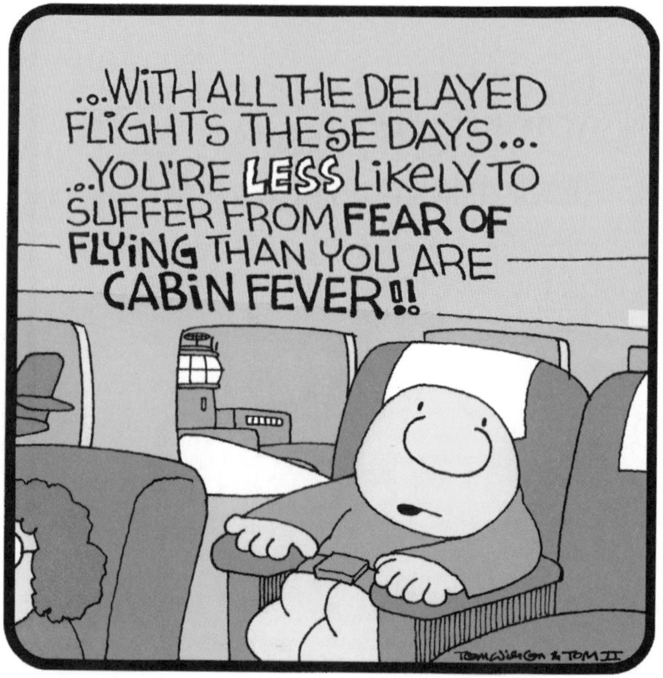
...WITH ALL THE DELAYED FLIGHTS THESE DAYS...
...YOU'RE LESS LIKELY TO SUFFER FROM FEAR OF FLYING THAN YOU ARE CABIN FEVER!!
TOM WILSON & TOM II

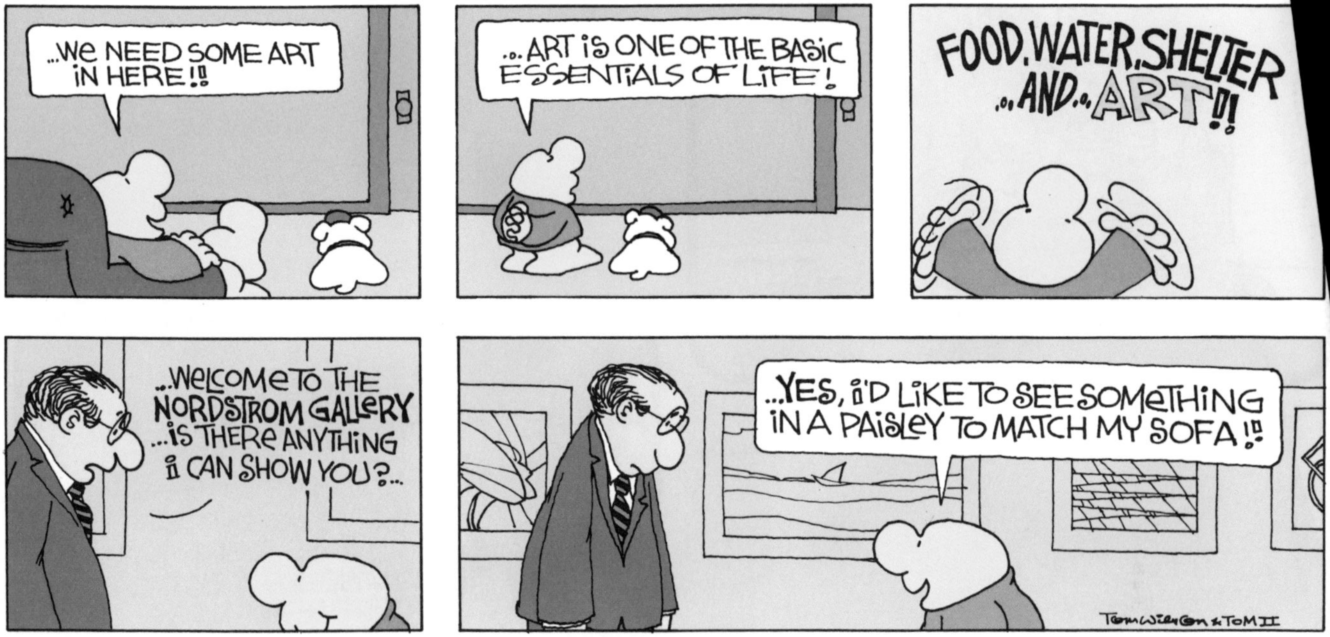
...WE NEED SOME ART IN HERE!!
..o..ART IS ONE OF THE BASIC ESSENTIALS OF LIFE!
FOOD, WATER, SHELTER ..o.. AND..o.. ART!!
...WELCOME TO THE NORDSTROM GALLERY ...IS THERE ANYTHING I CAN SHOW YOU?...
...YES, I'D LIKE TO SEE SOMETHING IN A PAISLEY TO MATCH MY SOFA!!
TOM WILSON & TOM II

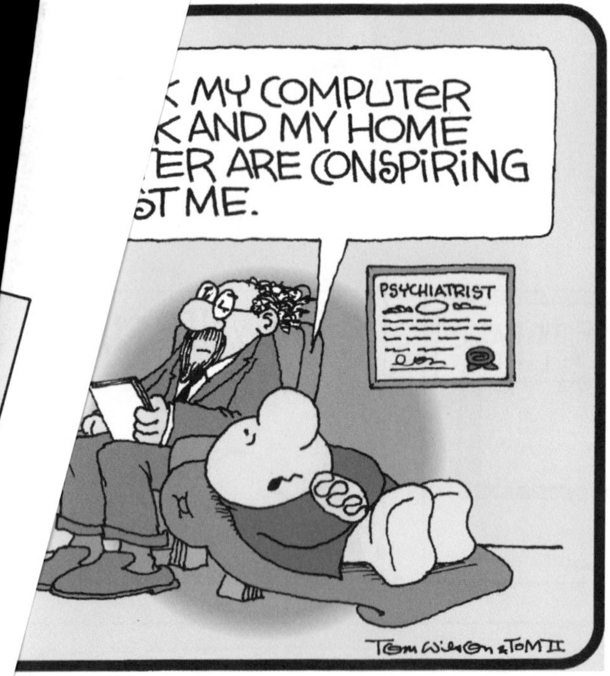
K MY COMPUTER
K AND MY HOME
TER ARE CONSPIRING
ST ME.
PSYCHIATRIST
Tom Wilson & TOM II

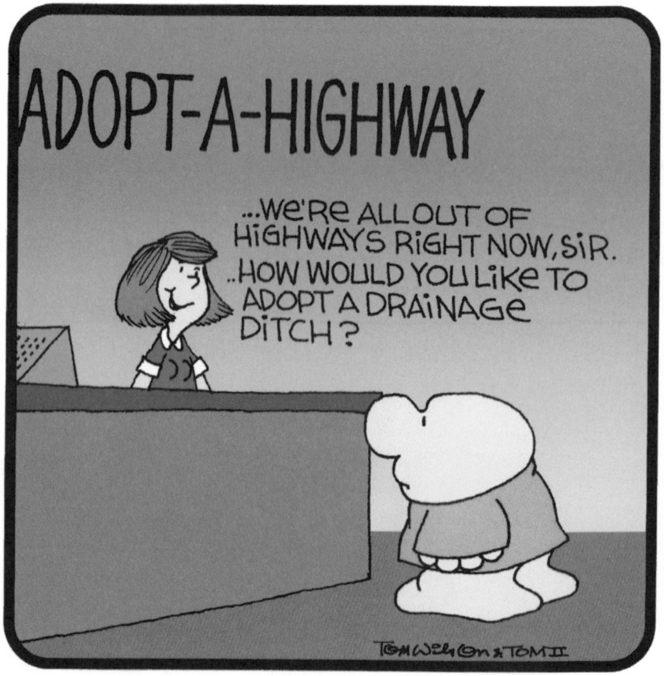
ADOPT-A-HIGHWAY
...WE'RE ALL OUT OF HIGHWAYS RIGHT NOW, SIR. ..HOW WOULD YOU LIKE TO ADOPT A DRAINAGE DITCH?
Tom Wilson & TOM II

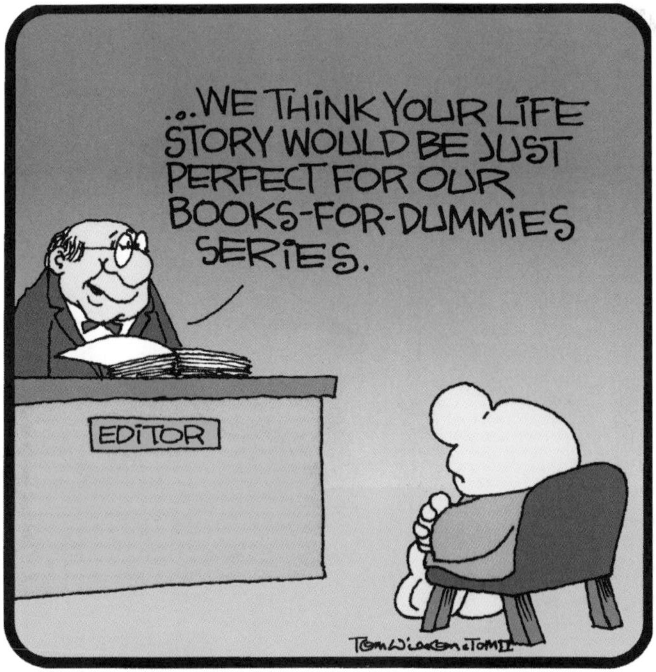
...WE THINK YOUR LIFE STORY WOULD BE JUST PERFECT FOR OUR BOOKS-FOR-DUMMIES SERIES.
EDITOR
TOM WILSON & TOM II

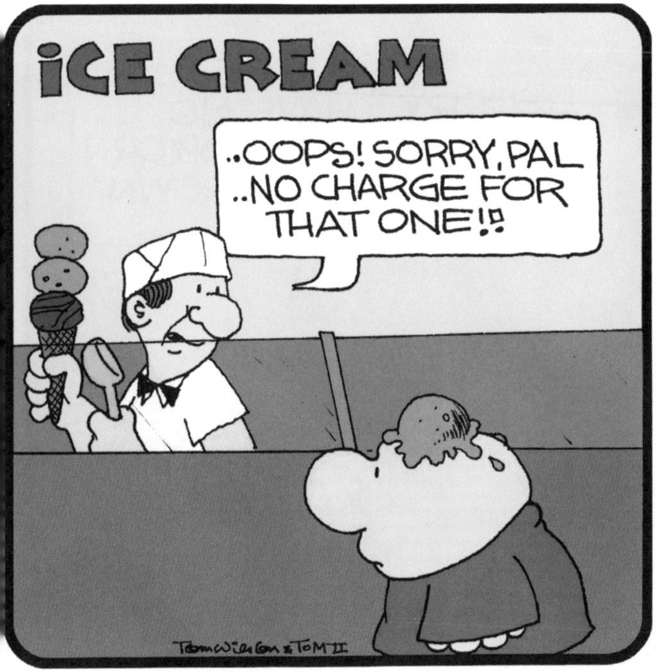
ICE CREAM
..OOPS! SORRY, PAL ..NO CHARGE FOR THAT ONE!!?
TOM WILSON & TOM II

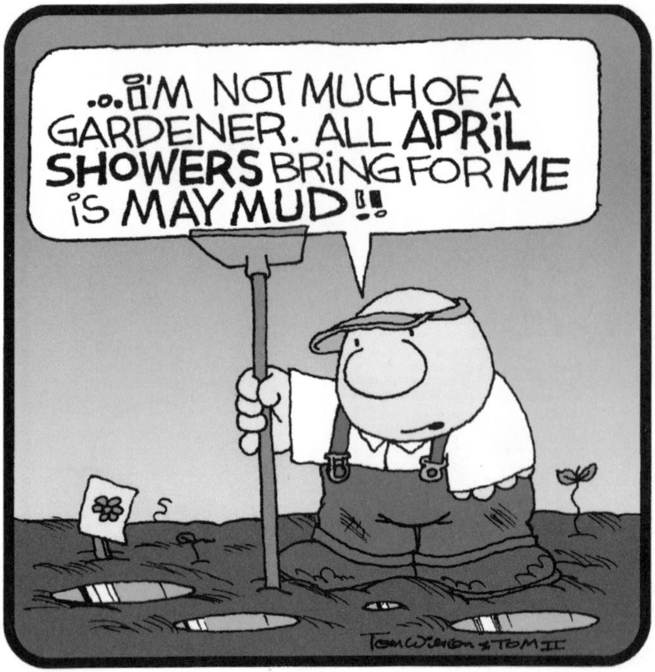
..o.I'M NOT MUCH OF A GARDENER. ALL APRIL SHOWERS BRING FOR ME IS MAY MUD!!
TOM WILSON & TOM II

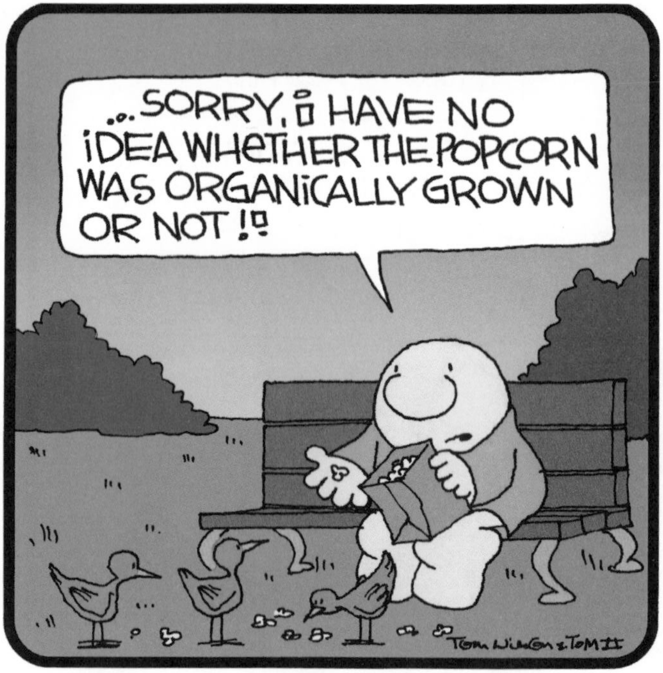
..o.SORRY, I HAVE NO IDEA WHETHER THE POPCORN WAS ORGANICALLY GROWN OR NOT!?
TOM WILSON & TOM II

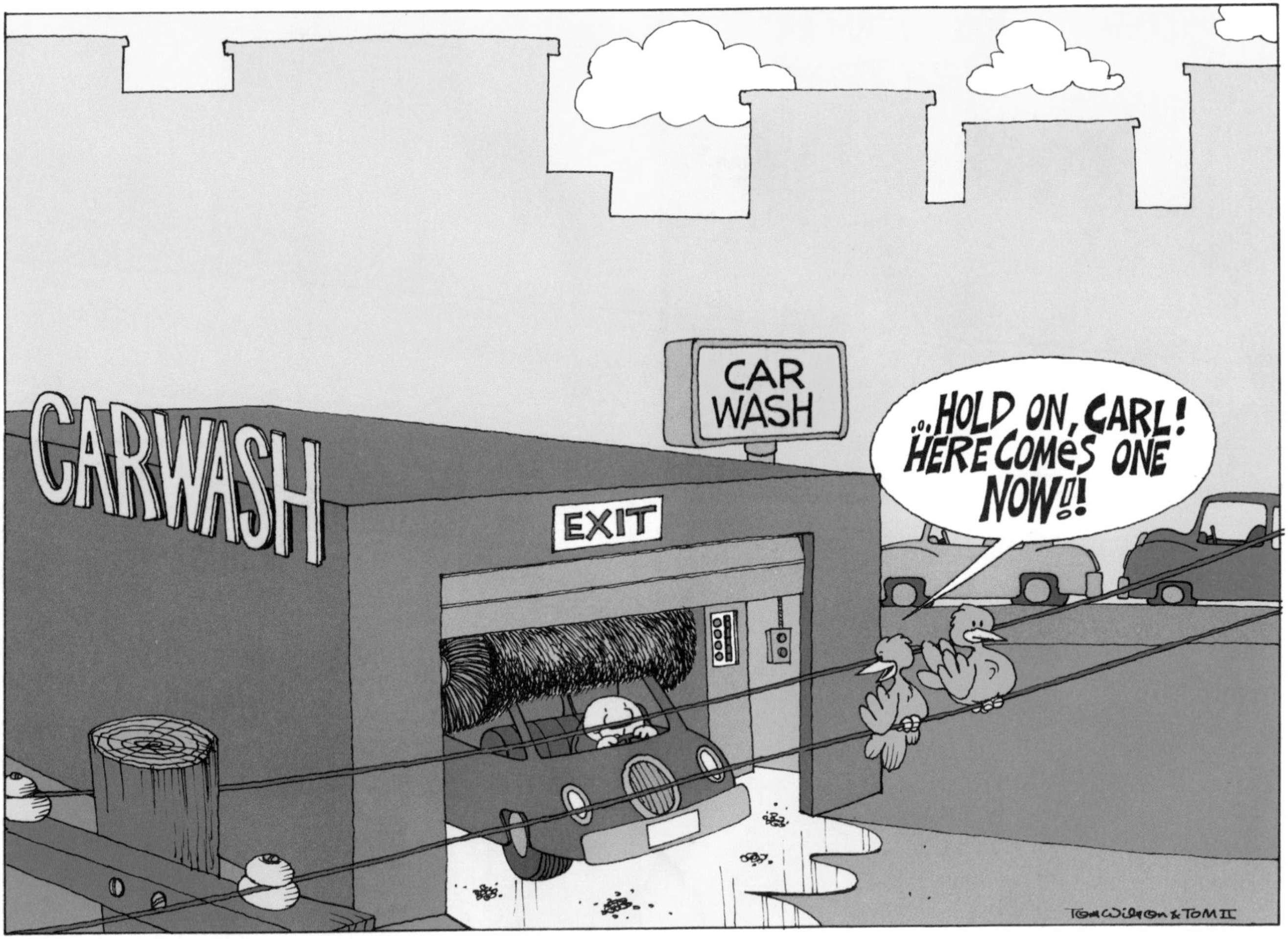
CARWASH
CAR WASH
EXIT
..HOLD ON, CARL! HERE COMES ONE NOW!!
TOM WILSON & TOM II

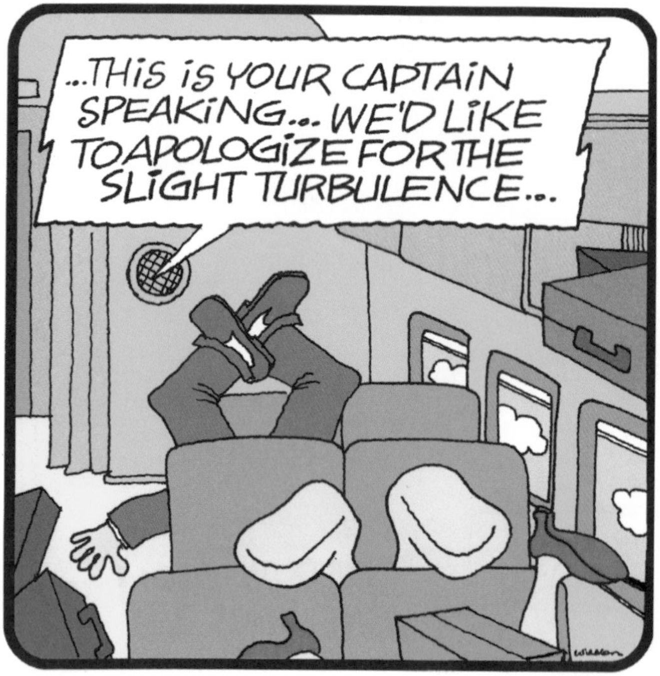
..THIS IS YOUR CAPTAIN SPEAKING... WE'D LIKE TO APOLOGIZE FOR THE SLIGHT TURBULENCE...

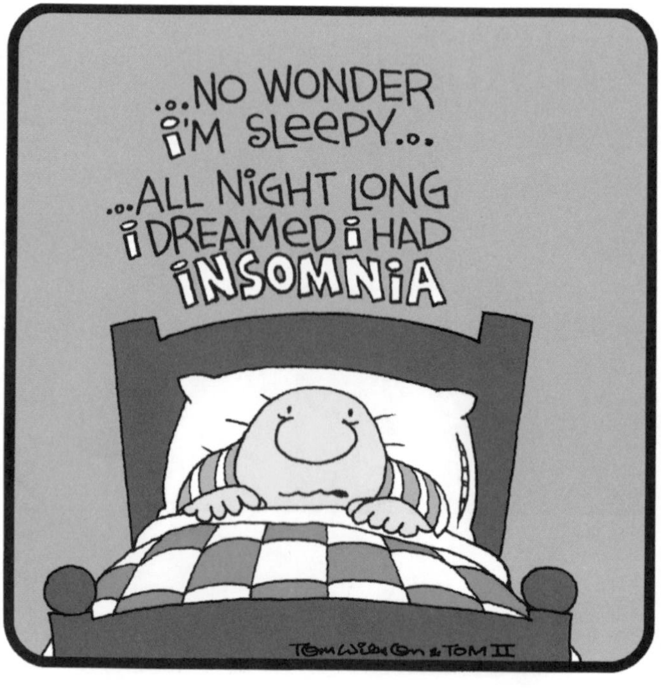
...NO WONDER I'M SLEEPY...
...ALL NIGHT LONG I DREAMED I HAD INSOMNIA
TOM WILSON & TOM II

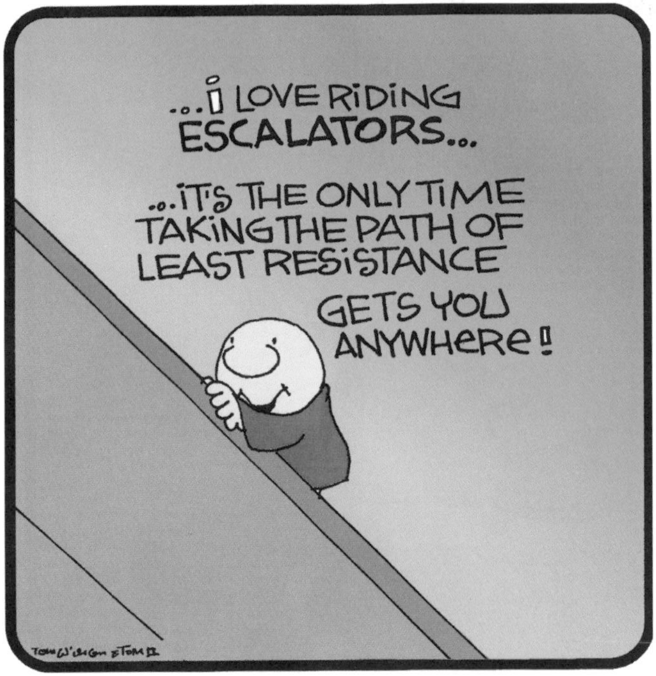
...I LOVE RIDING ESCALATORS...
...IT'S THE ONLY TIME TAKING THE PATH OF LEAST RESISTANCE
GETS YOU ANYWHERE!

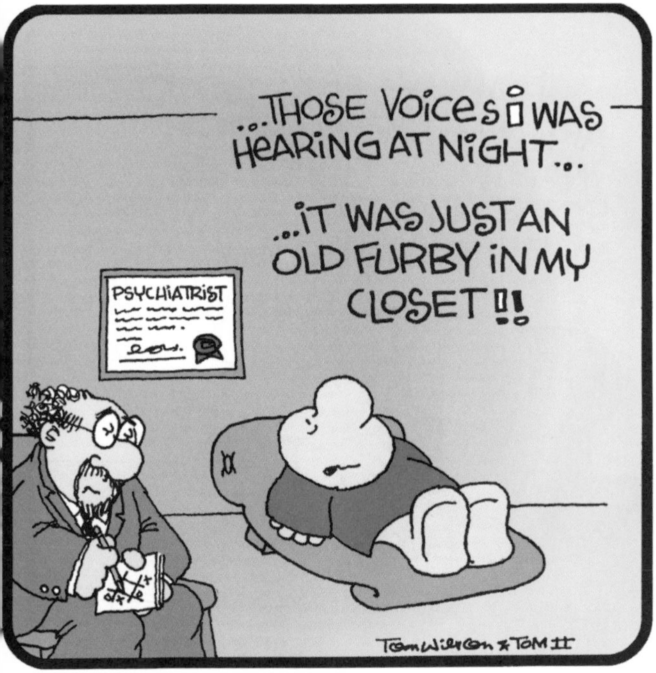
...THOSE VOICES I WAS HEARING AT NIGHT...
...IT WAS JUST AN OLD FURBY IN MY CLOSET!!
PSYCHIATRIST

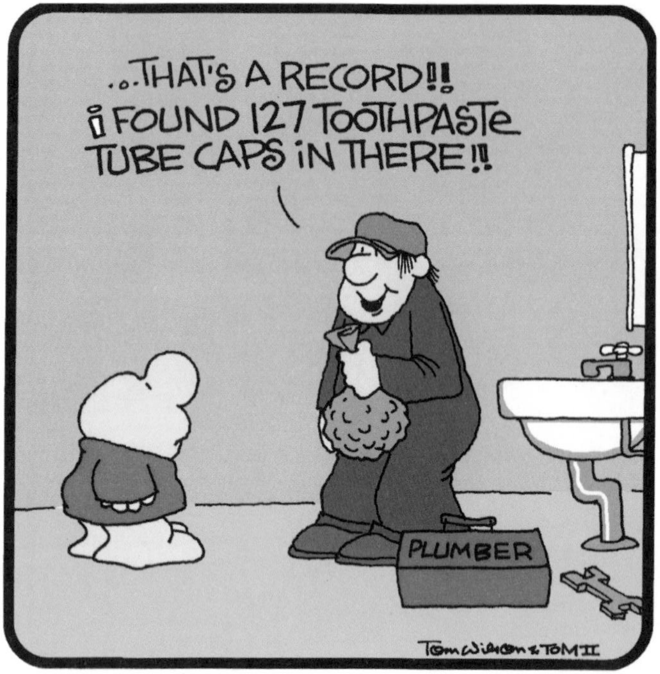
...THAT'S A RECORD!!
I FOUND 127 TOOTHPASTE TUBE CAPS IN THERE!!
PLUMBER
Tom Wilson & TOM II

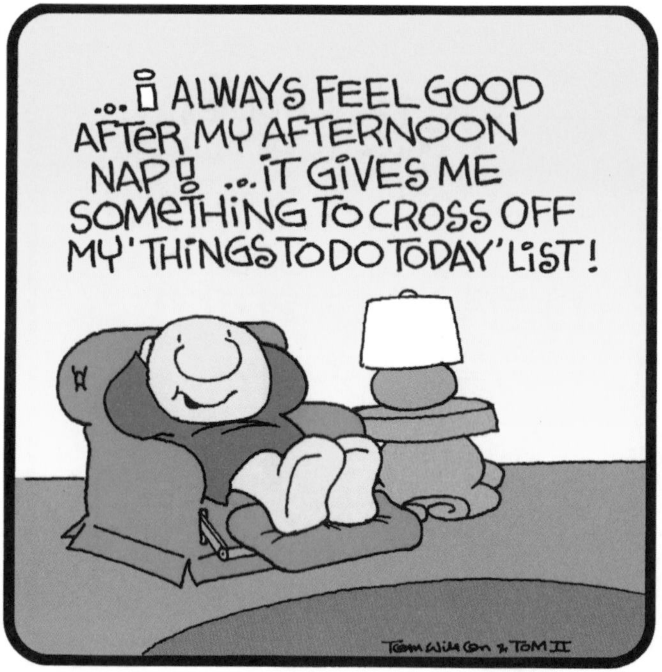
... I ALWAYS FEEL GOOD AFTER MY AFTERNOON NAP! ... IT GIVES ME SOMETHING TO CROSS OFF MY 'THINGS TO DO TODAY' LIST!
Tom Wilson & TOM II

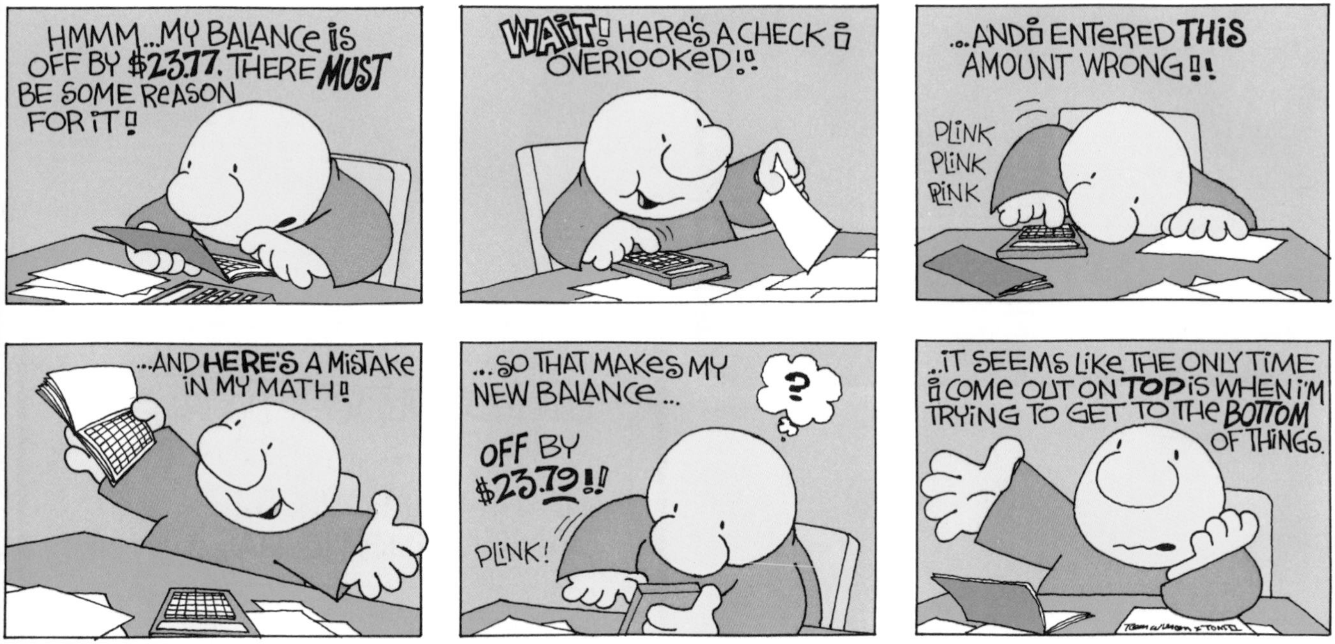
HMMM...MY BALANCE IS OFF BY $23.77. THERE MUST BE SOME REASON FOR IT!
WAIT! HERE'S A CHECK I OVERLOOKED!!
...AND I ENTERED THIS AMOUNT WRONG!!
PLINK
PLINK
PLINK
...AND HERE'S A MISTAKE IN MY MATH!
...SO THAT MAKES MY NEW BALANCE...
?
OFF BY $23.79!!
PLINK!
...IT SEEMS LIKE THE ONLY TIME I COME OUT ON TOP IS WHEN I'M TRYING TO GET TO THE BOTTOM OF THINGS.

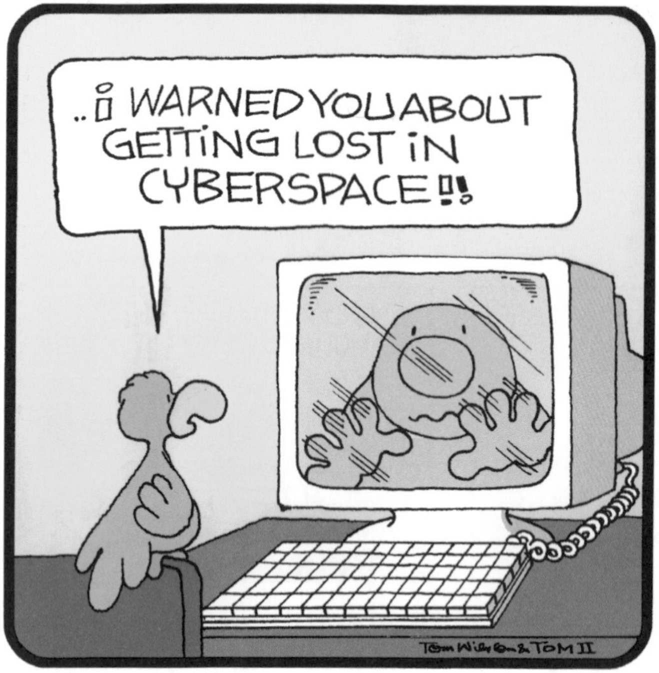
..I WARNED YOU ABOUT GETTING LOST IN CYBERSPACE!!
TOM WILSON & TOM II

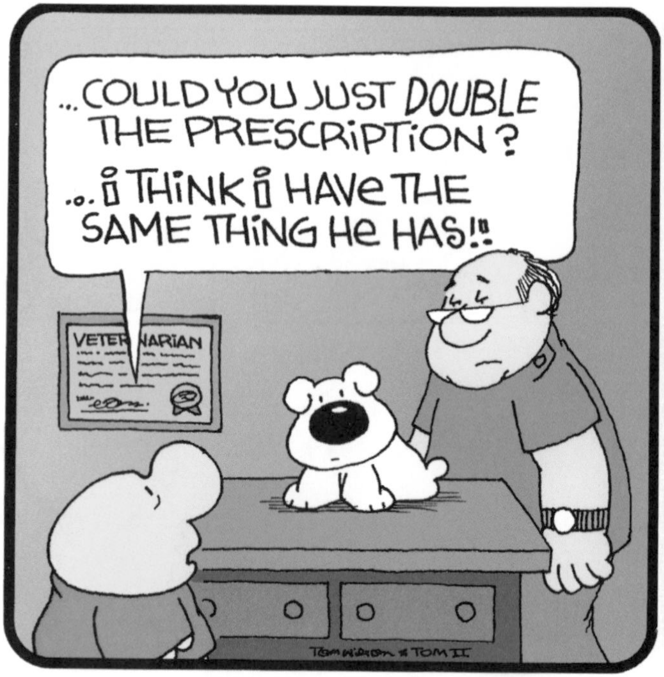
...COULD YOU JUST DOUBLE THE PRESCRIPTION? ...I THINK I HAVE THE SAME THING HE HAS!!
VETERINARIAN
TOM WILSON & TOM II

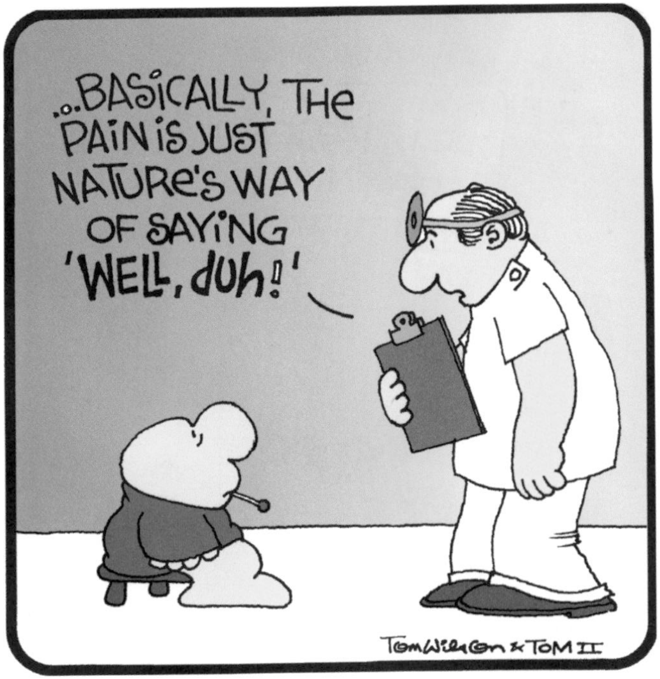
...BASICALLY, THE PAIN IS JUST NATURE'S WAY OF SAYING 'WELL, duh!'
TOM WILSON & TOM II

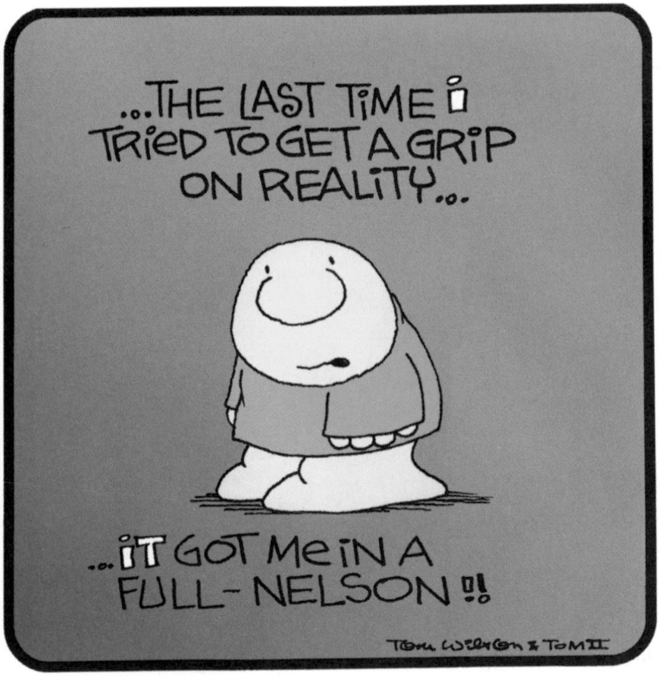
...THE LAST TIME I TRIED TO GET A GRIP ON REALITY...
...IT GOT ME IN A FULL-NELSON!!
TOM WILSON & TOM II

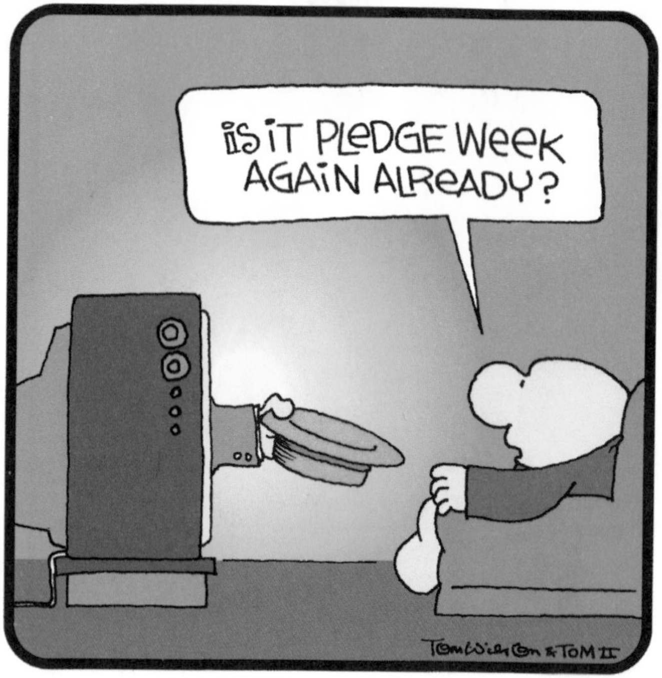
IS IT PLEDGE WEEK AGAIN ALREADY?
TOM WILSON & TOM II

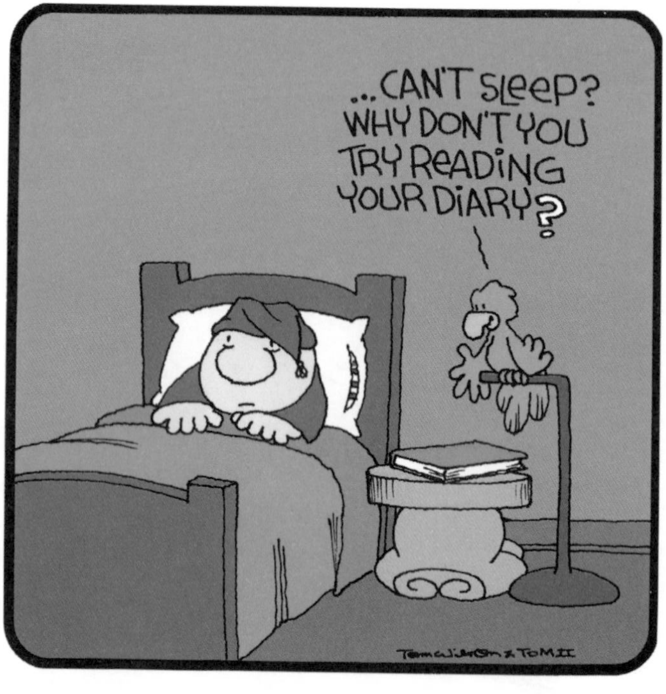
...CAN'T SLEEP? WHY DON'T YOU TRY READING YOUR DIARY?
TOM WILSON & TOM II

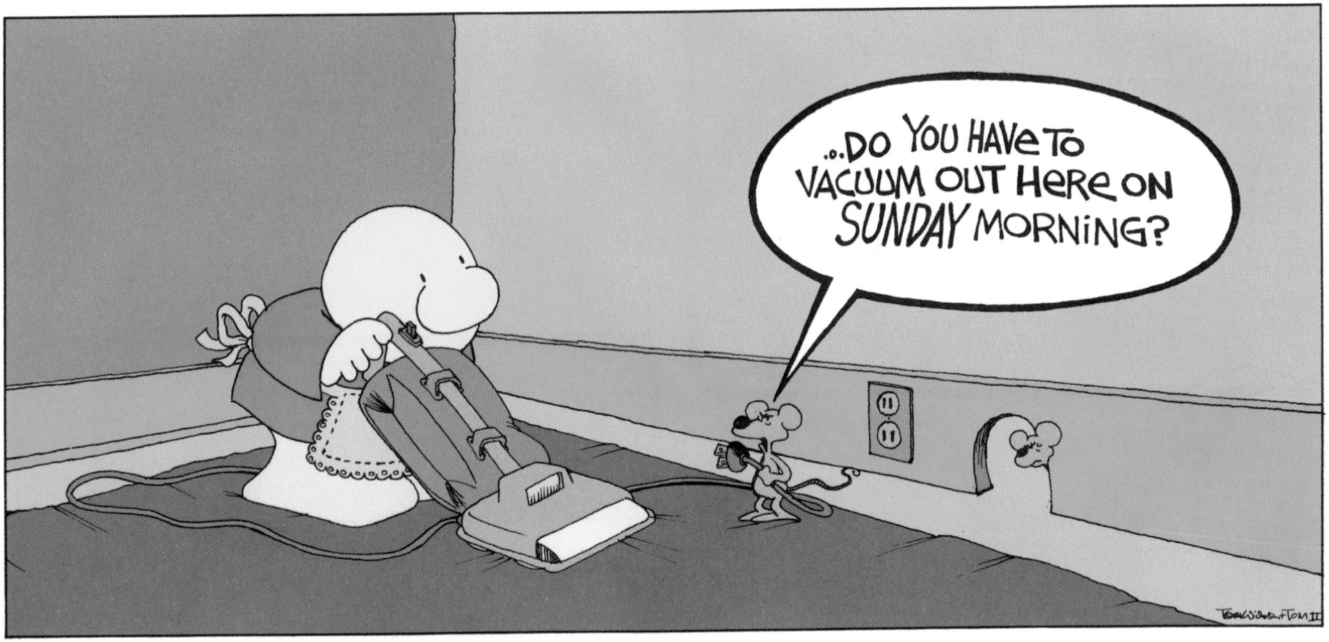
..DO YOU HAVE TO VACUUM OUT HERE ON SUNDAY MORNING?

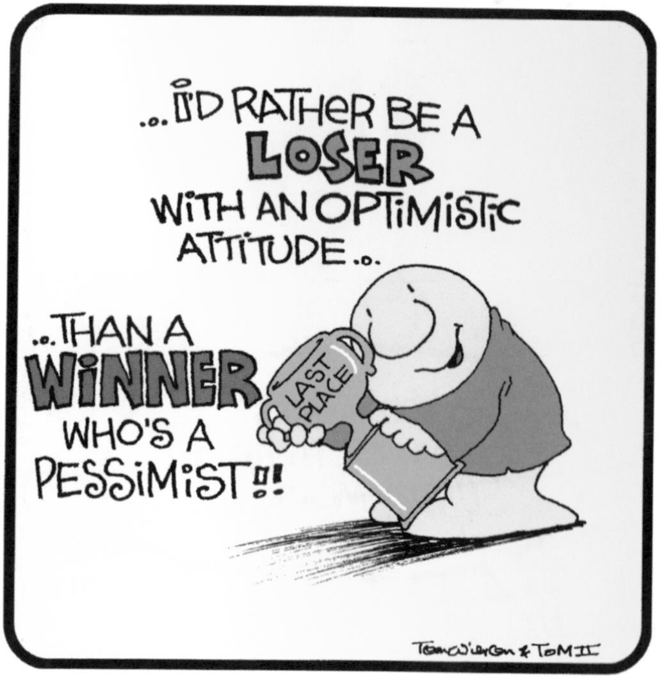
...I'D RATHER BE A
LOSER
WITH AN OPTIMISTIC
ATTITUDE...
...THAN A
WINNER
WHO'S A
PESSIMIST!!
LAST PLACE

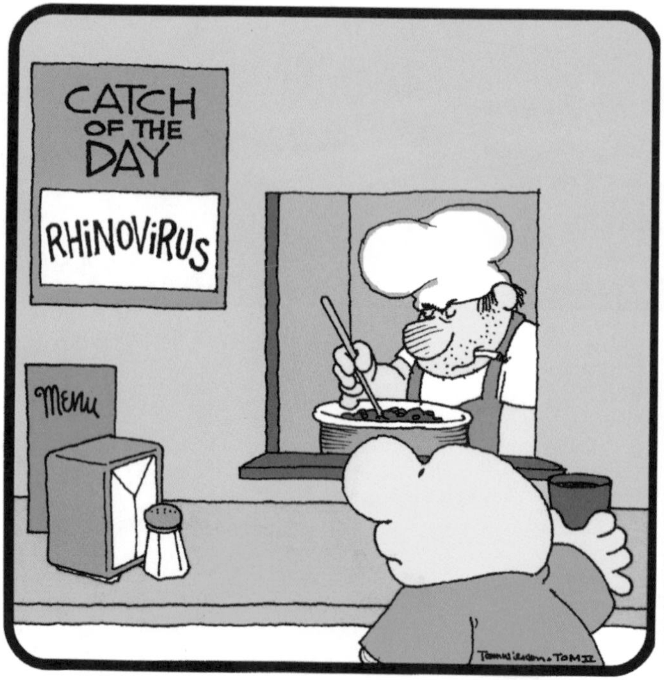
CATCH OF THE DAY
RHINOVIRUS
Menu

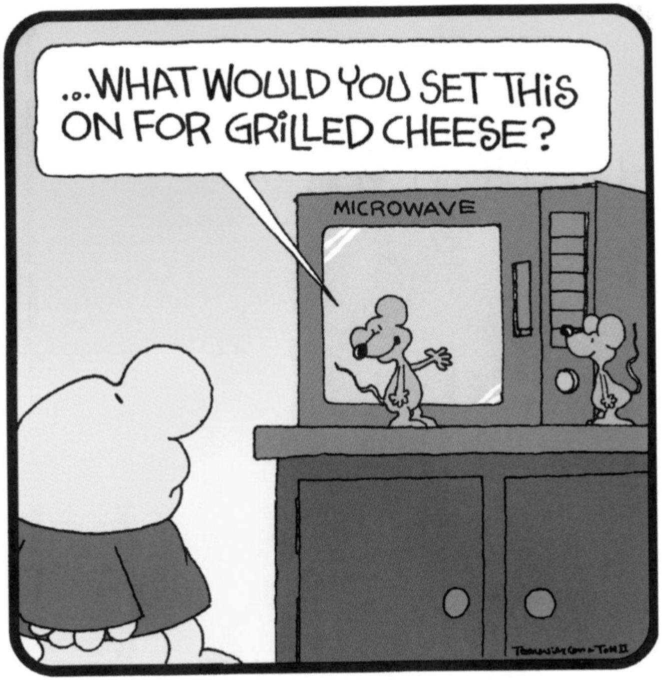
..WHAT WOULD YOU SET THIS ON FOR GRILLED CHEESE?
MICROWAVE
TOM WILSON & TOM II

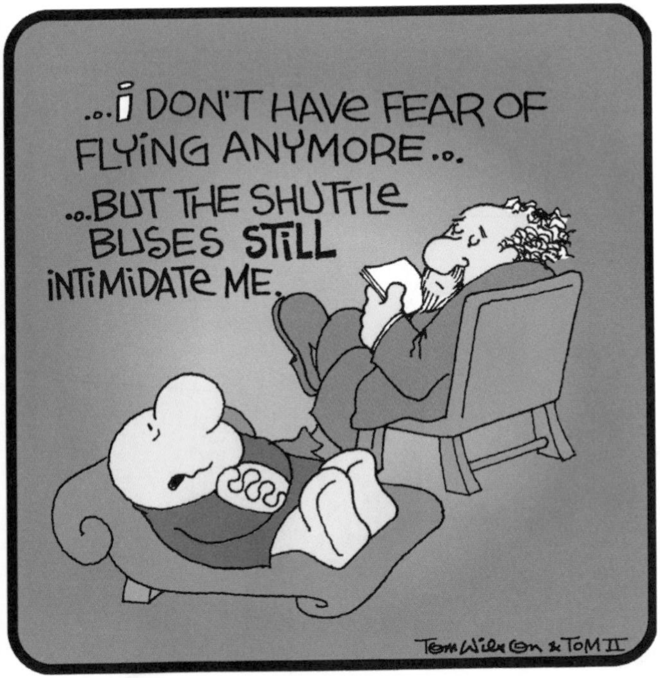
..I DON'T HAVE FEAR OF FLYING ANYMORE..
..BUT THE SHUTTLE BUSES STILL INTIMIDATE ME.
TOM WILSON & TOM II

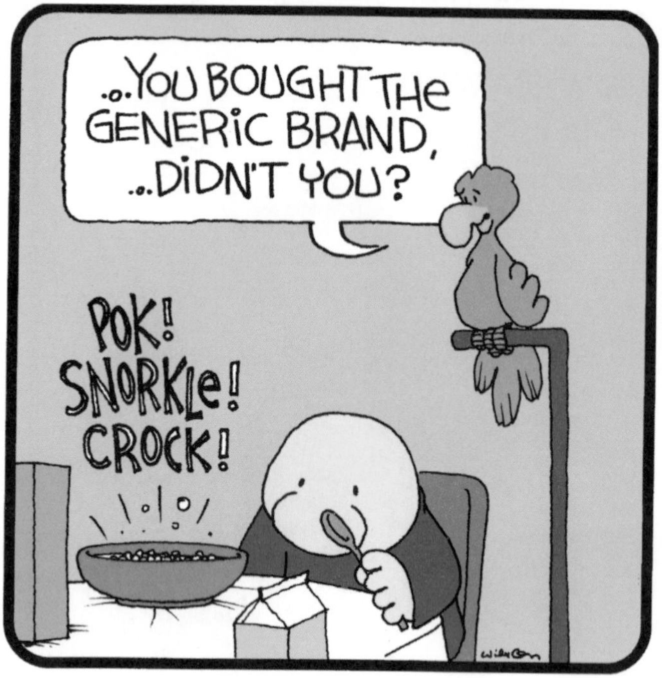
..YOU BOUGHT THE GENERIC BRAND, ..DIDN'T YOU?
POK! SNORKLE! CROCK!

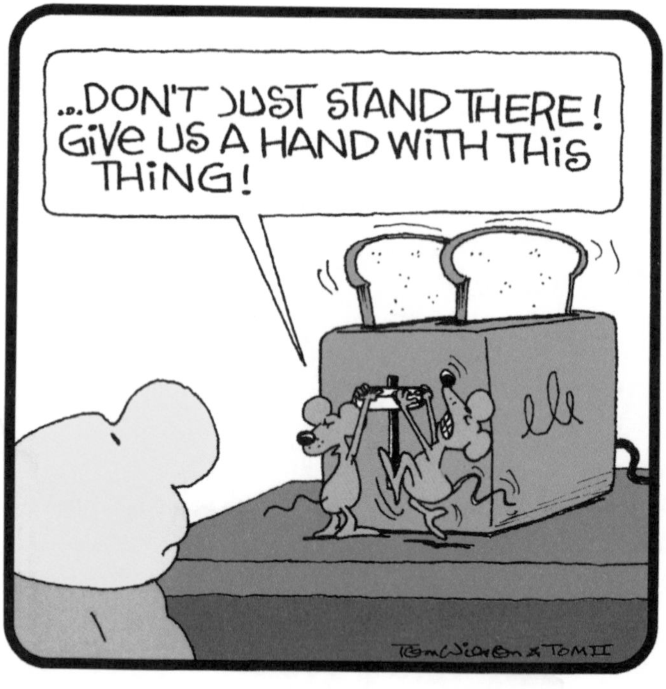
..DON'T JUST STAND THERE! GIVE US A HAND WITH THIS THING!
TOM WILSON & TOM II

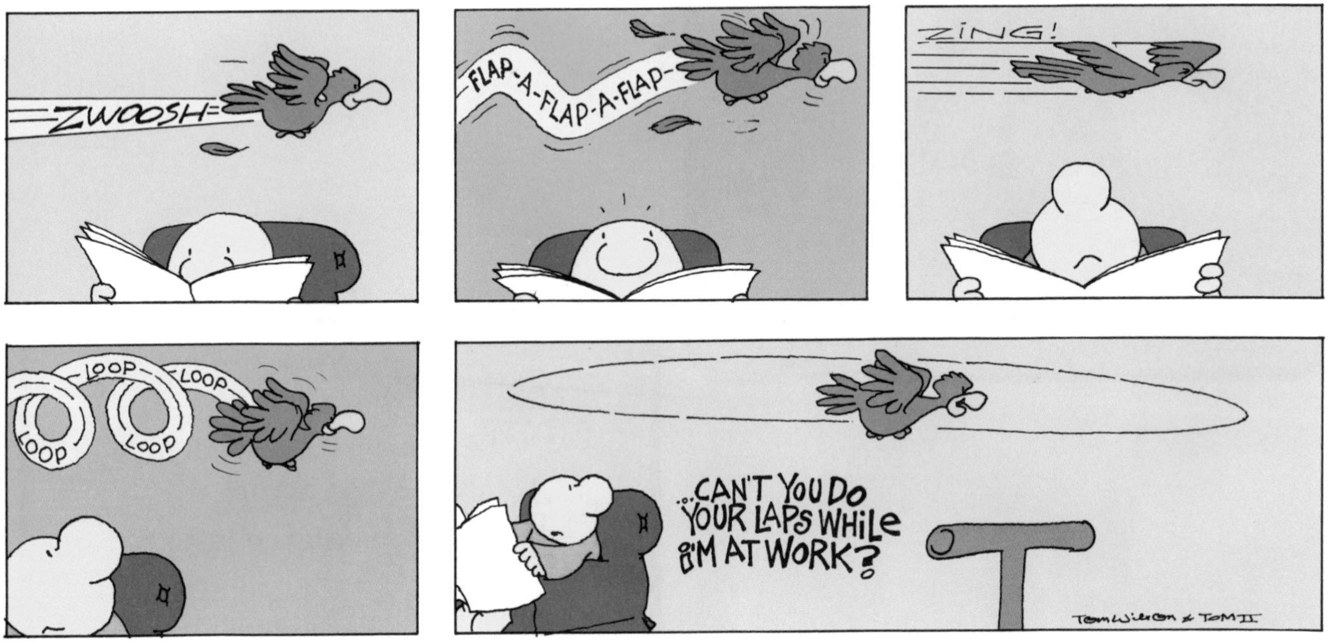
ZWOOSH
FLAP-A-FLAP-A-FLAP
ZING!
LOOP LOOP LOOP LOOP
...CAN'T YOU DO YOUR LAPS WHILE I'M AT WORK?

..NO BIG WISHES, OKAY? ... I'M JUST A DWARF STAR, YOU KNOW!
TOM WILSON & TOM II

..THE FOOTBALL GAME STARTS IN THREE MINUTES!
...I'LL GIVE YOU FULL ACCESS TO THE REFRIGERATOR FOR THE REMOTE!!
TOM WILSON & TOM II

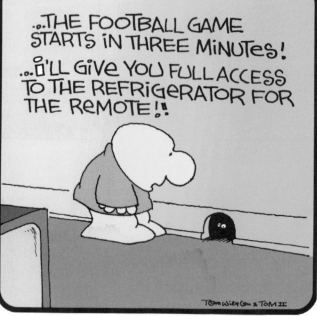

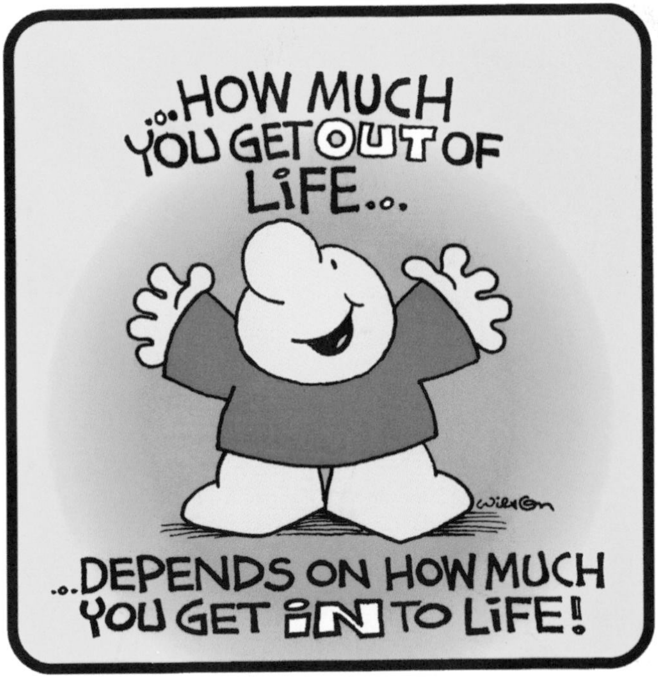
..HOW MUCH YOU GET OUT OF LIFE..
..DEPENDS ON HOW MUCH YOU GET IN TO LIFE!
WILSON

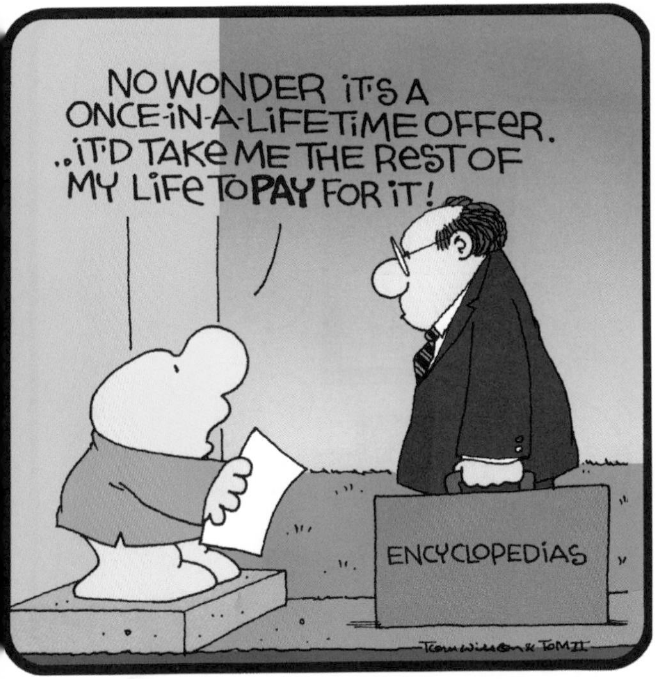
NO WONDER IT'S A ONCE-IN-A-LIFETIME OFFER. ..IT'D TAKE ME THE REST OF MY LIFE TO PAY FOR IT!
ENCYCLOPEDIAS

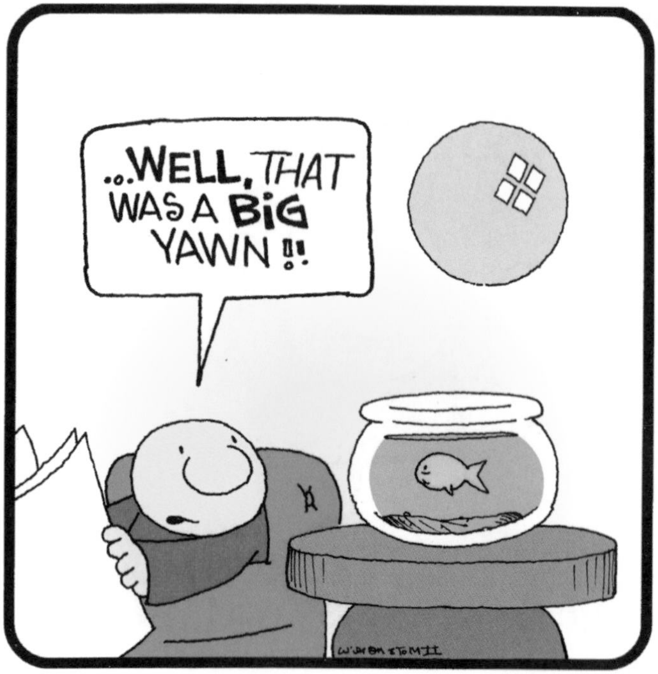
..WELL, THAT WAS A BIG YAWN !!

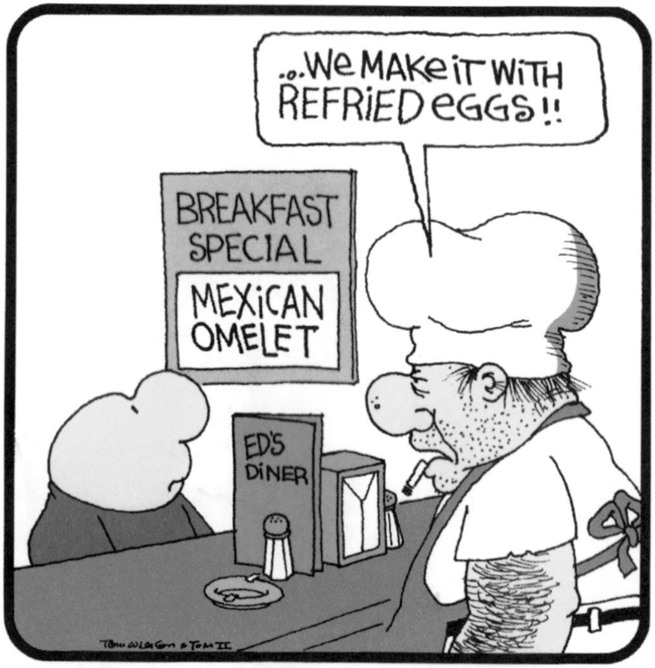
..We MAKE IT WITH REFRIED eGGS !!
BREAKFAST SPECIAL
MEXICAN OMELET
ED'S DINER

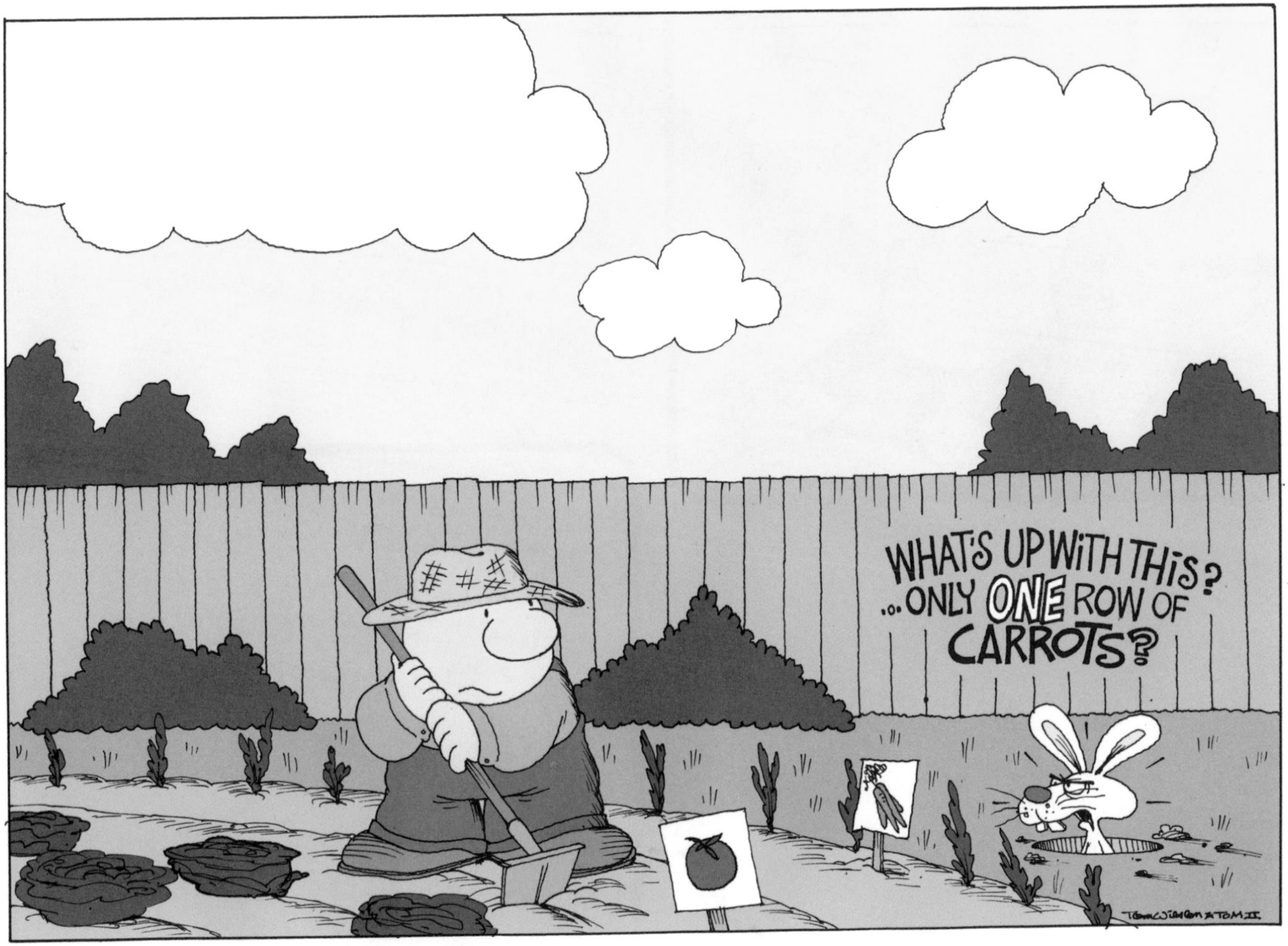
WHAT'S UP WITH THIS?
..ONLY ONE ROW OF
CARROTS?

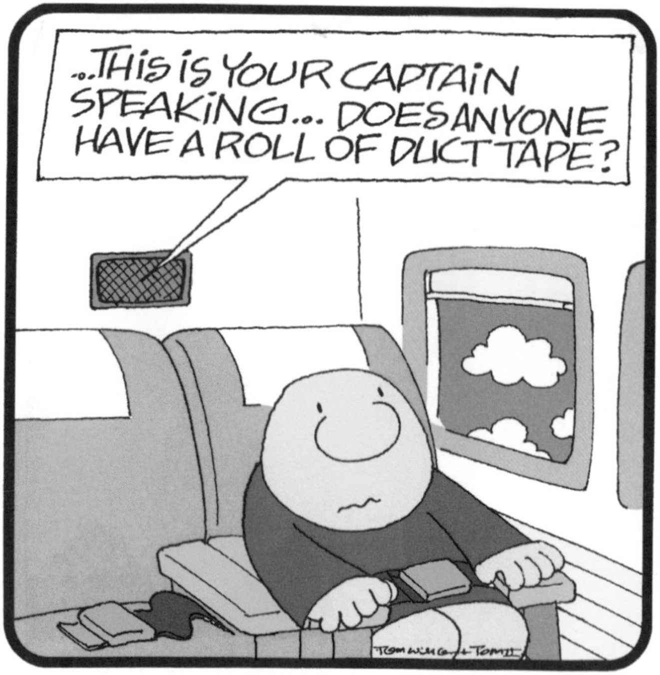
..THIS IS YOUR CAPTAIN SPEAKING... DOES ANYONE HAVE A ROLL OF DUCT TAPE?

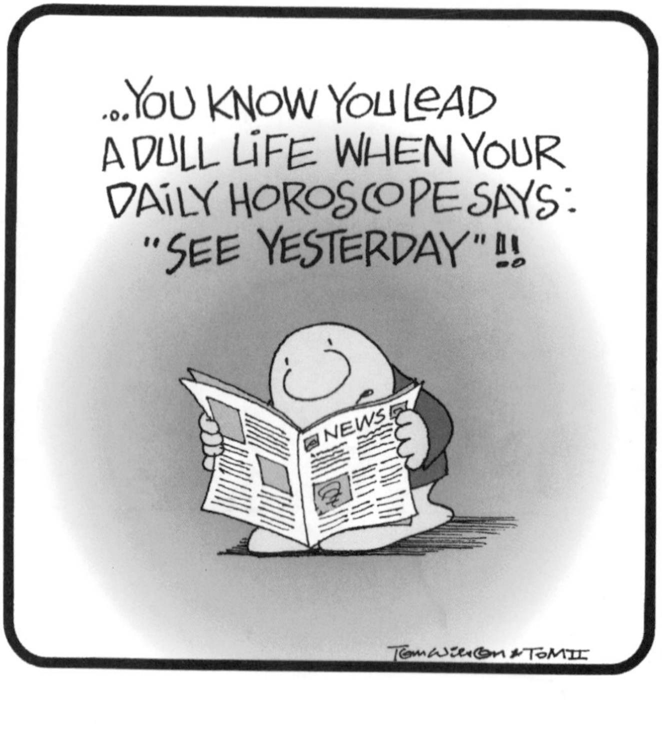
..YOU KNOW YOU LEAD A DULL LIFE WHEN YOUR DAILY HOROSCOPE SAYS: "SEE YESTERDAY"!!
NEWS

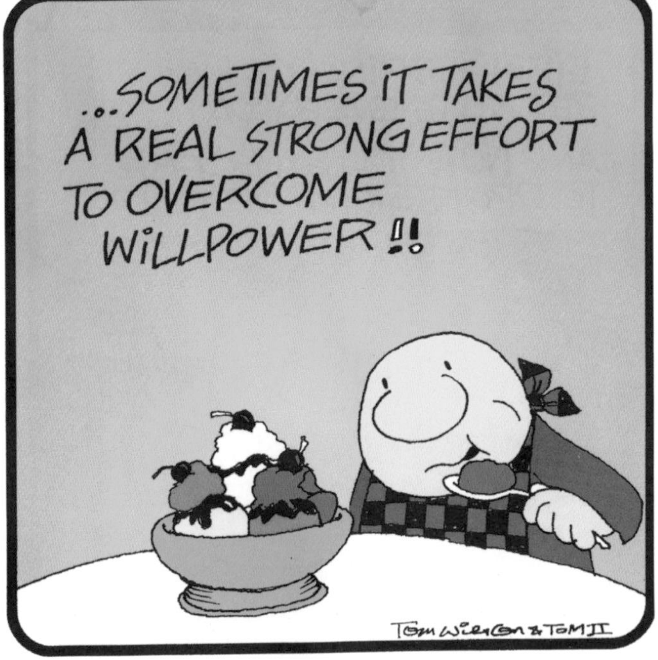
...SOMETIMES IT TAKES A REAL STRONG EFFORT TO OVERCOME WILLPOWER!!
TOM WILSON & TOM II

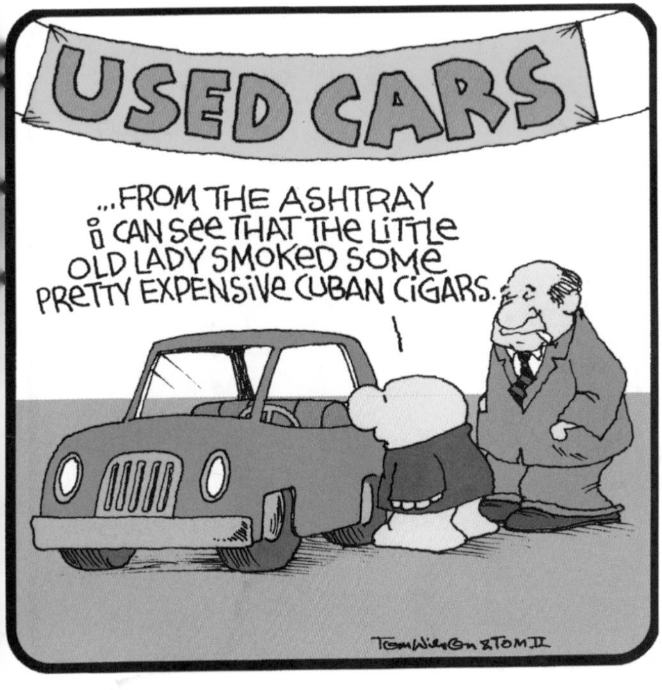
USED CARS
...FROM THE ASHTRAY I CAN SEE THAT THE LITTLE OLD LADY SMOKED SOME PRETTY EXPENSIVE CUBAN CIGARS.
TOM WILSON & TOM II

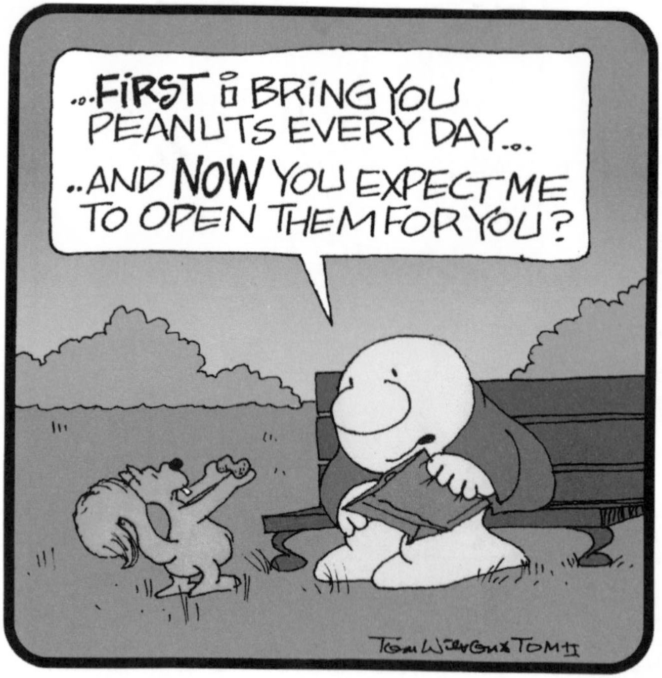
..FIRST I BRING YOU PEANUTS EVERY DAY...
..AND NOW YOU EXPECT ME TO OPEN THEM FOR YOU?

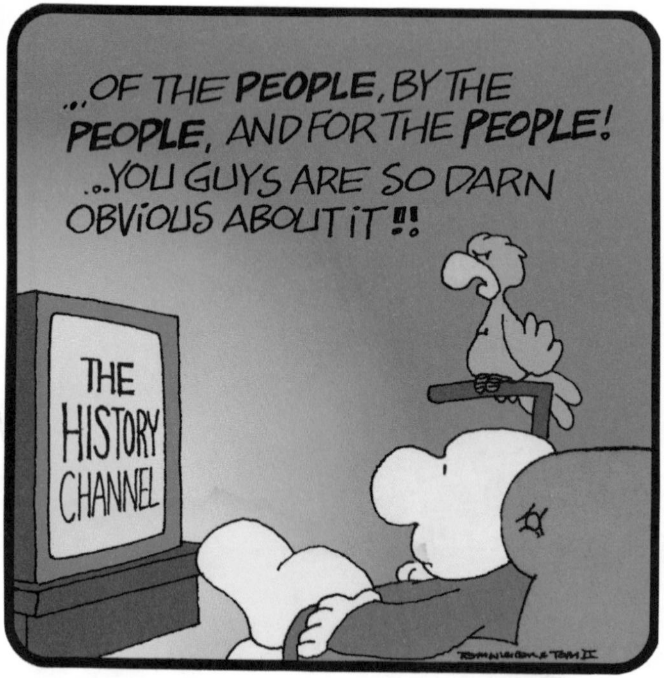
...OF THE PEOPLE, BY THE PEOPLE, AND FOR THE PEOPLE!
..YOU GUYS ARE SO DARN OBVIOUS ABOUT IT!!
THE HISTORY CHANNEL

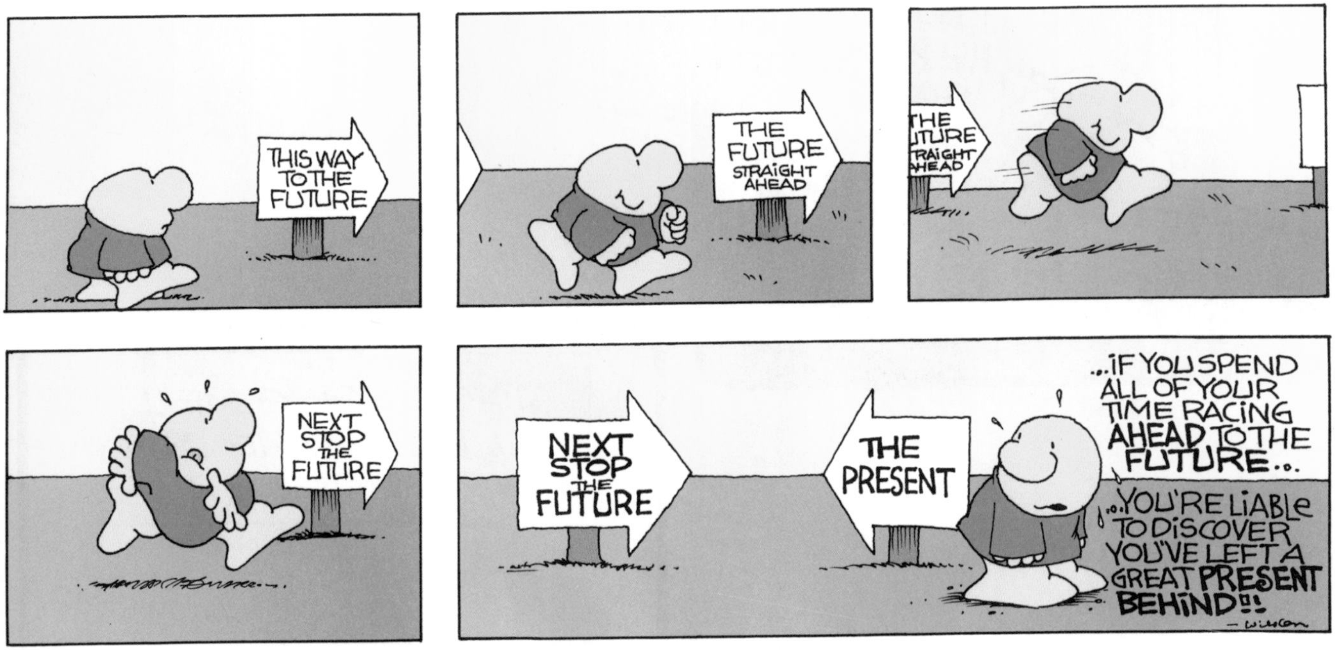
THIS WAY TO THE FUTURE
THE FUTURE STRAIGHT AHEAD
NEXT STOP THE FUTURE
NEXT STOP THE FUTURE
THE PRESENT
...IF YOU SPEND ALL OF YOUR TIME RACING AHEAD TO THE FUTURE...
...YOU'RE LIABLE TO DISCOVER YOU'VE LEFT A GREAT PRESENT BEHIND!!

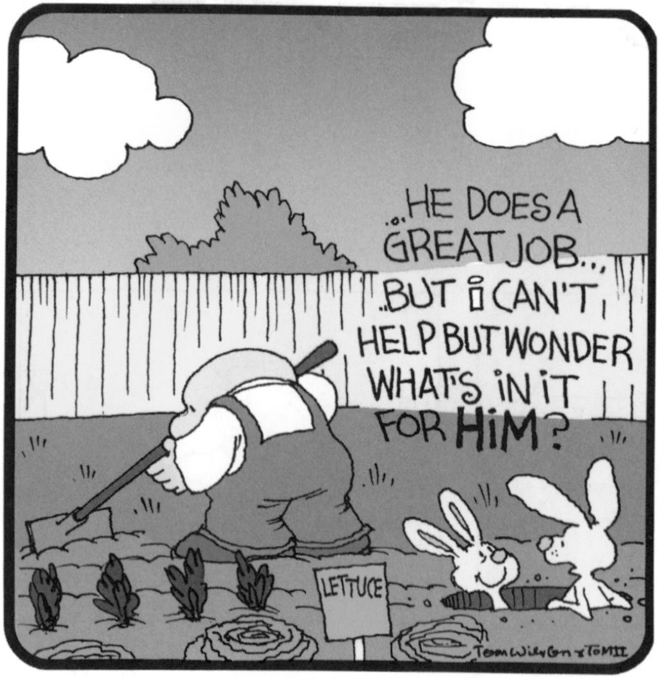
...HE DOES A GREAT JOB...
...BUT I CAN'T HELP BUT WONDER WHAT'S IN IT FOR HIM?
LETTUCE
Tom Wilson & TOM II

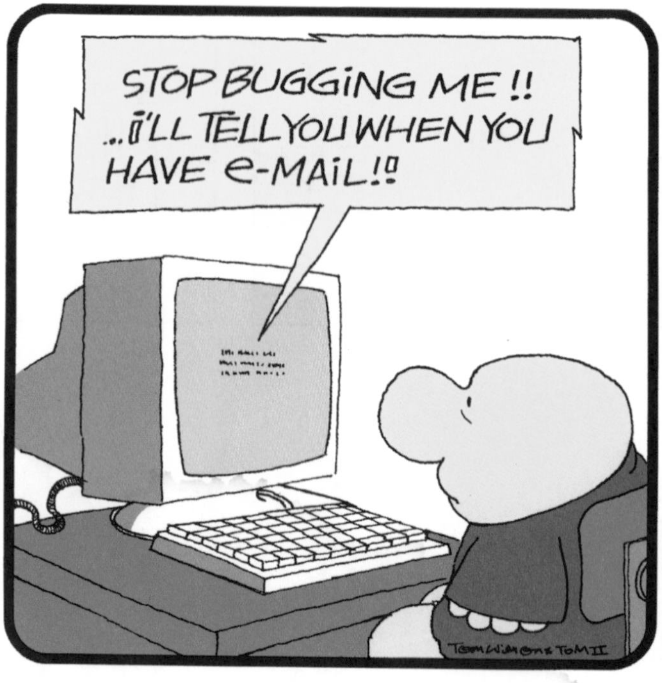
STOP BUGGING ME!! ...I'LL TELL YOU WHEN YOU HAVE E-MAIL!!
Tom Wilson & TOM II

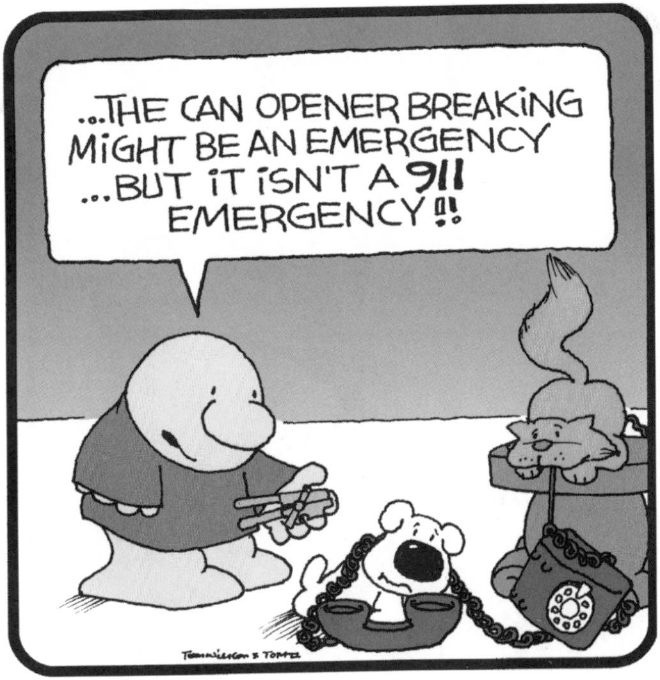
...THE CAN OPENER BREAKING MIGHT BE AN EMERGENCY ...BUT IT ISN'T A 911 EMERGENCY!!
Tom Wilson & Tom II

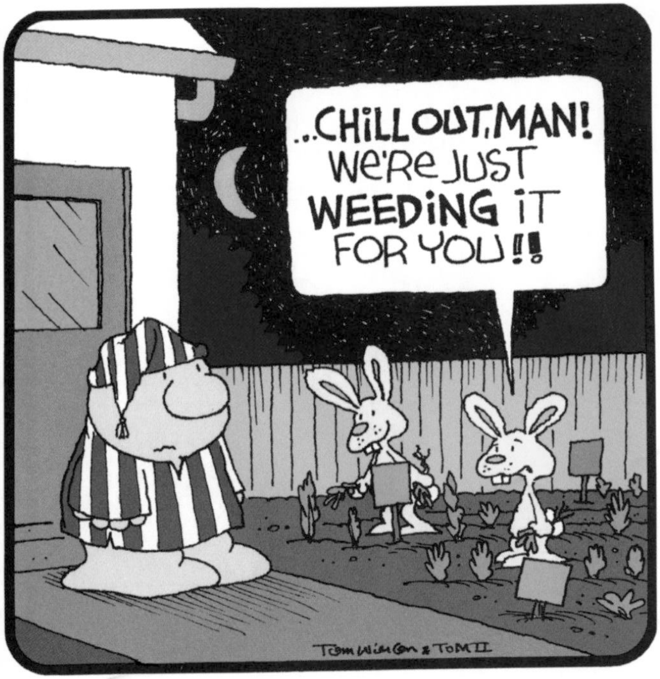
...CHILL OUT, MAN! WE'RE JUST WEEDING IT FOR YOU!!
Tom Wilson & Tom II

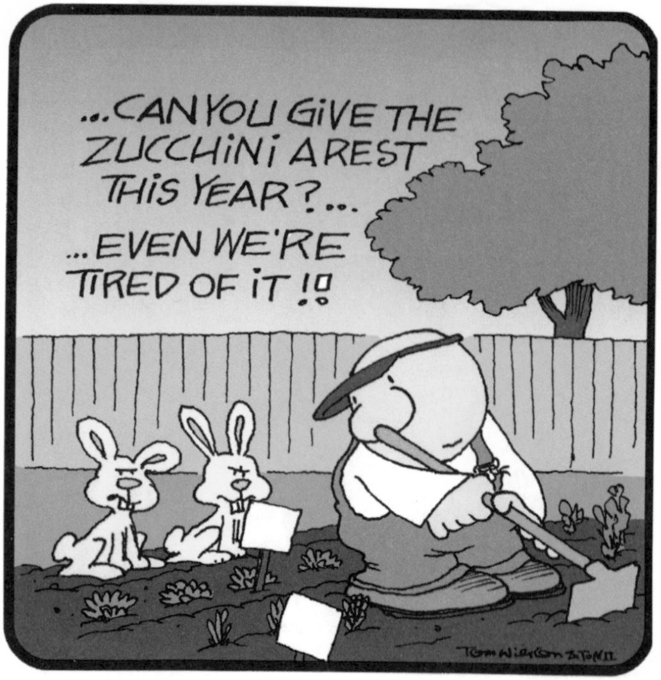
...CAN YOU GIVE THE ZUCCHINI A REST THIS YEAR?...
...EVEN WE'RE TIRED OF IT!!

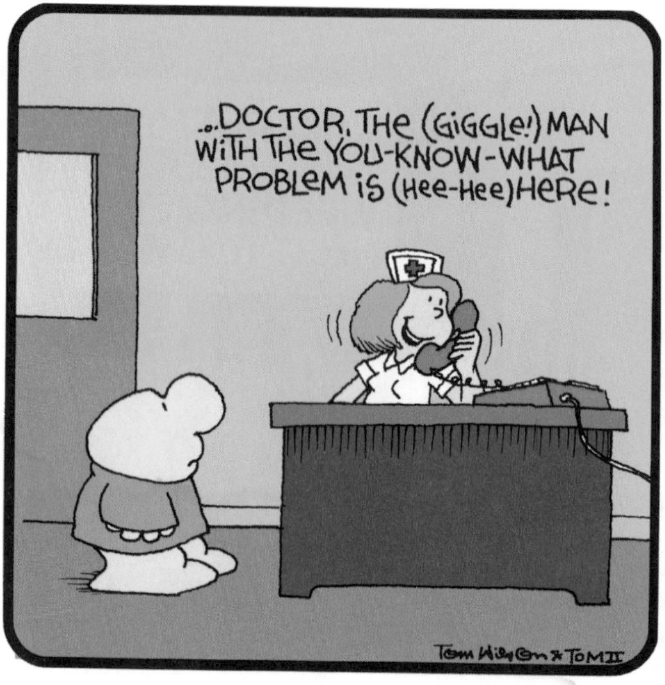
..DOCTOR, THE (GIGGLE!) MAN WITH THE YOU-KNOW-WHAT PROBLEM IS (HEE-HEE) HERE!

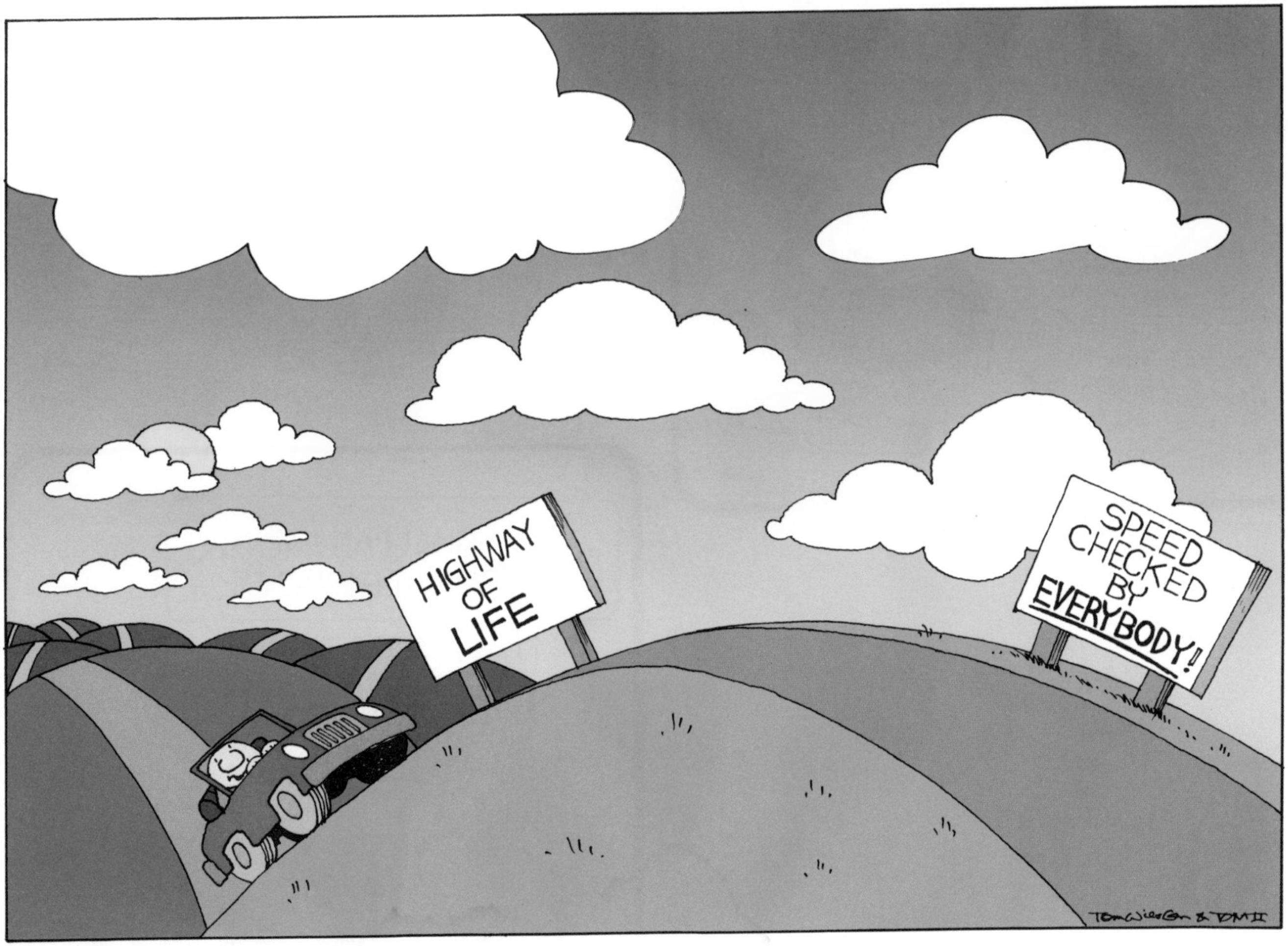
HIGHWAY
OF
LIFE
SPEED
CHECKED
BY
EVERYBODY!

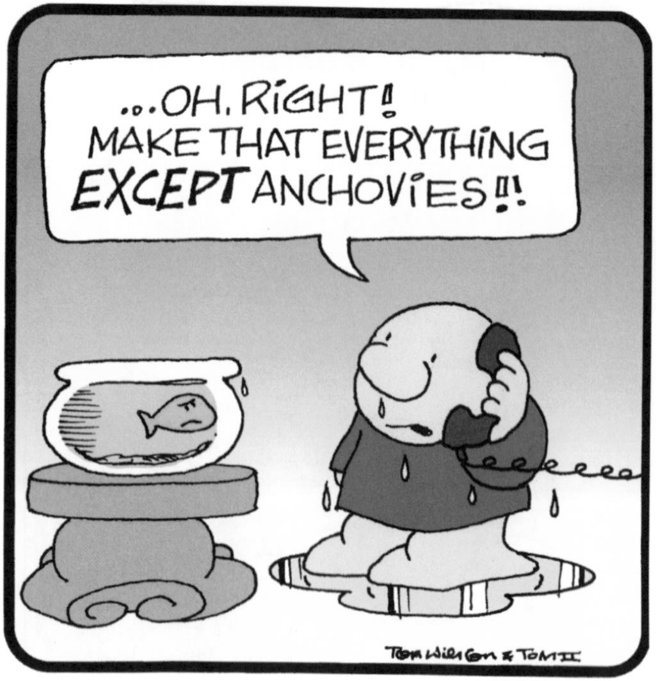
...OH, RIGHT!
MAKE THAT EVERYTHING
EXCEPT ANCHOVIES!!!

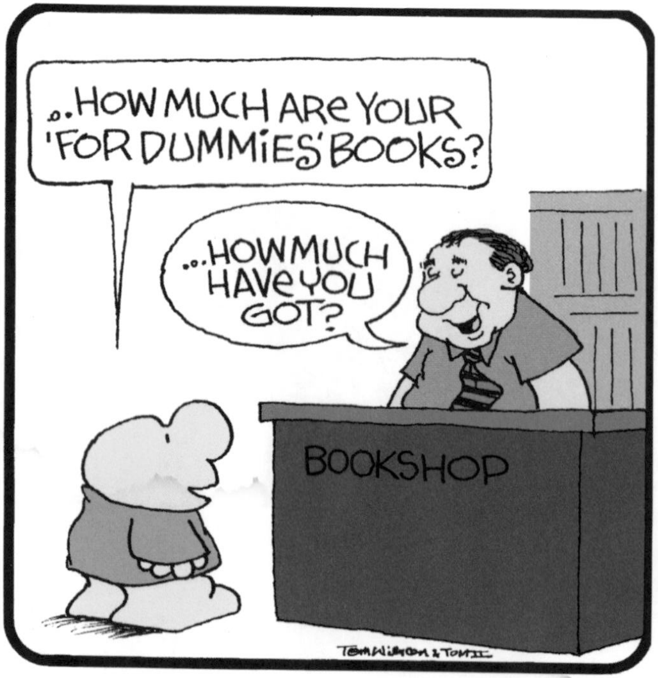
..HOW MUCH ARE YOUR
'FOR DUMMIES' BOOKS?
...HOW MUCH
HAVE YOU
GOT?
BOOKSHOP

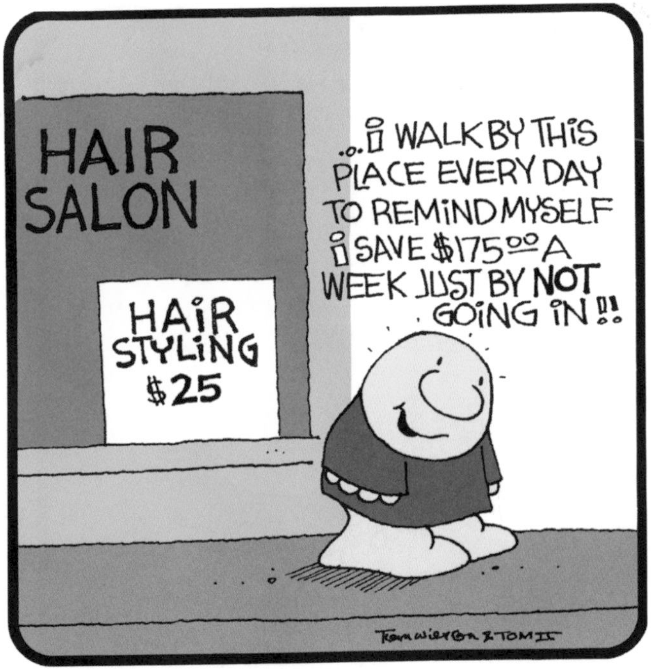
HAIR
SALON
HAIR
STYLING
$25
..i WALK BY THIS PLACE EVERY DAY TO REMIND MYSELF i SAVE $175.00 A WEEK JUST BY NOT GOING IN!!
Tom Wilson & Tom II

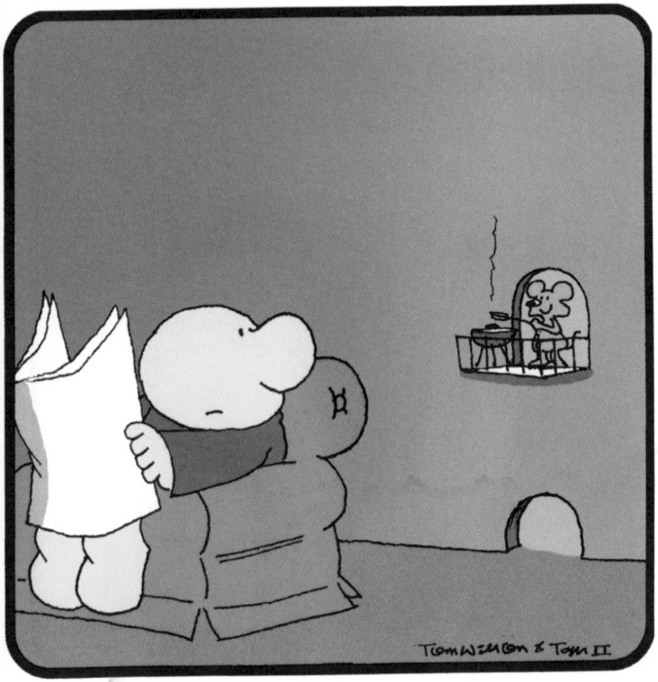
Tom Wilson & Tom II

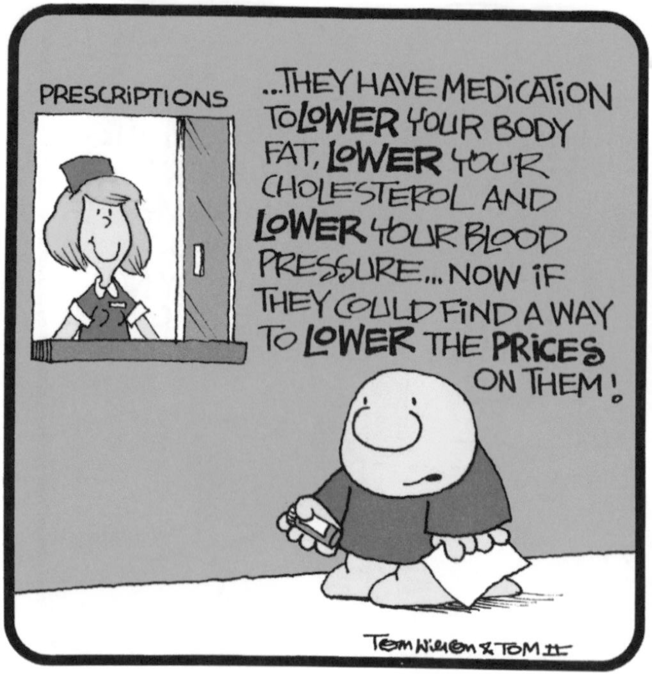
PRESCRIPTIONS
...THEY HAVE MEDICATION TO LOWER YOUR BODY FAT, LOWER YOUR CHOLESTEROL AND LOWER YOUR BLOOD PRESSURE... NOW IF THEY COULD FIND A WAY TO LOWER THE PRICES ON THEM!
Tom Wilson & Tom II

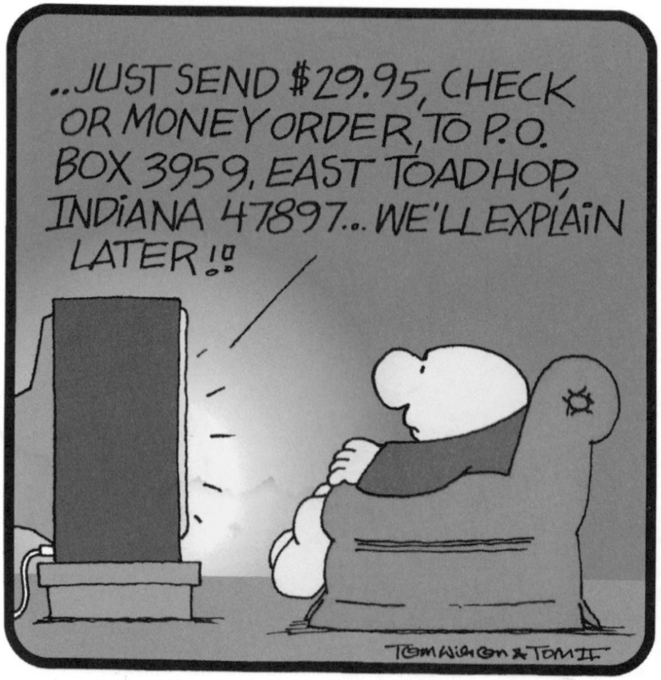
..JUST SEND $29.95, CHECK OR MONEY ORDER, TO P.O. BOX 3959, EAST TOADHOP, INDIANA 47897.. WE'LL EXPLAIN LATER!!
Tom Wilson & Tom II

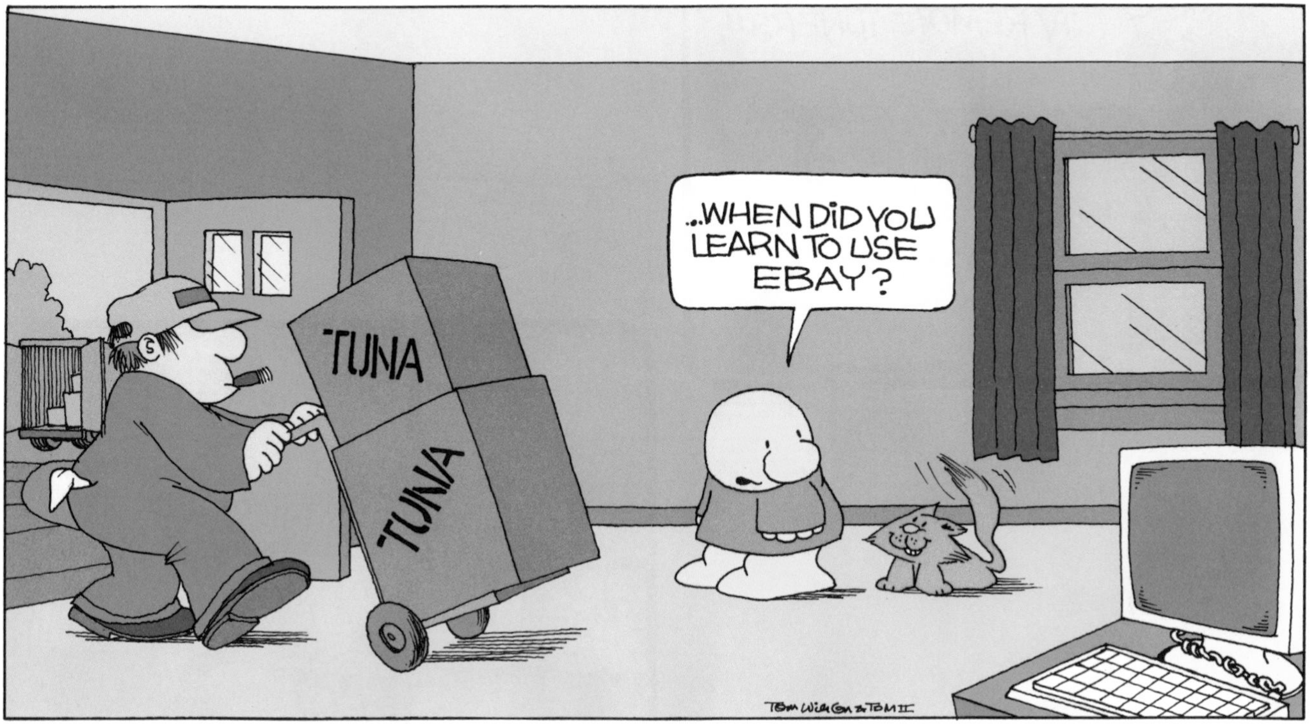

TUNA
TUNA
..WHEN DID YOU LEARN TO USE EBAY?
TOM WILSON & TOM II

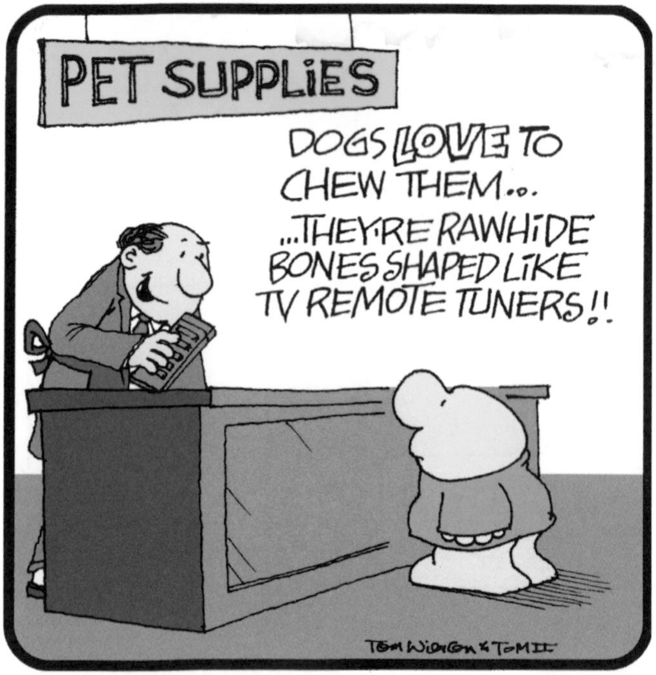
PET SUPPLIES
DOGS LOVE TO CHEW THEM...
...THEY'RE RAWHIDE BONES SHAPED LIKE TV REMOTE TUNERS!!

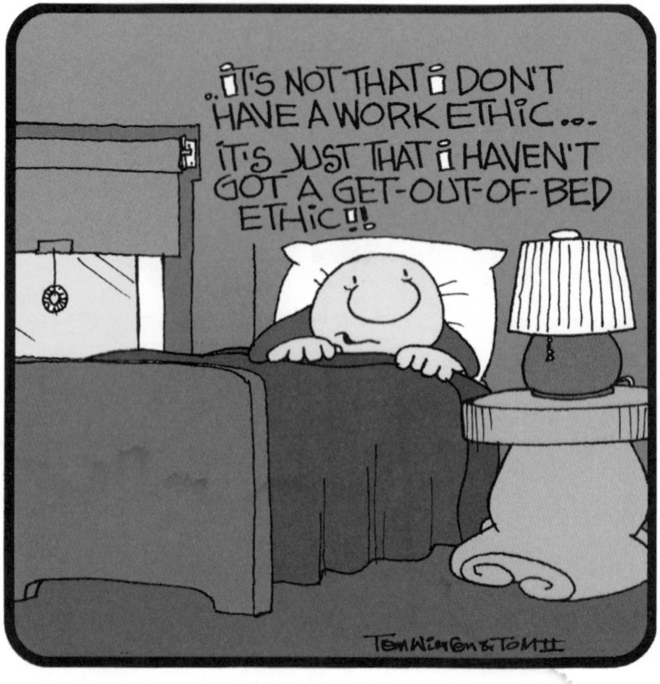
..IT'S NOT THAT I DON'T HAVE A WORK ETHIC...
IT'S JUST THAT I HAVEN'T GOT A GET-OUT-OF-BED ETHIC!!

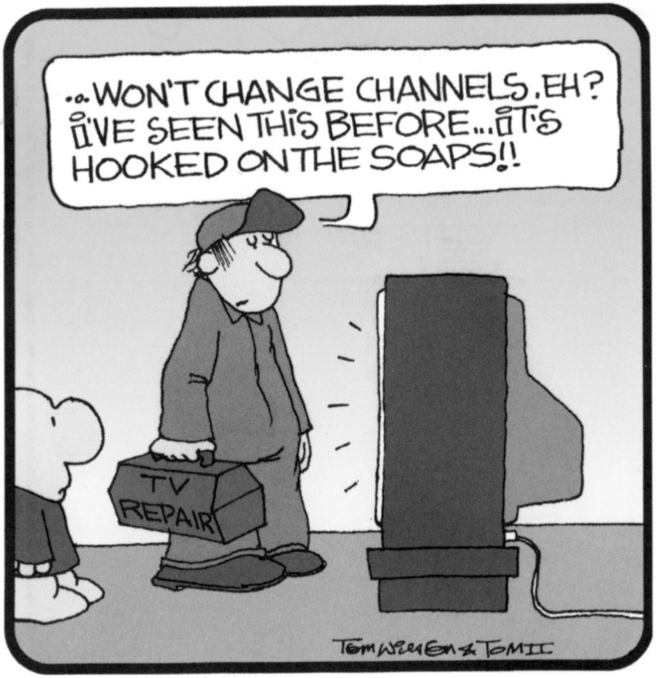
..WON'T CHANGE CHANNELS, EH? I'VE SEEN THIS BEFORE...IT'S HOOKED ON THE SOAPS!!
TV REPAIR
Tom Wilson & Tom II

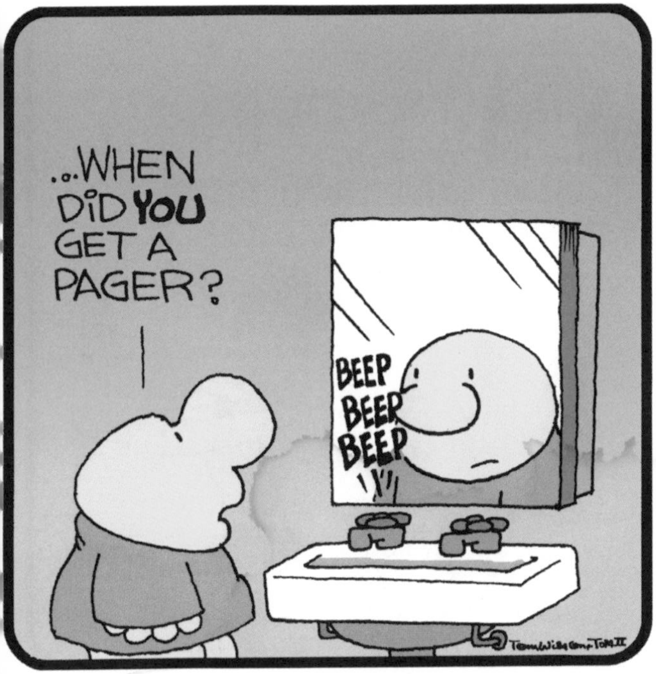
..WHEN DID YOU GET A PAGER?
BEEP BEEP BEEP
Tom Wilson & Tom II

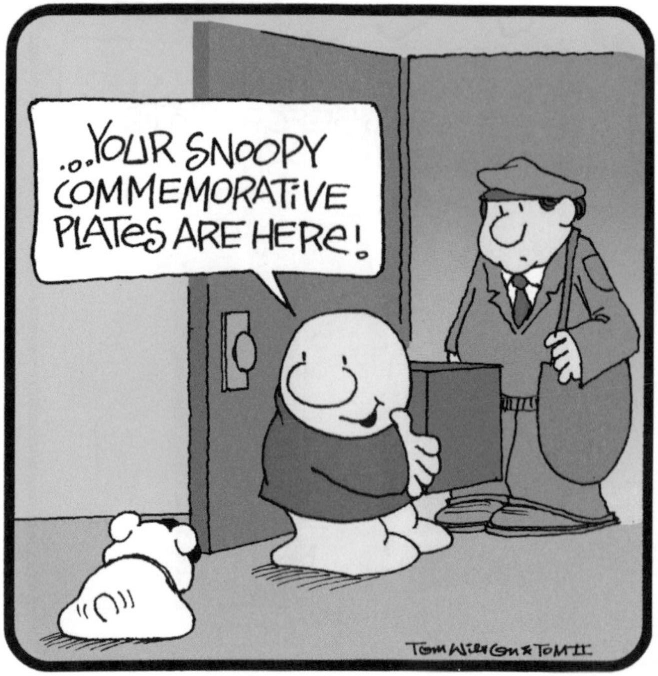
..o..YOUR SNOOPY COMMEMORATIVE PLATES ARE HERE!
TOM WILSON & TOM II

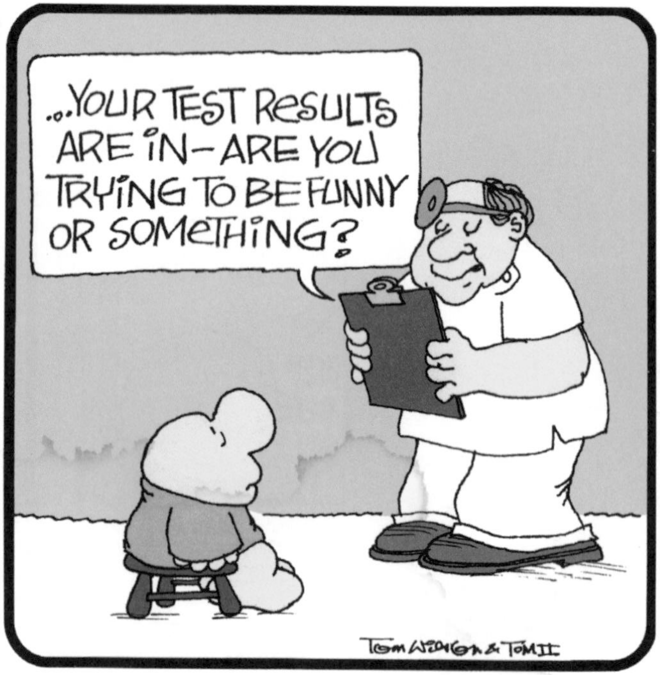
..o..YOUR TEST RESULTS ARE IN–ARE YOU TRYING TO BE FUNNY OR SOMETHING?
TOM WILSON & TOM II

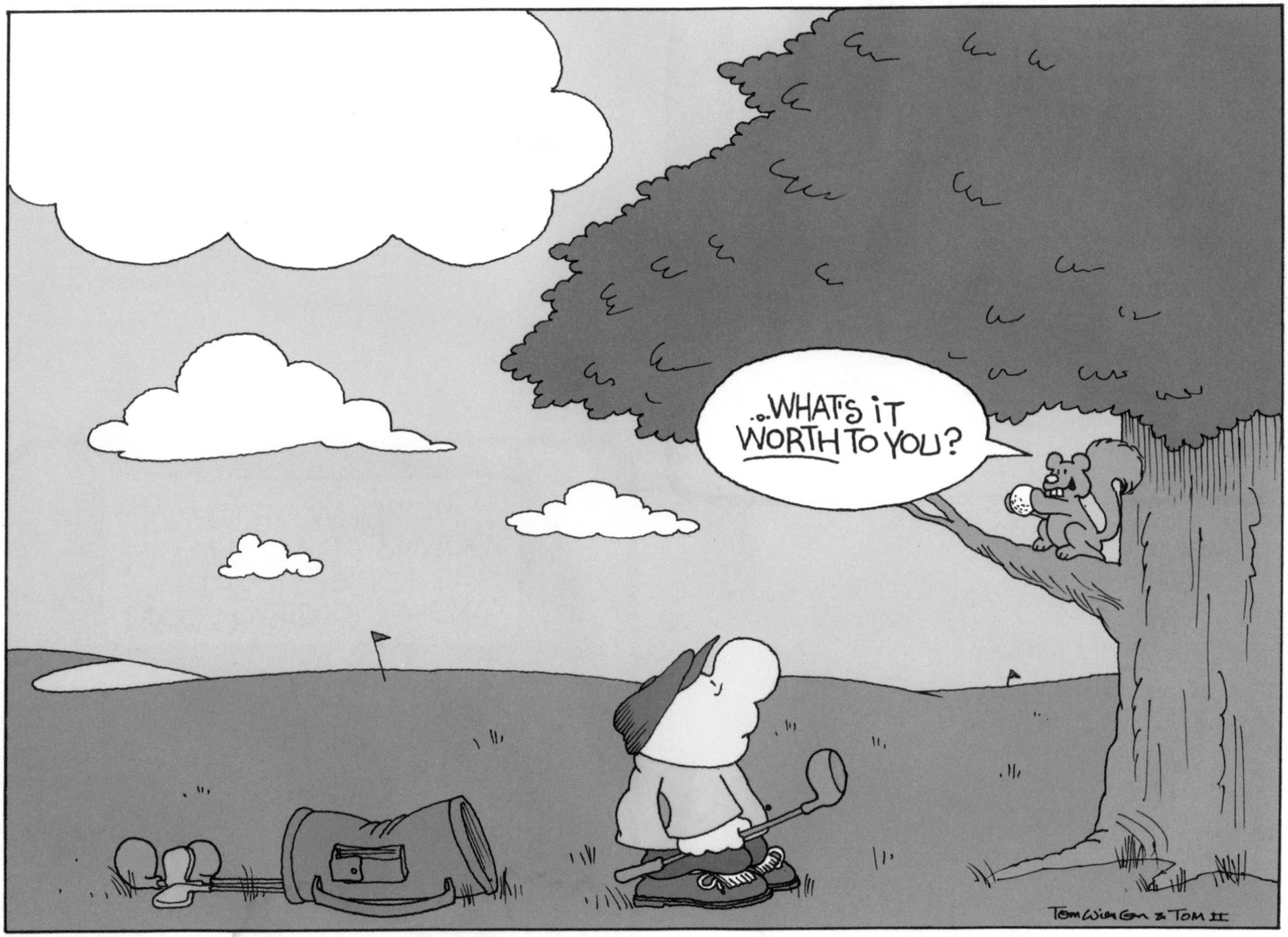
..WHAT'S IT WORTH TO YOU?
TOM WILSON & TOM II

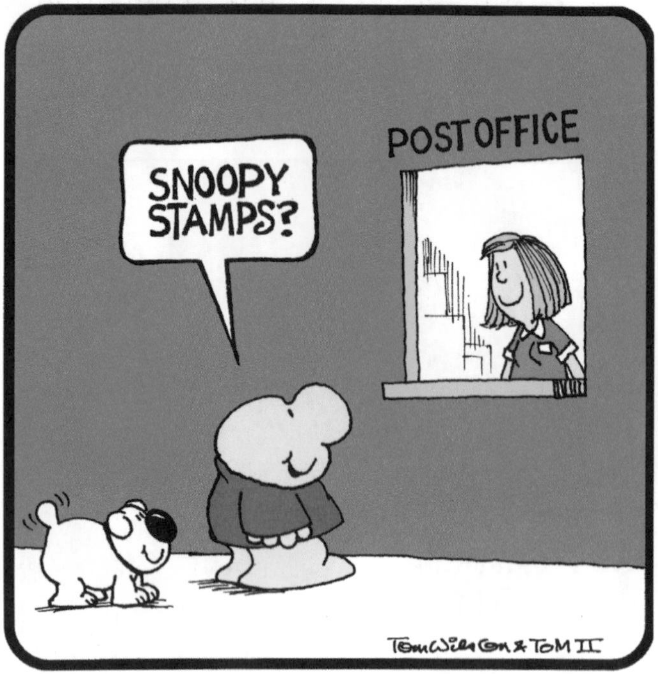
POST OFFICE
SNOOPY STAMPS?
TOM WILSON & TOM II

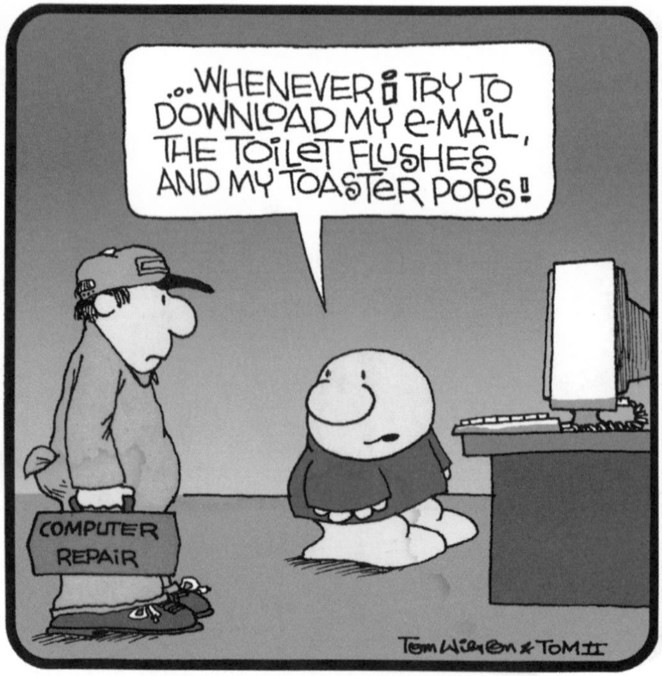
...WHENEVER I TRY TO DOWNLOAD MY e-MAIL, THE TOILET FLUSHES AND MY TOASTER POPS!
COMPUTER REPAIR
TOM WILSON & TOM II

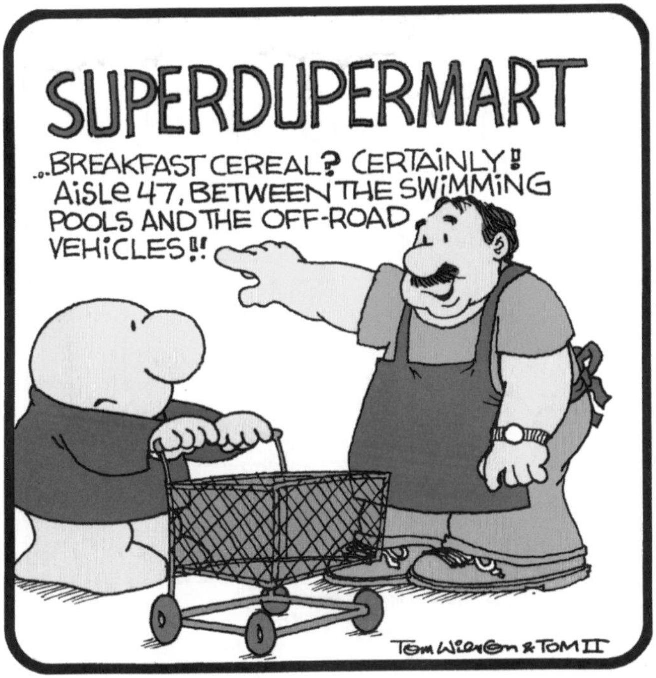
SUPERDUPERMART
..o..BREAKFAST CEREAL? CERTAINLY! AiSLe 47, BETWEEN THE SWiMMiNG POOLS AND THE OFF-ROAD VEHiCLES!!
TOM WILSON & TOM II

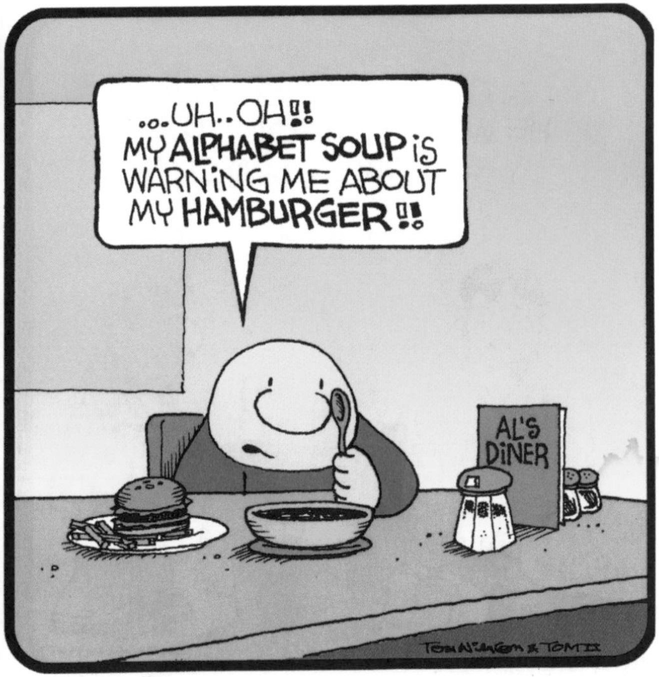
..o..UH..OH!!
MY ALPHABET SOUP iS WARNiNG ME ABOUT MY HAMBURGER!!
AL'S DiNER
TOM WILSON & TOM II

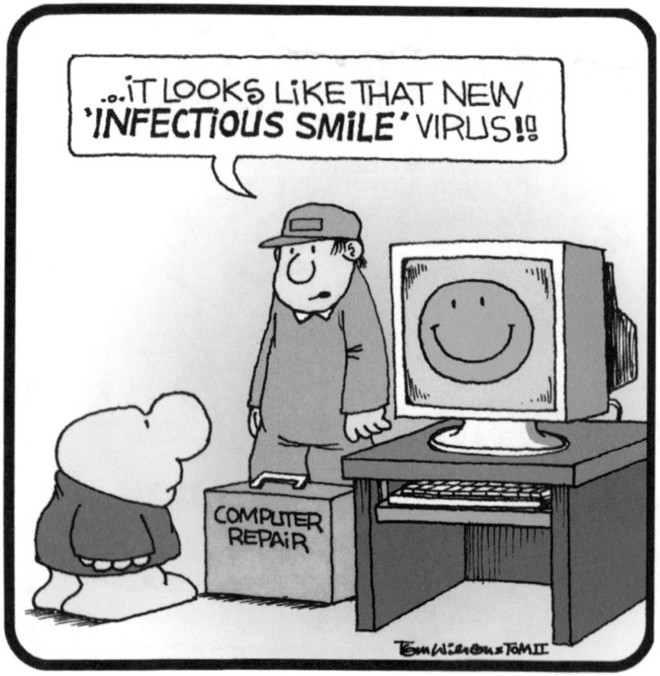
..IT LOOKS LIKE THAT NEW 'INFECTIOUS SMILE' VIRUS!!
COMPUTER REPAIR

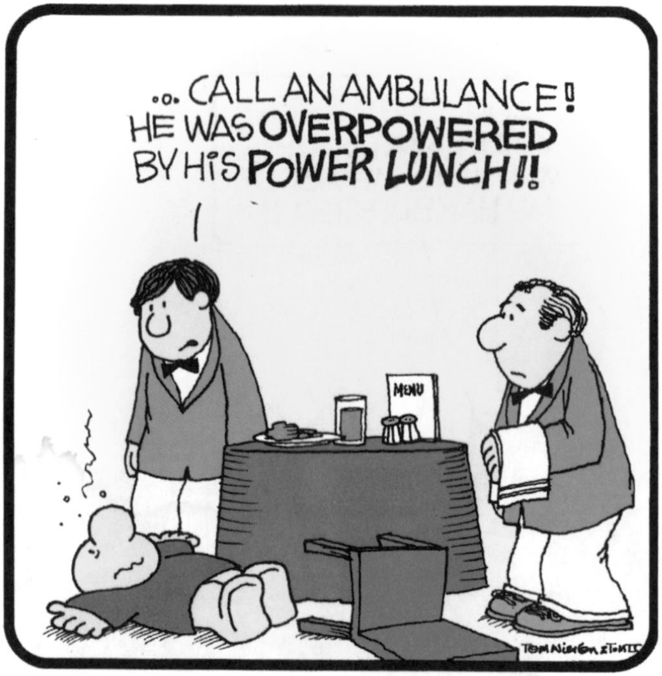
.. CALL AN AMBULANCE! HE WAS OVERPOWERED BY HIS POWER LUNCH!!
MENU

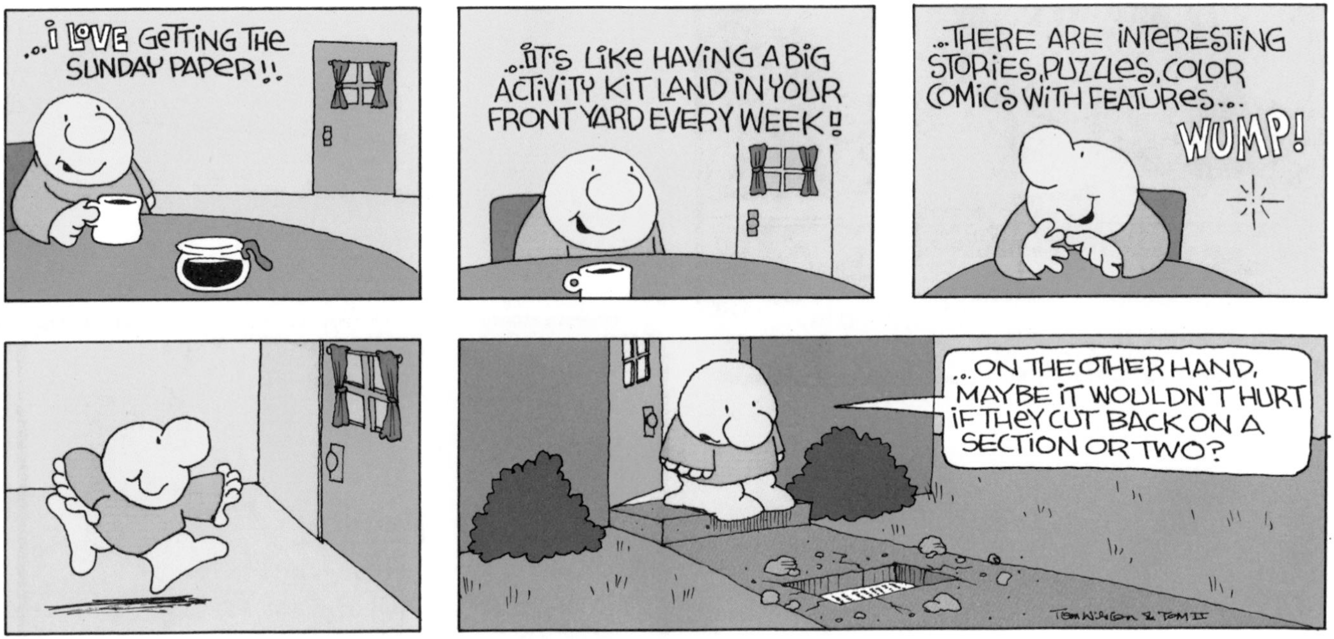
..I LOVE GETTING THE SUNDAY PAPER!!
..IT'S LIKE HAVING A BIG ACTIVITY KIT LAND IN YOUR FRONT YARD EVERY WEEK!
..THERE ARE INTERESTING STORIES, PUZZLES, COLOR COMICS WITH FEATURES...
WUMP!
..ON THE OTHER HAND, MAYBE IT WOULDN'T HURT IF THEY CUT BACK ON A SECTION OR TWO?
Tom Wilson & Tom II

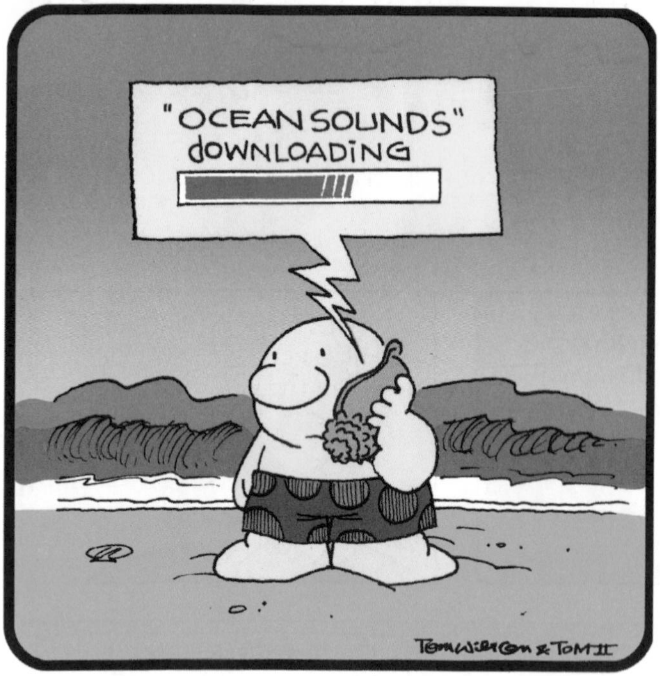
"OCEAN SOUNDS" DOWNLOADING
TOM WILSON & TOM II

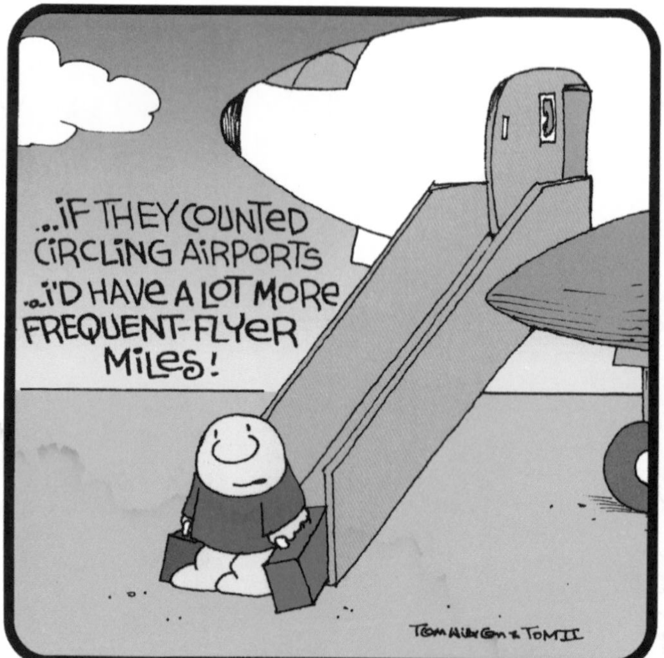
..IF THEY COUNTED CIRCLING AIRPORTS ..I'D HAVE A LOT MORE FREQUENT-FLYER MILES!
TOM WILSON & TOM II

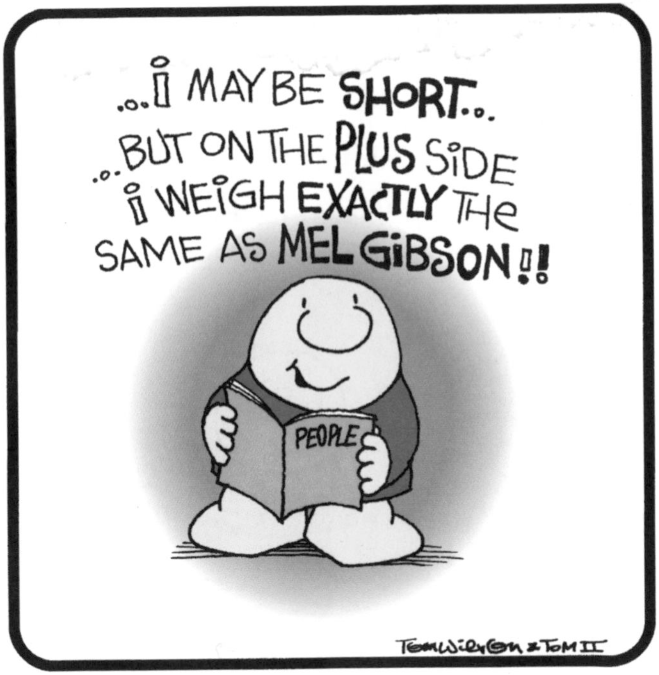
...i MAY BE SHORT...
...BUT ON THE PLUS SiDE
i WEiGH EXACTLY THE
SAME AS MEL GiBSON!!
PEOPLE
TomWilson & TOM II

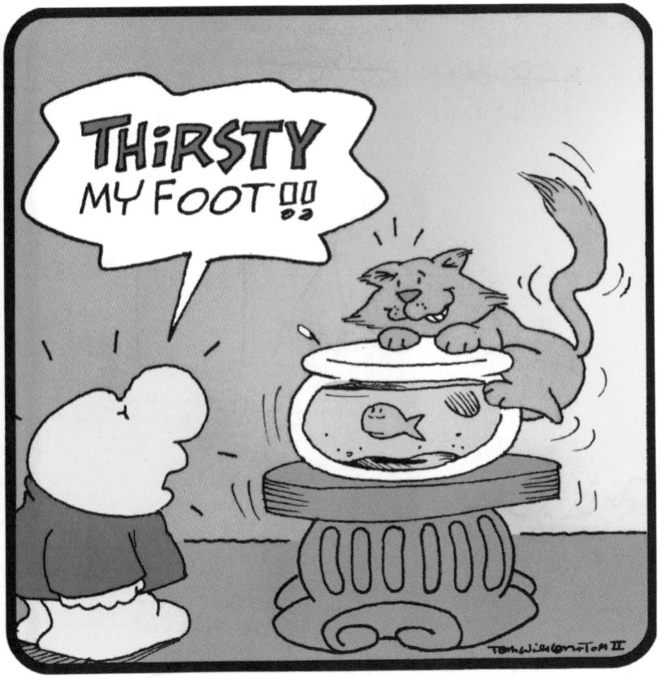
THiRSTY
MY FOOT!!
TomWilson & TOM II

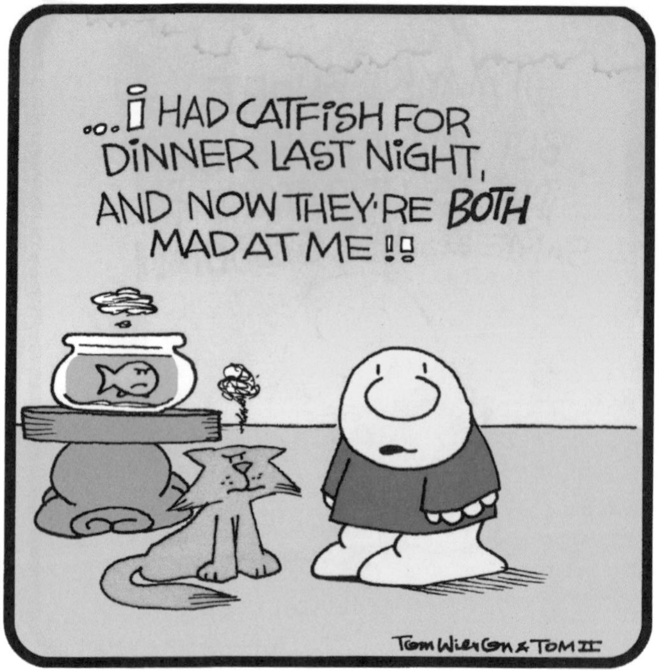
...I HAD CATFISH FOR DINNER LAST NIGHT, AND NOW THEY'RE BOTH MAD AT ME !!
Tom Wilson & TOM II

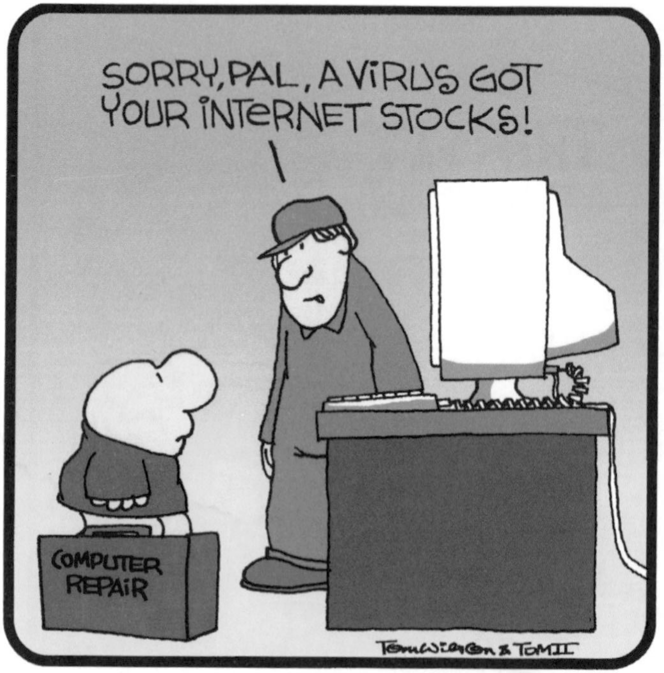
SORRY, PAL, A VIRUS GOT YOUR INTERNET STOCKS!
COMPUTER REPAIR
Tom Wilson & TOM II

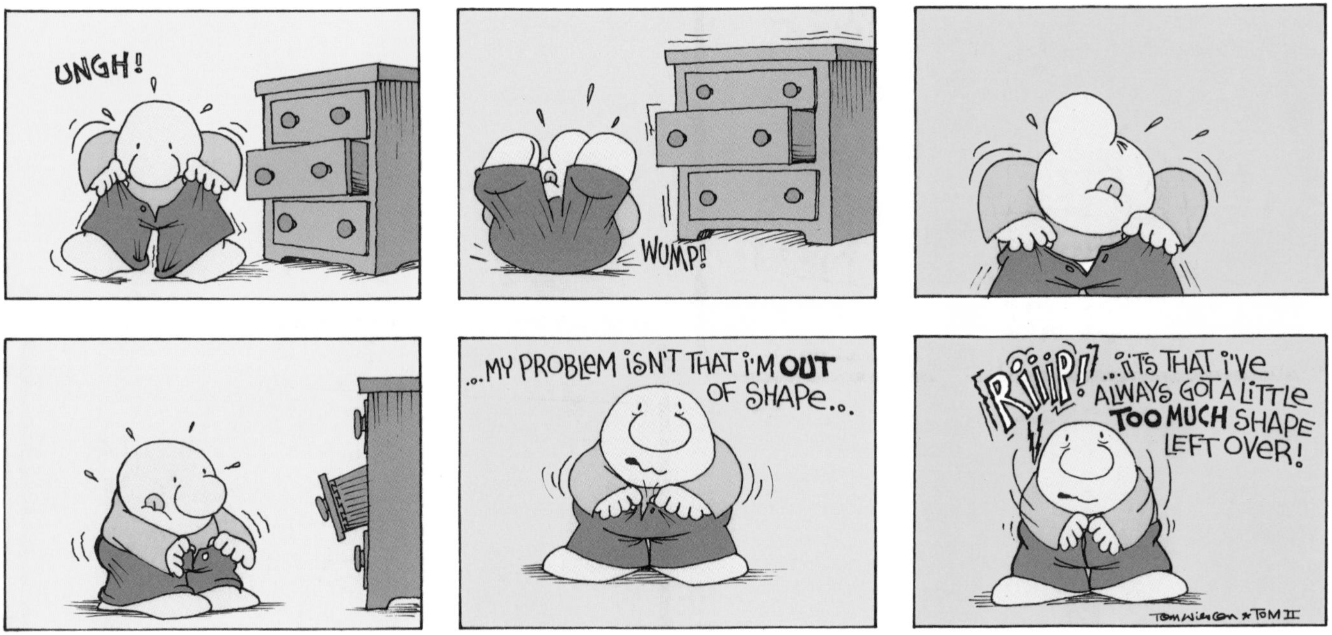
UNGH!
WUMP!
..MY PROBLEM ISN'T THAT I'M **OUT** OF SHAPE...
RIIIP!
...IT'S THAT I'VE ALWAYS GOT A LITTLE **TOO MUCH** SHAPE LEFT OVER!

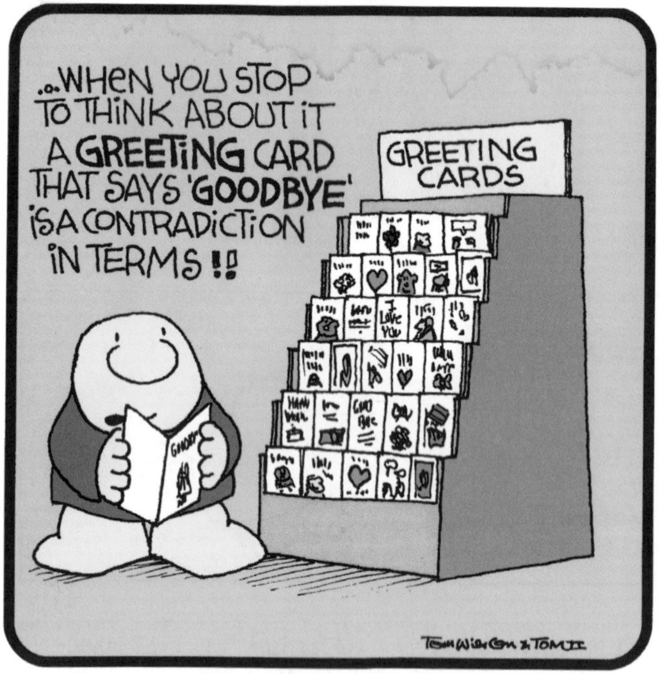
..WHEN YOU STOP TO THINK ABOUT IT A **GREETING** CARD THAT SAYS '**GOODBYE**' IS A CONTRADICTION IN TERMS !!
GREETING CARDS
TOM WILSON & TOM II

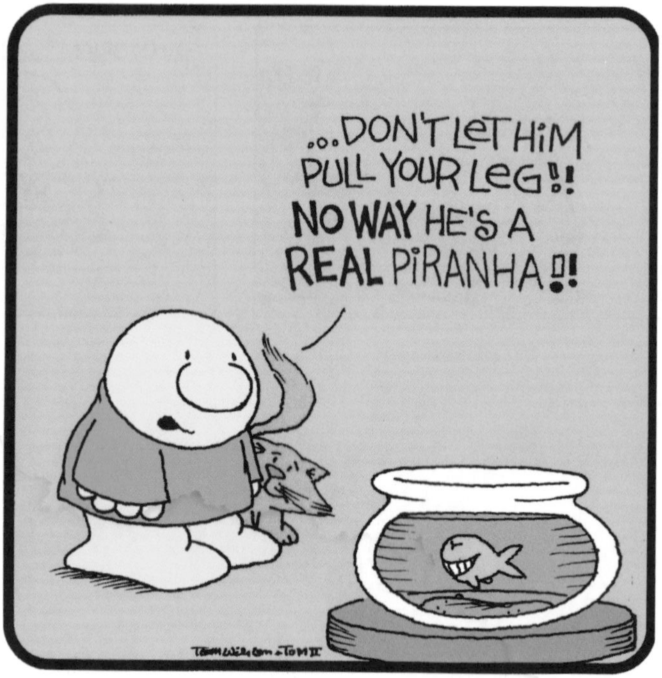
...DON'T LET HIM PULL YOUR LEG!! **NO WAY** HE'S A **REAL** PIRANHA!!
TOM WILSON & TOM II

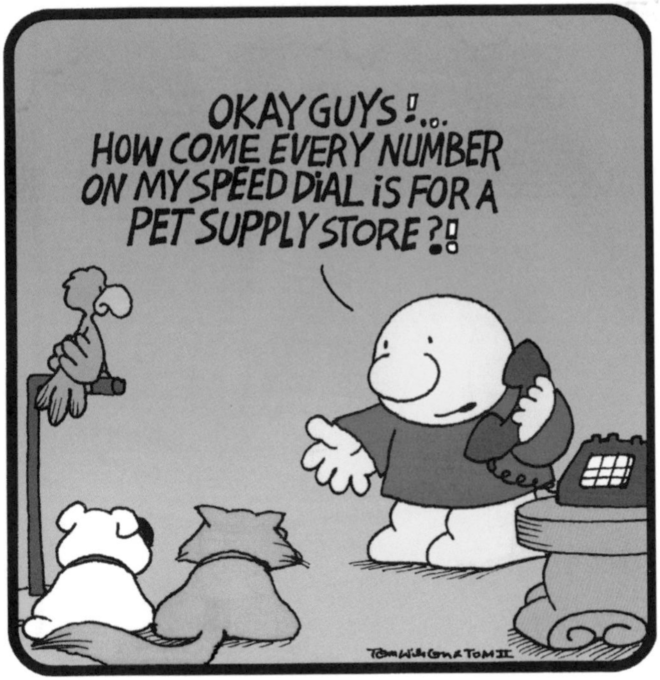
OKAY GUYS !...
HOW COME EVERY NUMBER ON MY SPEED DIAL IS FOR A PET SUPPLY STORE ?!
TOM WILSON & TOM II

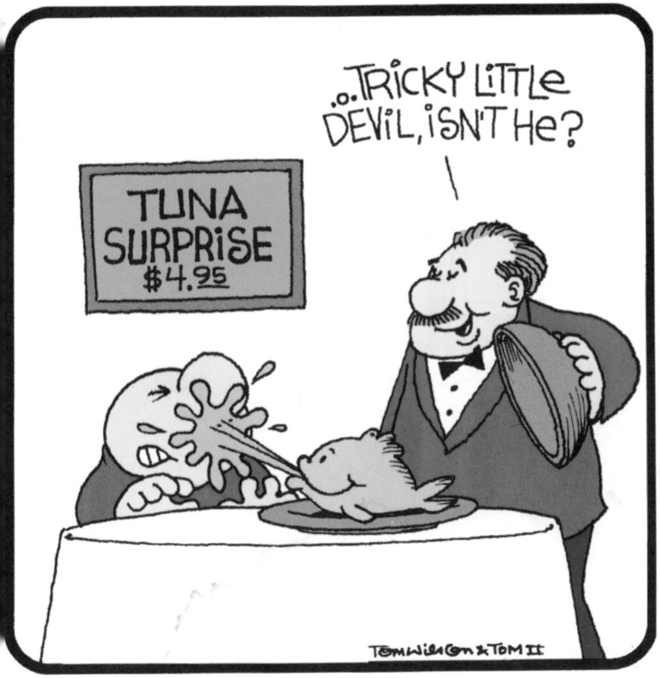
..o..TRICKY LITTLE DEVIL, ISN'T HE?
TUNA SURPRISE $4.95
TOM WILSON & TOM II

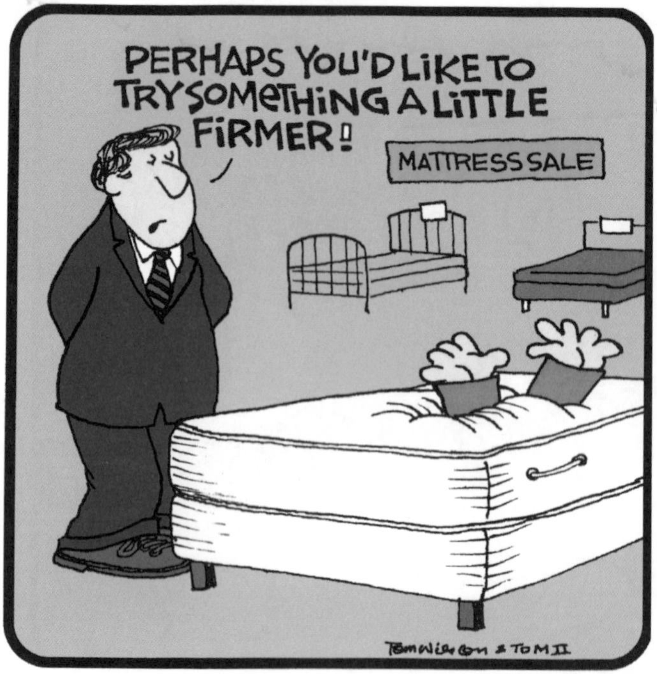
PERHAPS YOU'D LIKE TO TRY SOMETHING A LITTLE FIRMER!
MATTRESS SALE

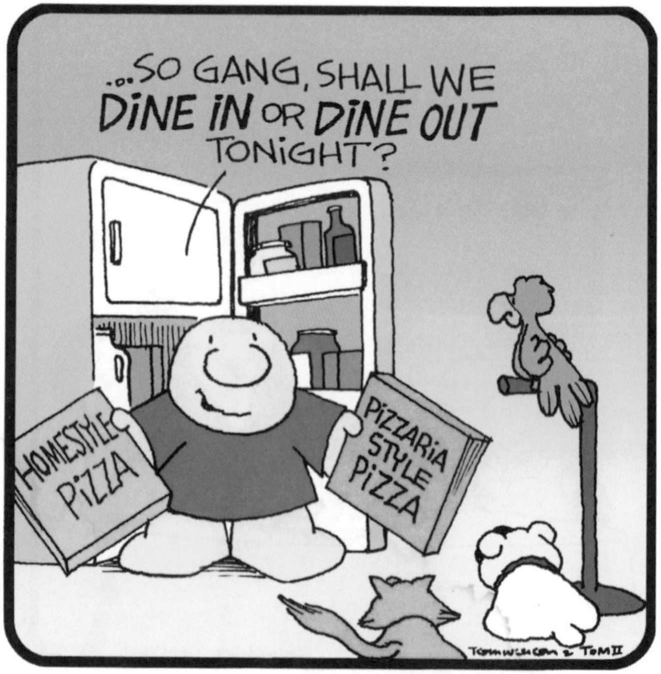
...SO GANG, SHALL WE DINE IN OR DINE OUT TONIGHT?
HOMESTYLE PIZZA
PIZZARIA STYLE PIZZA

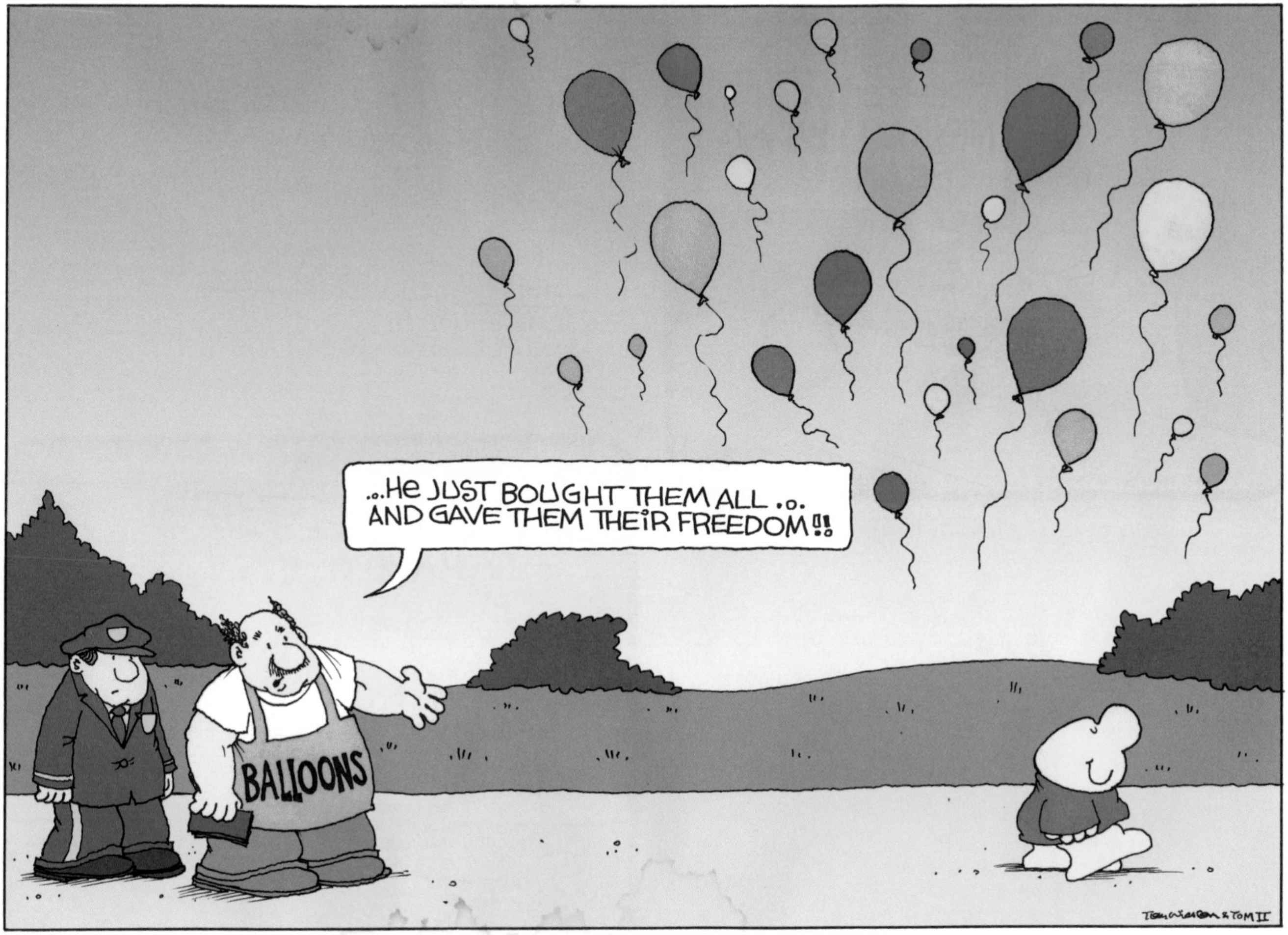
..He JUST BOUGHT THEM ALL .o.
AND GAVE THEM THEiR FREEDOM!!
BALLOONS

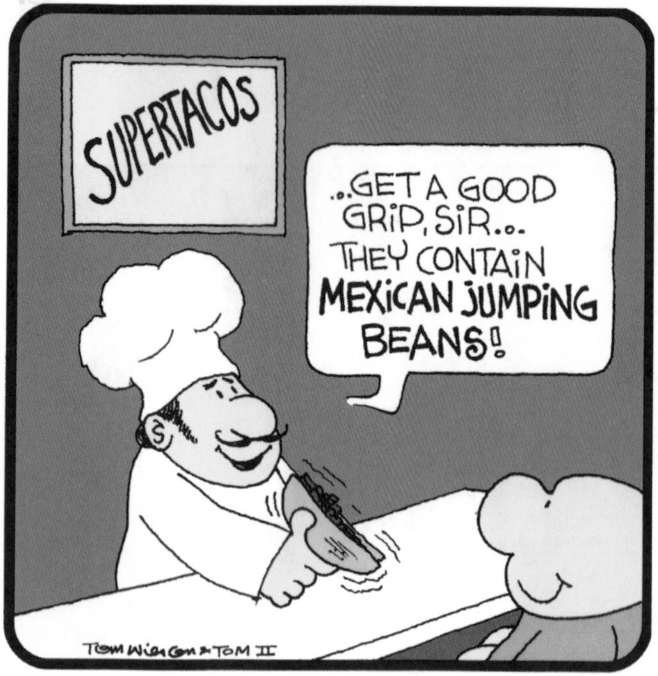
SUPERTACOS
..GET A GOOD GRIP, SIR.... THEY CONTAIN MEXICAN JUMPING BEANS!
TOM WILSON & TOM II

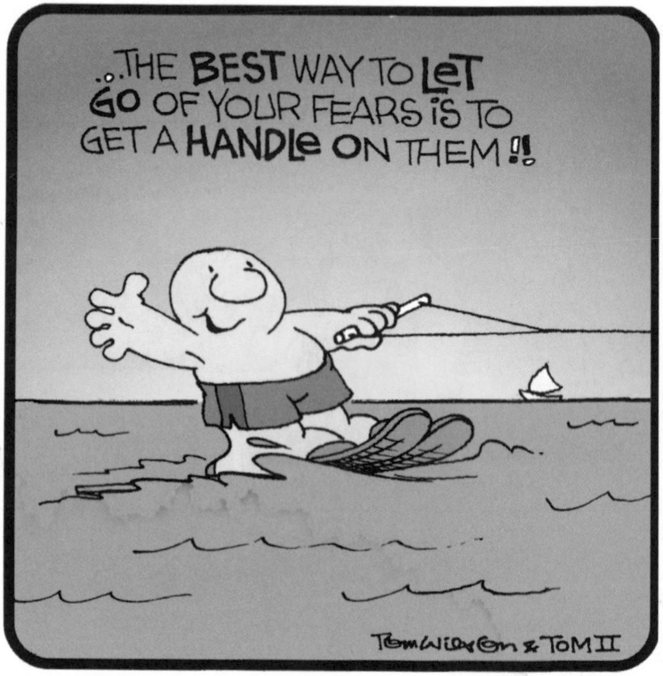
..THE BEST WAY TO LET GO OF YOUR FEARS IS TO GET A HANDLE ON THEM!!
TOM WILSON & TOM II

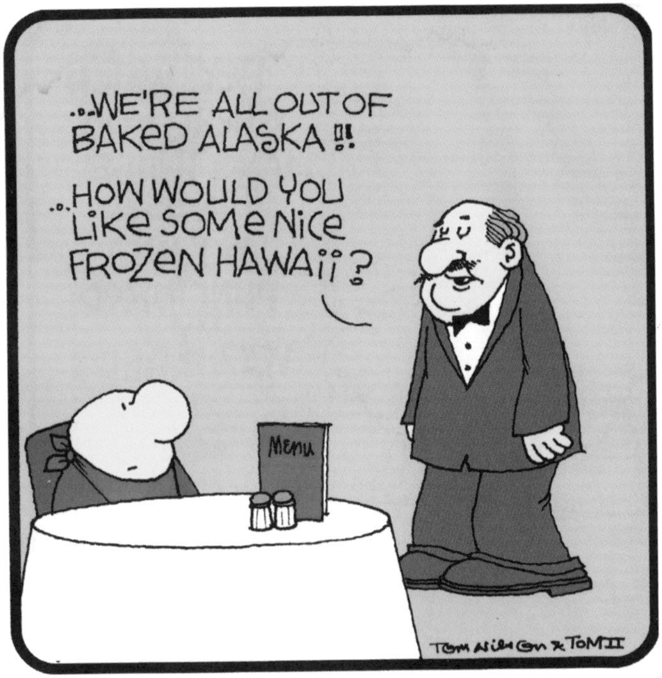
..WE'RE ALL OUT OF BAKED ALASKA !!
..HOW WOULD YOU LIKE SOME NICE FROZEN HAWAII?
Menu
TOM WILSON & TOM II

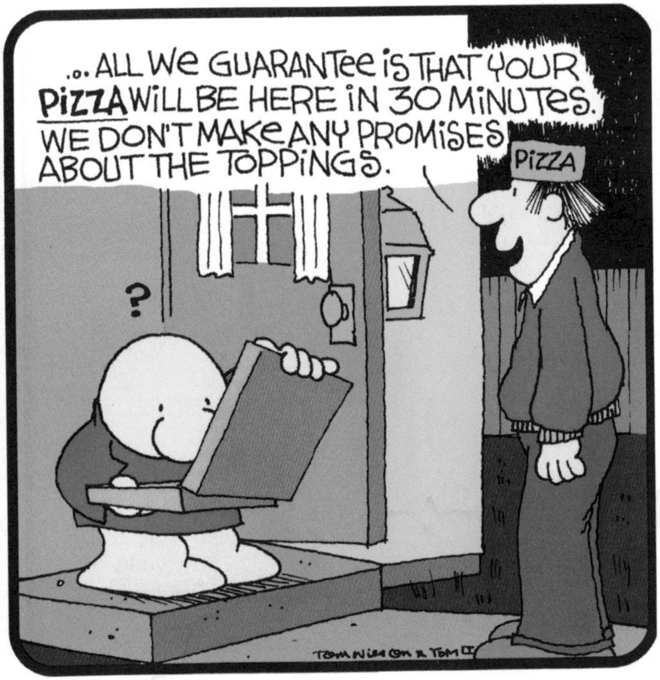
..ALL WE GUARANTEE IS THAT YOUR PIZZA WILL BE HERE IN 30 MINUTES. WE DON'T MAKE ANY PROMISES ABOUT THE TOPPINGS.
PIZZA
?
TOM WILSON & TOM II

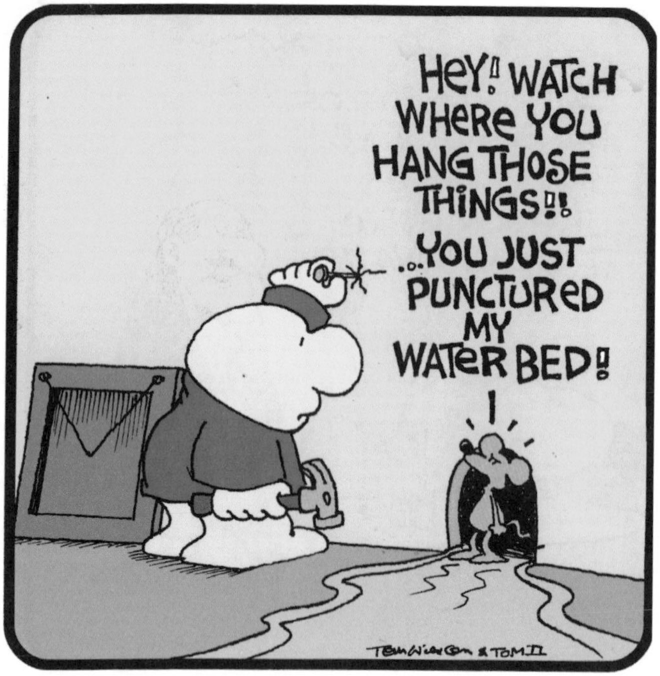
HEY! WATCH WHERE YOU HANG THOSE THINGS!!
..YOU JUST PUNCTURED MY WATER BED!
TOM WILSON & TOM II

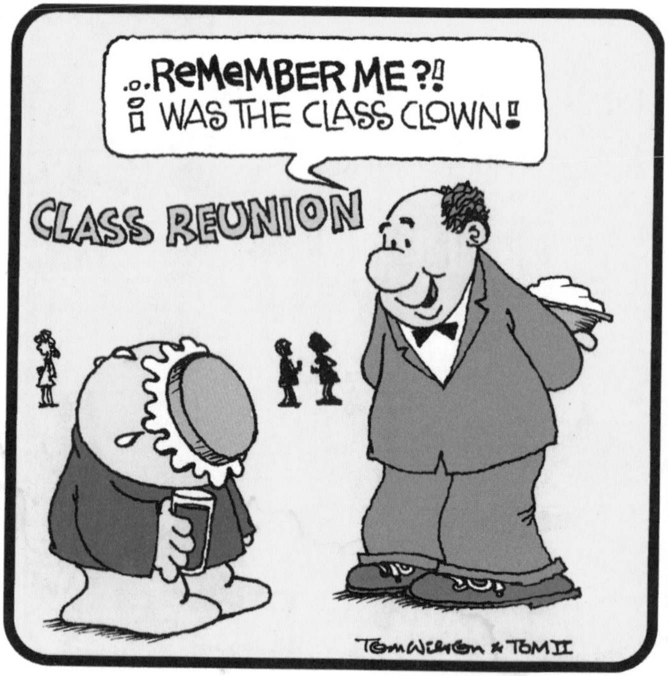
..REMEMBER ME?!
I WAS THE CLASS CLOWN!
CLASS REUNION
TOM WILSON & TOM II